Promotional Cultures

For Hannah, Miriam and Kezia

Promotional Cultures

The Rise and Spread of Advertising, Public Relations, Marketing and Branding

Aeron Davis

polity

First published in 2013 by Polity Press
Reprinted 2015

Polity Press
65 Bridge Street
Cambridge CB2 1UR, UK

Polity Press
350 Main Street
Malden, MA 02148, USA

ISBN-13: 978-0-7456-3982-6
ISBN-13: 978-0-7456-3983-3 (pb)

A catalogue record for this book is available from the British Library.

Typeset in 10.5 on 12 pt Plantin
by Servis Filmsetting Ltd, Stockport, Cheshire
Printed and bound in Great Britain by Clays Ltd, St Ives plc

For further information on Polity, visit our website: www.politybooks.com

Contents

Detailed Contents   vi
Preface and Acknowledgements   x

1   Introduction   1

Part I: Producers, Consumers and Texts

2   Production: Industry and its Critics   15
3   Audiences and Consumers   34
4   Texts: Situating the Text in Promotional Culture   51

Part II: Commodities, Media and Celebrity

5   Commodities: Promotional Influences on the Creation of
     Stuff   73
6   News Media and Popular Culture: Promotion and Creative
     Autonomy   92
7   Celebrity Culture and Symbolic Power   112

Part III: Politics, Markets and Society

8   Politics and Political Representation   135
9   Conflict and Pluralism in Civil Society   154
10   Economies, Speculative Markets and Value   173

11   Conclusions   191

References   203
Index   237

Detailed Contents

Preface and Acknowledgements   x

1   Introduction   1
    Defining promotional culture and promotional intermediaries   1
    The book's core argument and approach   3
    Chapter outline and wider themes   8

Part I: Producers, Consumers and Texts

2   Production: Industry and its Critics   15
    Introduction   15
    The rise of promotional culture: an industry perspective   16
        A history of professional development   16
        The 'professions' in history: markets, democracies and media   19
    The rise of promotional culture: critical perspectives   23
        Alternative professional histories   24
        Professions and the reshaping of markets, democracies and media 27
    Conclusion   32

3   Audiences and Consumers   34
    Introduction   34
    Countering the productionist thesis and relocating the consumer-
        audience   35
    Promotional culture as co-created culture   37
    Consumer reappropriation and uses of material and promotional
        culture   40
    Reappraising the consumer-audience position   44
    Conclusion   50

4   Texts: Situating the Text in Promotional Culture   51
      Introduction   51
      Methodological differences in analysing promotional texts   52
      Texts as autonomous reflections   56
      Critical analyses of texts and power   58
      Audiences and open and writerly texts   62
      Poststructuralism, postmodernism and sign-saturated texts   64
      Texts and a return to the material, power and the ideological? 67
      Conclusion   68

Part II: Commodities, Media and Celebrity

5   Commodities: Promotional Influences on the Creation of
    Stuff   73
      Introduction   73
      Top-down and bottom-up perspectives on the creation and
        promotion of stuff   74
      Promotional culture and the reshaping of commodity uses, firms
        and markets   77
        Promotional influences on the construction of commodities and
          the retail experience   77
        Promotional influences on the firm   79
        Promotion and the shaping of markets   81
      Promotion, clothes and fashion: from haute couture to the high
        street   83
      Promotion and hi-tech goods: from the printing press to the
        Microsoft–Apple computer wars   87
      Conclusion   91

6   News Media and Popular Culture: Promotion and Creative
    Autonomy   92
      Introduction   92
      Promotional culture and independent news journalism   93
      Promotion and entertainment media: music and television   98
        Promotional constraints on creative autonomy and cultural
          outputs   98
        Creativity and autonomy retained   103
      Promotional culture and creative autonomy in the Hollywood film
        industry   105
      Conclusion   111

7   Celebrity Culture and Symbolic Power   112
     Introduction   112
     The growth of celebrity culture and the celebrity industry   113
     Celebrities as a powerless elite   116
     Celebrities, accumulating symbolic capital and forms of power 119
     Celebrity, symbolic capital and political capital: the case of David
          Cameron   123
     Celebrity, symbolic capital and ideological power: the case of
          Jennifer 'J. Lo' Lopez   126
     Celebrity, symbolic capital and economic capital: the case of Tiger
          Woods   129

Part III: Politics, Markets and Society

8   Politics and Political Representation   135
     Introduction   135
     Democracies, promotional politics and the crisis of representation 136
          A crisis of representation in democracies   136
          The rise of promotional culture in politics   138
     Promotional politics, managed media and citizenship   140
     US party politics, political marketing and representation   143
     UK politics, promotional professionalization and the mediatization
          of parties and politicians   148
     Conclusion   153

9   Conflict and Pluralism in Civil Society   154
     Introduction   154
     The rise and spread of professional campaigning in promotional
          civil society   155
          The plurality issue in political sociology debates   156
          The plurality issue in media sociology debates   159
     Trade unions and the promotional battle against Post Office
          privatization in the UK   163
     Interest groups and the challenge to global poverty: the Make
          Poverty History campaign   165
     Taking on the power of global finance and the 1 per cent: the
          Occupy movement   168
     Conclusion   171

10   Economies, Speculative Markets and Value   173
       Introduction   173
       Markets, actors and value: economic rationality, sociological
          irrationality and promotional markets   174
       Neo-classical, orthodox economics   174
       Heterodox economics, social and cultural perspectives   177
       Promotion and markets   179
       The promotion of financial products, financial markets and
          financialization   181
       Selling financial markets, free markets and financialization to
          governments   181
       The over-promotion of companies and stock markets to outside
          investors: the 2000 dot.com boom   185
       The over-promotion of credit, debt and financial products to
          financiers: the 2008 financial crisis   186
       Conclusion   189

11   Conclusions   191
       Individualism as a dominant discourse   193
       Trust, certainty and values   195
       Media logic, mediation and mediatization   196
       Marketization, neo-liberalism and Anglo-American promotional
          capitalism   197
       Risk, creativity and innovation   199
       Democracy, politics, information and power   200
       Final thoughts? What now?   202

References   203
Index   237

Preface and Acknowledgements

Promotional Cultures has been many years in the making and has had multiple inspirations and sources of advice. My early research focused on public relations, news media and political communication. Since then I have looked at promotional practices and mediated consumption in several settings, including the trade union movement, the corporate and financial sectors, and party politics. At the same time, my teaching and interests have wandered across popular culture, the cultural industries, literary theory, social and industrial history, anthropology, and economic and political sociology. In 2003 I began putting these varied interests together in a course called 'Promotional Culture' (taking the title from Andrew Wernick's 1991 book). My knowledge of advertising, marketing and branding was extended, as was my reading around promotion in media, culture, consumption and everyday commodities markets. The course, like this book, offers only brief introductions to the actual practices of these professions. Its main aim is to try and observe and think about them historically and socially. How have they grown and come to influence people, media, culture, organizations, occupational fields and social networks? These are the core concerns driving this book.

This book will appeal to anyone interested in the rise of promotional culture. It should also draw in anyone interested in seeing how promotional imperatives and practices influence social relations professionally and personally. Promotion is always there, working visibly or invisibly, whether one is drawn to celebrities and fashion, popular music and film, politics and campaigning, or goods markets and high finance (and many other things besides). The book is written for advanced students and scholars in departments of media and culture, sociology, politics, anthropology and social history. Although not designed specifically for practitioners and business school-style courses, it should still have much to offer them. It is full of industry histories and sources, statistical information, and case studies.

I have many people to thank. The first of these are Andrea Drugan, Lauren Mulholland and everyone at Polity. As well as offering useful advice and encouragement, Andrea persevered with me over several years of delayed delivery. The many friends, colleagues and external advisors who have offered advice, assistance and/or moral support along the way include Peter van Aelst, Olivier Baisnee, Rod Benson, Lisa Blackman, Andy Chadwick, Nick Couldry, Rosemary Crompton, James Curran, Will Dinan, Lee Edwards, Natalie Fenton, Bob Franklin, Des Freedman, Julie Froud, Jonathan Hardy, David Hesmondhalgh, Sukhdev Johal, Anu Kantola, Mike Kaye, Gholam Khiabany, Adam Leaver, Bong-hyun Lee, Jacqui L'Etang, Colin Leys, Celia Lury, Liz McFall, Angela McRobbie, David Miller, Pat Moloney, Liz Moor, Mick Moran, Angela Phillips, Michael Pickering, Mike Savage, Emily Seymour, Nick Sireau, Gerry Sussman, Grahame Thompson, Peter Thompson, Daya Thussu, Catherine Walsh, Karel Williams and Dwayne Winseck. Last of all I must, of course, mention my family, who have had to compete more than they would have liked with this book: Anne, Hannah, Miriam, Kezia, Kelly, Helen and Neville.

Aeron Davis
October 2012

1

Introduction

This book investigates the rise of what Andrew Wernick (1991) first termed promotional culture. It begins by tracing the twentieth-century history of the promotional professions of public relations, lobbying, advertising, marketing and branding. Other early chapters look at promotional texts and consumer interactions with promotional culture. The book then goes on to observe how the professions and practices of promotion have spread and come to influence society more generally.

Throughout, the book asks what part promotion has played in historical transformations and in evolving social relations. Promotional practice was once fairly ad hoc and driven primarily by the selling of goods and services. Now it is professional and systematic. It is also about selling organizations, professions, ideas and people. For industry practitioners, everything is promotable: big or small, public or private, complex or simple, exclusive or common, solid or intangible, present or future. For individuals, too, promotion is part of everyday practices, both in work and in leisure. Over time, promotional imperatives have come to influence the behaviours of whole organizations, professions and institutions. Industry, politics, civil society, media, culture, markets and finance have all accommodated promotional developments, just as they have evolving new technologies or demographic shifts. In so doing, they have changed. The question is how?

Defining promotional culture and promotional intermediaries

To start, some clarification of the terms *promotional culture* and *promotional intermediaries* is needed. My *definitions relate to active practices.*

When Wernick (1991) first used the term 'promotional culture', he offered a rather broad definition. He argued that 'culture' generally had become 'saturated in the medium of promotion'. No object (image, product or form of communication) could be separated from the promotion of itself and all objects linked to it through communications. All objects are thus connected by 'an endless chain of mutual reference and implication'. Bourdieu (1984: 359) first used the term 'cultural intermediaries', which I have adapted to 'promotional intermediaries'. In his explanation, he referred to the 'new petit bourgeoisie' which were employed 'in all the occupations involving presentation and representation', 'in all the institutions providing symbolic goods and services ... and in cultural production and organization' – in other words, a wide section of society employed in a large range of symbolic activities. My use of these terms is narrower and relates to active promotional practices.

It is the *promotional industries* which have done most to define *promotional practices*. The industries include public relations, lobbying, advertising, marketing and branding, as well as those in related professional fields (e.g., pollsters, publicists, speech writers and agents). *Promotional intermediaries* are those who work in one of these occupations, either for a promotional company, in-house for an organization, or as an independent consultant. Although such occupations can be multifaceted and quite distinct from one another, they also overlap and converge in certain ways. Each is concerned to identify *a saleable product* (a commodity, message, idea or individual), *a potential audience* (citizen, consumer, social group, elite decision-maker), *a communications medium* (formal, informal, mass, digital) and *a message*. For industry historians, these occupations established themselves as 'professions', with identifiable institutions, norms and practices, through the course of the twentieth century (see chapter 2). According to the US Bureau of Labor Statistics (2010), in 2008 there were 623,800 people employed as 'managers' in 'advertising, marketing, promotions, public relations and sales'. This was predicted to rise to 704,000 by 2018. According to the UK Office of National Statistics (ONS, 2011), in 2011, 432,000 people were employed directly in marketing, advertising and public relations.* These figures do not include the hundreds of thousands

* ONS (2011) includes 'marketing and sales directors', 'advertising and public relations directors', 'public relations professionals', 'advertising accounts managers and creative directors', 'marketing associate professionals' and 'market research interviewees'.

more employed in junior roles or those who work in linked or server professions.

However, promotional culture is not simply reducible to a few recognized professions. As will become apparent, promotional practices have been adopted, to a greater or lesser extent, by many non-promotional occupations. Lawyers, journalists, campaigners, religious leaders and industrialists, to name a few, gain promotional advice and training, and are all capable of using promotional techniques. At another level, ordinary individuals, in their day-to-day experiences, have both grown accustomed to a promotion-rich society and come to internalize and reproduce basic promotional practices. This is not the same thing as saying everything is promotional and everyone is a promotional intermediary. Rather, the point is that active promotional practices are rather more widespread and systematic than they once were. They have become absorbed into day-to-day culture.

The book's core argument and approach

The book explains and engages with various perspectives on promotional culture. Some of these are quite dismissive when it comes to considering the significance and impact of promotion. Those derived from orthodox economics, or audience or consumer studies, strongly question the influence or effectiveness of promotional practices. Others, in cultural studies and parts of the industry itself, suggest that promotional culture is simply part of wider culture and thus cannot be an independent shaping force. Each therefore downplays the significance of the promotional professions and their activities.

In contrast, I argue that promotional culture's impact has been rather more substantive. The argument is not just based on the idea that promotional techniques persuade individuals to believe in or buy things they would not otherwise do. This is often the case, although, as decades of effects and audience studies have found, the issues are complex. Promotion frequently fails and may well be more influential in various indirect ways. For example, advertising messages may not convince people to buy a product that promises to make them more attractive or improve their social lives. But such adverts may extend brand awareness, help define what is attractive, or link acts of consumption to social relationships. However, such debates are a relatively small part of the book's broader position.

The larger point about promotional culture's influence is based on the notion that individuals and organizations have become more promotionally oriented. That is to say, they give promotion a greater priority, more resources and more time. Similarly, promotional practices have spread to a number of occupations and settings which once had little or no promotional function. In many instances, strategic decisions to promote specific things are consciously made. But, in many respects, the need to promote has simply become unconsciously internalized by people and institutions. Over time this has had a subtle 'social-shaping' influence on those who adopt it. Politics, markets, popular culture and media, civil society, work and individual social relations have all adapted to promotional needs and practices.

At an institutional level, promotional intermediaries and resources are now employed in many areas of society and by many types of organization. Political parties, charities, news organizations, legal firms and police authorities are just as likely to turn to media managers and brand consultants as the producers of soft drinks or widgets. Heads of marketing, advertising and public relations sit on company boards and hold equivalent senior management positions elsewhere. Their objectives are given higher organizational priority. Budgets now routinely include promotional costs. Indeed, the promotional budget in many diverse types of organization has grown several-fold over the decades. For example, between 1987 and 1997, Nike's promotional budget grew tenfold, to reach almost $1 billion annually (Goldman and Papson, 1998: 4). In 2005, the average Hollywood studio film had come to devote 38 per cent of its budget, or $39 million, to its promotion and distribution. It had been 12 per cent in the 1940s (Epstein, 2005: 7–9). In the UK, over the last three decades, the number of information officers employed in the Ministry of Defence has quadrupled while those in the Metropolitan Police increased elevenfold (COI, 2012). In 2008 the combined campaign expenditure for US presidential candidates, political party committees and political action groups reached $5.98 billion (Magleby, 2011: 19).

Organizational strategy and decision-making, in turn, is influenced by promotional imperatives. Heads of marketing have a significant say on which musical acts, authors, television productions and stars should be supported. Politicians and policies rise and fall, in part, as a consequence of decisions based on expectations of media coverage, focus group and survey data. Promotional skill-sets are increasingly valued within organizations. Individuals, whose primary occupation is not promotion, regularly undergo promotional skills training. It is now common for public figures, be they politicians, CEOs or heads of charities, to have media relations training. Marketing knowledge is now highly desirable for those wishing to move into professions such as financial management or fashion design.

On a personal level, people in mature capitalist democracies both move in promotion-rich environments and have themselves absorbed the practices and cultures of promotion. Everywhere we look and travel we are besieged by promotional images. According to estimates, individuals are bombarded with over 3,000 adverts a day (Twitchell, 1996). These are on billboards, television channels, films, websites, radio stations, public transport and sports stadia. Many everyday objects contain the logos and imagery of their producers. Gap T-shirts, Levi jeans, Apple phones and Chanel perfumes scream out at their consumer-owners with each use. Sponsorship deals and product placements pop up in Hollywood films and television shows. Fast food comes in packaging sporting the latest Disney or Pixar characters.

At the same time, individuals have internalized the practices of self-promotion. Many service companies exploit the 'emotional labour' of their employees. How workers dress, their mannerisms, behaviour and scripted speeches are all regarded as key promotional elements of the firm (Hochschild, 1983). Self-promotion continues outside of work too. As Bauman (2007) notes, in order to operate in today's consumer society, people turn themselves into promotional commodities. Choices of clothes and goods promote the 'commodity-self' to others, whether at work or in leisure. CVs, blogs and social networking sites are also used more consciously to present the individual self to a wider audience.

Thus, slowly, and often imperceptibly, promotion has seeped into all areas of society, at the organizational, social and individual levels. In the twenty-first century, promotion has become ubiquitous. It appears everywhere and, at the same time, we no longer notice its presence. Products and product lines have shifted. Organizational structures, budgets and the balance of personnel employed have changed. Ideas, norms and values have altered, influencing elite and wider public understanding and decision-making. Mainstream public media and popular culture have been reshaped.

Investigating the nature and significance of such individual, social and organizational changes is what directs discussion in most of the chapters that follow. These never assume that promotion is an autonomous all-powerful force that 'determines' or 'performs' all it touches. In fact, the book's approach involves exploring just how promotion interacts with individuals, organizations and other influences in a more co-determining or dialectical way. Promotion combines and interacts with social, economic, technical and other forces.

Most of the chapters convey a sense of modern history and change in which promotion plays a part. Chapters 2 and 3 look at the histories of the promotional industries as well as evolving patterns of consumption in history. Other chapters delve into the histories of film, fashion, television, electrical goods, celebrity, journalism, political parties, interest groups, the trade union movement and financial markets. In some cases, the history leaps erratically through the twentieth century. In others, it dwells very much on the last three decades, a time when Anglo-American, extreme forms of free-market capitalism have been in the ascendancy. At such a time of market 'disembeddedness' (Polanyi, 1944), it is unsurprising that promotional industries and practices have flourished. Much of the time, the focus is on an evolving market, political or cultural field. Biographies, historical overviews and news pieces often combine with academic accounts to fill out these histories. In that respect, a large proportion of the texts cited are not concerned primarily with promotional culture per se but, in diverse ways, still offer insights on its presence and influences.

Under such circumstances, many of the sector studies locate the influences of promotional culture within the general evolution of those fields. It soon becomes clear that the promotional intermediaries employed, and the means by which promotion interacts with a sector, vary considerably. For example, in consumer electronics markets, one crucial aspect of promotion is driven by companies lobbying one another and regulators in an attempt to establish their preferred industry standards and platforms (chapter 5). In the music and film industries, personal agents and company image managers are key to the promotion of new music releases and movies through their stars (chapters 6 and 7). In financial markets, investor relations specialists are vital for finessing company reports and accounting data in order to impress big institutional investors (chapter 10). In politics and civil society (chapters 8 and 9), the need to manage public news media has reshaped organizational campaign strategies and policy preferences. In party politics (chapter 8), film and network television (chapter 6), and the clothing industry (chapter 5), where fashions are volatile, marketing managers are a powerful day-to-day force. But, in all cases, one or more types of promotional intermediary and forms of promotional practice have directly or subtly altered a sector.

At the same time, one can also locate promotional similarities and patterns emerging across the quite diverse occupational fields discussed. For example, Hollywood big budget films and haute couture fashion both share a similar promotional market dynamic with Wedgwood's eighteenth-century top ceramic ranges. This involves producing high-profile, loss-making products which serve to promote high-volume sales of cheaper, associated goods. Similarly, individual showmanship can be found in many occupational fields. Great economists, such as John Maynard Keynes and Milton Friedman, spread their new economic orthodoxies as much through popular media as through academic papers. John Paul Gaultier, Steve Jobs and David Cameron have all put great emphasis on impressive media launches, building on personal presentation, to promote their 'products'. From another promotional perspective, financial products, such as complex derivatives, have much in common with film stars, dotcom companies and modern art. All have become 'sign-saturated' goods which generate financial value out of the 'symbolic value' (Baudrillard, 1988b) that promotional activity produces. Each may be packaged up to encourage large investment, creating high economic valuations out of myths, narratives and speculation. Clearly, the practices of P. T. Barnum are still alive, and snake-oil salesmen come in many guises.

Before continuing, it is necessary to put down a few provisos and acknowledge some failings. First, although the promotional professions are often discussed as one, they are separate occupations that can operate in very different ways. They share many similar and overlapping functions, but one cannot assume they are the same. Some of the more general points made may be more applicable to certain promotional industries than others. Likewise, some chapters focus more on certain promotional professions than others. Second, this is not a text for budding spin doctors and advertising executives. Industry perspectives are presented and there are lots of useful examples, figures and case studies. However, it is not a how-to-do book that explains the core principles of the promotional disciplines and lays out clear advice on best practice. Nor is it an uncritical, pro-industry account. Third, it is not possible to cover every promotional topic adequately in such a text. Several subjects, such as media effects, agents and publicists, or web-based promotion and social media, could have had a whole chapter but, instead, are dealt with within other discussions. There will also be many key industry figures and scholars who are mentioned only fleetingly or not included at all. Similar gaps and omissions will be apparent in the various sector studies, from fashion and finance to politics and popular culture.

Such is the consequence of attempting to cover a wide range of professions and disparate subject matters. I am happy to admit all these faults but hope these will be balanced up by the book's larger argument and broad subject coverage.

Chapter outline and wider themes

The main argument and approach outlined above runs through the chapters that follow. Each chapter, while contributing to the larger argument, also offers a self-contained review of a subject that can be read alone and often contains alternative interpretive frameworks for understanding and evaluating promotional culture. The first part, *Producers, Consumers and Texts*, focuses very much on the promotional industries themselves and their outputs as well as consumer responses to promotion. It is in this part that several of the classic texts on promotional culture are presented and juxtaposed.

Chapter 2 looks at conflicting histories of promotional culture, pitting *industry accounts* against (post-)Marxist and other critiques. Practitioners view their industries as developing from ad hoc and self-serving occupations into respectable 'professions' that now serve organizations and their publics equally. Industry histories also characterize these emerging professions as vital cogs in the development of much that we now take for granted: democracy and its institutions, mature consumer-oriented markets, and mass media. In stark contrast, *(post-)Marxists and others* essentially tie promotional culture to wider critical evaluations of capitalist democracies. Promotional intermediaries are employed primarily to fulfil state and corporate objectives. Their activities manipulate publics into acting against their own self-interests, obscure true social and industrial conditions, reinforce social prejudices, and are deployed falsely to justify wars and environmental degradation.

Chapter 3 draws on work in sociology, anthropology and media studies to focus on *consumer and audience perspectives*. It offers a critical re-evaluation of those critics of promotional culture that tend to focus on producers and economic determinism. Countering the 'productionist thesis' of history, authors reinsert consumers and consumption back into the evolving cycles of past and present production. Similarly, they directly counter the passive audience-consumer model assumed by critiques. Instead, individuals actively 'reappropriate', 'decommodify' and 'recontextualize' commodities and promotional texts as they establish their own identities and social relations. The final part of the chapter sets out the counter-criticisms of the audience-consumer society thesis. These suggest that the notion of 'consumer sovereignty' is itself a trope generated by modern capitalism that promotes misconceptions of work, leisure and consumer power. The sustainability and consequences of 'the consumer society' are also questioned.

Chapter 4 looks specifically at the texts, signs, symbols and discourses of promotional culture. It presents key methodological approaches for analysing adverts and promotionally influenced news texts. It then discusses how these have been employed by different traditions: industry-applied forms of analysis; critical, mainly (post-) Marxist and feminist critiques; audience and readerly conceptions of texts; and *poststructuralist and postmodern perspectives*. In this last, more detailed account, there is a strong sense that promotion has helped to transform capitalism and social relations. Both 'exchange value' and 'use value' have become subordinated to 'symbolic value'. Processes of production, exchange and consumption are now occupied more with signs than with material objects. Such discussions highlight wider philosophical questions about what exactly promotional texts represent and where they are to be located in society and culture.

Chapters 2, 3 and 4, while offering a dialogue with alternative perspectives on promotional culture, also restate the book's core position. This emphasizes both the increasing promotional orientation of society and that promotion has had a significant 'social-shaping' influence on those who either adopt it or engage with it. Indeed, promotional intermediaries, practices and texts retain considerable discursive and symbolic influence. They thus have a bearing on social relations and material power. The chapters in the second and third parts of the book follow this line of reasoning. Each records the emerging influence of promotional intermediaries and practices within the sector. Each also evaluates a core issue that emerges as promotional culture becomes a more central part of a field. These include commodity production itself, creative autonomy, symbolic power, citizen representation, plurality in civil society, and value.

Part II covers *Commodities, Media and Popular Culture, and Celebrity*. Chapter 5 looks at *the construction and promotion of everyday commodities*, or 'stuff', and introduces a further perspective on promotional culture: *new economic sociology* and its variants (*cultural economy, actor network theory*). This work looks at the role of promotion in industrial history, in markets, and in the behaviour of market participants. It does so using sociological rather than economic perspectives. In most relevant literature on commodity promotion, the influence of promotion on the production of goods per se appears minimal. However, as the chapter argues, promotional influence works in a number of less visible ways that then affect production indirectly. Promotional imperatives can reshape corporations, retailers and markets quite significantly. They may also focus on business-to-business relations in order to establish standards, norms and fashion parameters. Thus, by influencing producers and market structures, promotion can also influence production processes. The larger discussion is followed by extended case studies of commodities markets in haute couture and high-street clothing fashions, electrical goods and home computers. The examples of *Microsoft* and *Apple* are given particular attention.

Chapter 6 turns to the sectors of *mass news media and popular culture*. The theme is one of *worker autonomy* in these industries. The focus is on how promotional considerations and personnel conflict with news journalists and creative artists. From the start, the cultural industries have been reliant on advertising. Over the decades, both public relations and marketing have also become strongly interconnected with media and cultural production. Whether this co-dependency between the promotional and cultural industries has had an all-too-powerful influence on the creative process, and therefore the shape of news and cultural products, is examined. The discussion is applied in greater depth to the cases of *news media, popular music, television* and *Hollywood film*.

Chapter 7 brings together literature from sociology, media, politics and business to investigate the topic of *celebrity*. Celebrities have multiple roles in promotional societies. They promote themselves, are used to promote their host organizations and products, and promote other organizations and products. The theme explored is *symbolic capital and power*. Many accounts see celebrity, fame and the symbolic as rather superficial, transitory and powerless things. However, as the chapter argues, the symbolic capital generated by celebrities and their intermediaries is exchangeable for substantial levels of economic, political and ideological forms of power. This has a series of consequences, both for the organizations involved and for wider society, politics and markets. The general discussion is followed by extended case studies of *David Cameron, Jennifer Lopez* and *Tiger Woods*.

Part III, *Politics, Markets and Society*, turns towards other sectors of society in which the role of promotional culture has grown and, accordingly, contributed to the reshaping of those fields. Chapter 8 draws on studies in *political communication* and *media and politics* to record how institutional politics has been affected by promotional needs. The key theme is *citizen representation*. This investigates how the formal institutions of democracy – parties and governments – have become more or less representative of their publics. Advocates and critics of political marketing, advertising and public relations come to quite different conclusions on the issue. As the chapter goes on to argue, the promotional needs of parties and governments have, in turn, helped to reshape political news coverage, political parties and legislative agendas. Three case areas are discussed in some detail: *news media management*, *political marketing in recent US presidential elections*, and *the mediatization of UK political parties* and personnel.

Chapter 9 looks at work in political sociology and media sociology to consider promotion in *civil society*. It has become clear that a wide range of organizations, institutions, interest groups and social movements have adopted promotional techniques and personnel to achieve a range of political, legal and economic goals. Churches, charities, consumer groups and local councils have joined others in attempting to influence news content and powerful decision-makers in government and business. The key theme of the chapter is *plurality* and the question of whether or not a more promotional society is also a more pluralist society. The larger discussion is followed by extended case studies of *UK union battles* against Post Office privatization, the international *Make Poverty History* campaign, and the global *Occupy movement*.

Chapter 10 introduces a further perspective on promotional culture: *neo-classical economics*. Economics has an ambiguous relationship with promotional culture. On the one hand, advertising and marketing appear to be essential components for linking producers and consumers and for reconciling supply and demand. On the other, orthodox economic theory likes to assume that market actors are rational and to exclude social, cultural and other external factors, including promotional culture. The chapter rejects such economic orthodoxy by drawing on alternative work in *economic sociology*, *cultural economy* and *heterodox economics*. The discussion then focuses on the role of promotion in the construction of speculative markets in finance and elsewhere. The theme of the chapter is value and how promotion is implicated in new *constructions of 'value'*. It goes on to argue that promotional intermediaries and activities can have a significant influence on volatile values, extreme market behaviours, bubbles and crashes. The cases discussed in more depth are *the financial lobby*, the *2000 dotcom boom and bust*, and the more recent *property and financial market bubbles and crashes*.

Chapter 11 offers general conclusions about our promotional times and also pulls together some of the wider themes that have emerged through the preceding chapters. These include discussions of marketization and promotional capitalism; media logic and mediatization; democracy, information and power; risk and innovation; individualism; and trust, certainty and values.

Part I

Producers, Consumers and Texts

2

Production: Industry and its Critics

Introduction

This chapter presents two contrasting accounts of the promotional industries in terms of their history and place in contemporary society. It focuses on the occupations of advertising, public relations and marketing as they emerged over the course of the twentieth century. The first part relays how the promotional industries define and present themselves. It combines some detailed histories with the views of industry practitioners as relayed in personal accounts and textbooks. This presents a history that combines rapid growth with an evolving sense of 'professionalization'. It also suggests that the promotional occupations have been vital constituent elements in the establishment of markets, democracy and mass media. The second part draws together promotional culture's varied critics, who question the 'professionalization' narrative. Instead they argue that such occupations have rather problematic historical evolutions, including the use of mass propaganda and the employment of unethical and questionable practices. Professional promotion has been used to serve elite corporate and state objectives rather than the public interest and to sustain corrupt and unjust forms of capitalist democracy. As such, promotional practices have negatively shaped markets, political institutions, media and culture.

The rise of promotional culture: an industry perspective

A history of professional development

For practitioners and industry historians, the history of the promotional industries is to be marked by an evolving sense of 'professional' development (e.g., Cutlip et al., 2000; L'Etang, 2004; Leiss et al., 2005; Newsom et al., 2007; Fletcher, 2008). Most writers acknowledge that examples of basic practices in advertising, public relations and branding can be traced back several centuries or millennia. However, in the main, historical narratives concentrate on the twentieth-century transformation of ad hoc practices into established professional occupations.

In each case, although details and time lines vary, historical accounts record a similar evolutionary path towards 'professional status'. Industries emerged out of the actions of dispersed individuals and small agencies. These were often engaged in dubious practices and instinctive decision-making. Over several decades each sector was transformed. Professional bodies, with codes of ethics and regulatory frameworks, were established. Educational programmes were developed, first within the firms and associations involved and then in higher education colleges. Complex research methodologies and rigorous social scientific procedures were cultivated. Industry trade magazines, academic journals and annual award ceremonies linked practitioners and disseminated 'best practice'. By the last decades of the century, transnational companies with global visions, networks and employees signalled how far these new industries had come.

Advertising (Leiss et al., 2005; Fletcher, 2008; see also Norris, 1990; Lears, 1995) very much conforms to this pattern as, over time, it became a 'scientifically informed' and 'regulated' profession. Advertising agents had existed since the mid-nineteenth century in the US and the UK but did no more than buy and sell advertising space in the press. That began to change in the early twentieth century. After advertising was made tax-free in the US in 1913, larger, stable advertising agencies emerged, each offering a range of creative and advisory services. By 1917, 95 per cent of national advertising was handled by such agencies (Leiss et al., 2005: 136). In 1926 both the UK and the US Advertising Association were founded, the latter with a mission 'to promote public confidence in advertising and advertised goods through the correction or suppression of abuses'. Both associations established codes of ethics and good practice as well as educational programmes. After the Second World War, advertising and ad agencies began to thrive. By the 1970s, pioneering firms, such as J. Walter Thompson in the US and Boase Massimi Pollitt in the UK, were offering integrated, research-based and creative 'account planning' services. Robust regulatory bodies emerged alongside industry expansion. In the UK in 1962, the Advertising Standards Authority was set up. In the 1970s it was strengthened with reputable advertisers contributing a 0.1 per cent levy of their revenues to its operation. It gained further powers under the media regulator Ofcom in 2006 (Fletcher, 2008: 249).

Marketing's history and growth is harder to define because of its changing functions and its overlap with economics and other promotional industries (see accounts in Bartels, 1988; McDonald, 1996; Kourdi, 2011). The National Association of Teachers of Advertising, established in 1915, became the American Marketing Association (AMA) in 1937. It began producing a monthly newsletter in 1946 and by the 1990s was publishing four journals. In the UK, the Chartered Institute of Marketing (CIM) began in 1911, originally as the Sales Managers Association. *Marketing* magazine started in 1931. In 1945 the association gained official government recognition, in 1973 it developed its first code of practice, and in 1983 it gained royal charter status. In 2001 the Marketing and Sales Standards Setting Body was created in conjunction with the Department for Education and Skills.

The development of industry research methods, education and training was also integral to the 'professionalization' of the marketing and advertising sectors. In 1908, Walter Dill Scott published *The Psychology of Advertising*, one of the early texts to draw on the social sciences in its approach. Charles Coolidge Parlin was credited with producing the first piece of market research, in 1911, presented as a 460-page 'commercial research' report. Several more followed in different industry sectors. In 1917, Ralph Starr Butler published *Marketing Methods*. George Gallup began producing public opinion surveys in the 1920s using proper sampling techniques. By the 1950s, agencies were making use of Nielson and Hooper audience ratings, as well as 'motivational research', 'consumer panels' and 'attitude measurement'. By the early 1960s, over 100 technical colleges were offering marketing diplomas in the UK. In 1962, the Designers and Art Directors Association emerged and launched a series of annual award ceremonies, educational programmes and publications. The Advertising Association sponsored the appointment of a chair of marketing at the London School of Economics in 1964 and the first MA degrees in marketing began the following year. In 1980 the IPA launched its Advertising Effectiveness awards. In 1998, the CIM presented its first Chartered Marketer awards (see also Nixon, 1996).

The historical development of professional public relations lagged a little behind advertising but followed a similar path (Tulloch, 1993; Ewen, 1996; Marchand, 1998; Cutlip et al., 2000; L'Etang, 2004; Newsom et al., 2007). The 'grandfathers' of the industry, Ivy Lee and Edward Bernays, set up offices and touted their services to businesses and government at the start of the twentieth century. Corporations, charities, churches and universities began organizing their 'publicity bureaus' before the First World War. The Democratic and Republican parties established their PR offices in 1928 and 1932 respectively. In the 1920s, UK government institutions, such as the Empire Marketing Board and the Ministry of Health, started employing press staff for public information campaigns. Like advertising, PR consultancies began growing more substantially in the US and the UK from the 1950s onwards.

Accounts also note the emergence of industry 'professionalism' in the form of associations, ethical codes, training and education. For many, nineteenth-century PR was typified by the kind of stunts and 'press agentry' of the showman P. T. Barnum (Grunig and Hunt, 1984). That began to change when, according to Newsom and his colleagues (2007: 29), Ivy Lee's new publicity bureau opened for business in 1906, with a 'Declaration of Principles'. In 1923, Edward Bernays's *Crystallizing Public Opinion* was among the first of many industry texts. Through the 1930s a number of early professional associations were founded. In 1947, Boston University opened the first school of public relations, and by 1949 some 100 colleges in the US were offering PR courses. In 1948, the Public Relations Society of America (PRSA) was established, and in 1954 it published its first code of ethics. The UK Institute of Public Relations (IPR) also began in 1948. It produced its first PR practice guide and offered its first qualifications in 1958; a more prescriptive 'Code of Practice' was published in 1963. In the 1980s the IPR (now CIPR) began presenting its own Excellence in Public Relations awards. In 1988 the first MA degree in public relations was offered, at Stirling University.

Since the 1950s each of these occupations has continued to expand. In the US in 2003, $249.2 billion was spent on advertising and the industry employed 165,000 people (Leiss et al., 2005: 3). PR practitioner numbers rose from 19,000 in 1950 to an estimated 258,000 in 2010 (Cutlip et al., 2000: 31; US Bureau of Labor Statistics, 2010). In 2002, the AMA estimated that 750,000 people were employed in marketing or marketing-related jobs. In the UK, in 1952, advertising expenditure was £123 million, equivalent to 0.77 per cent of GNP. In 2011, £15.9 billion, approaching 1.5 per cent of GNP, was spent on advertising (Fletcher, 2008; AA, 2011). By 2005, the PR sector employed directly an estimated 47,800 people, with many more employed indirectly in press cutting, media evaluation and other PR-servicing firms (Key Note, 2006). In 2011, £7.5 billion was spent on public relations (*PR Week*, 2011). Similarly, 60,000 people were members of the Chartered Institute of Marketing, and companies on average spent 7.29 per cent of their turnover on marketing services (CIM, 2011). Since the 1980s, large global communication conglomerates have formed, often combining these services. In 2008, WPP, the world's largest communications company, owning a range of marketing, public relations and advertising firms, employed 100,000 people in 2,000 offices across 106 countries. It generated $70 billion and had accounts with 340 of the world's largest top 500 companies (Fletcher, 2008: 195).

Across each of these promotional sectors the historical story is similar. Dubious, ad hoc and questionable occupations have evolved to become 'respectable' pillars of business and society. Public accountability, educational standards and ethical practices emerged out of a process of professionalization. In each case, self-serving organizational interests have come to be balanced by wider public interests. Thus, the UK CIPR declares that 'Public Relations practice is the planned and sustained effort to establish and maintain goodwill and mutual understanding between an organization and its publics.' As Newsom and his colleagues (2007: 2–3) state: 'Conscientiously planned programs that put the public interest in the forefront are the basis of sound public relations policy . . . A public relations practitioner should be measured by only one standard: ethical performance.' The American Marketing Association describes marketing as working 'to create exchanges that satisfy individual and organizational goals.' And, for Gibbons (2009: 47), 'Famous brands perform a naturally positive social role. Brands are a mark of standards, of quality and reliability . . . a mark of trust.'

The 'professions' in history: markets, democracies and media

Industry accounts also suggest that the promotional professions have been central to the positive evolution of modern free-market democracies. Histories, textbooks and personal accounts all contribute to the following narrative: markets, democracy and media are naturally good developments in human history; promotional occupations have been essential to their advancement; therefore promotion is an essential and positive part of contemporary society.

First, promotional culture has been, and remains, an essential shaping force in the development of healthy markets and economies. According to several of the above histories, promotional culture eased national economies through a number of necessary transitional stages. Eighteenth- and nineteenth-century industrialization required promotional culture to maintain markets for mass production and links with increasingly mobile and urbanized populations. During the twentieth century, promotional activity then played a central part in the shift from Fordist, mass-production-led economies to consumer-oriented ones (see also chapter 3). Marketers, in addition to selling ready-made products to general consumer markets, began selling detailed information about consumers to producers. This was to feed back into decision-making about product development and design. As Leiss and his colleagues (2005: 130) state, 'It was advertising that made businesspeople interested in what the consumer had to say.' Thus, in Marchand's (1998) history, Ford's mass-produced Model-T cars came to be replaced by General Motors's wider range of car models, drawing on the inputs of market researchers in their manufacture. In the postwar decades, as workers' wages rose, consumer credit became available and commercial competition intensified, so the need for the promotional industries increased. This need was further underlined during the post-1970s economic shift towards 'post-industrialism' or 'post-Fordism' (Piore and Sabel, 1984; Aglietta, 1987; Harvey, 1989; Lash and Urry, 1987, 1994). Accordingly, promotional culture continued to push producers towards further accommodating consumers rather than dictating to them. The range and variety of consumer goods continued to expand, as did the advanced monitoring, deciphering and segmenting of consumers by marketers and advertisers.

Digital media have further enhanced these trends (see Spurgeon, 2008; Grunig, 2009; Scott, 2010; Gillan, 2011). Electronic sales monitoring is central to the newer short-run production lines driven by flexible, reflexive and just-in-time production mechanisms. Search engines, such as Google, have linked advertising revenues to customer-led information searches, as opposed to traditional 'interruption' and 'persuasion' models of promotion. Online shopping sites, such as Amazon, cater to the multiple niche market interests of the emerging 'long tail economy'. They offer a consumer-oriented menu of information, including key word searches, lay reviews, links, tasters, customer rankings, and further suggestions for purchasing.

They and many other sites now track consumer movements and choices, building up micro-marketing data on a mass scale. Carefully honed brands maintain stable links between consumers and producers through ever evolving fashions and multi-platform media (Blackett, 2009; Lindemann, 2009; Gillan, 2011).

Thus the promotional professions have become essential to fast-changing, global, multi-mediated, consumer-oriented markets. For many in the professions, modern economies and markets could not function without them. Through all economic variations, multiple suppliers and buyers are connected productively via promotional activity. Thriving, competitive markets, with lots of 'rational', informed participating buyers and sellers, keep businesses efficient, costs down and prices low. As the Chartered Institute of Marketing declares, 'Marketing is the management process responsible for identifying, anticipating and satisfying customer requirements profitably.' For Tellis (2004: 4), 'advertising is essential for the efficient workings of competitive markets.' These facilitate thriving economies, which then produce jobs and taxes to support nations. For Gibbons (2009: 45), 'Strong economic growth goes hand-in-hand with strong recognizable brands.'

Second, industry accounts similarly suggest that the promotional professions have played a vital part in the evolution of stable democracies (see also chapter 8). With the transition from feudal and authoritarian regimes to democracies with universal suffrage, there developed wider communication needs. Consequently, the practices and personnel of the promotional industries have become an institutionalized feature of governments, parties and other state institutions (Blumler and Gurevitch, 1995; Maarek, 1995; Swanson and Mancini, 1996; L'Etang, 2004; Lilleker and Lees-Marshment, 2005). Governments and parties use market research techniques, from opinion polls to focus groups, to consult with citizens on their legislative agendas. Political organizations then use advertising and public relations to inform voter-citizens about electoral candidates, policy proposals and political affairs.

Practitioners argue that the application of political marketing automatically improves democracy. They view politics as an electoral marketplace where parties compete for citizen support. As with commodities markets, 'rational' citizens calculate the 'marginal utility' for them of voting for one party or another. According to Jennifer Lees-Marshment (2008, 2004; Lilleker and Lees-Marshment, 2005), 'successful' parties are those that have made the transition to being 'market-oriented parties' (MOPs). They have moved on from traditional parties which were interested more in selling than in listening. Instead, modern MOPs use marketing tools as part of the initial policy- and ideas-formation process. Therefore they become freed from the constraints of ideological dogma while also being more consultative and deliberative. Thus, Margaret Thatcher was a 'marketing pioneer' of MOP for the Conservatives in 1979, as was Tony Blair for Labour in 1997. The electoral highs and lows of these two parties are linked to their shifts between market- and sales-oriented behaviours.

Practitioners and some political communication scholars similarly argue that advertising and public relations are also beneficial. They offer targeted, cost-effective ways of producing citizen-oriented messages (Scammell, 1995, 2003; Newman, 1999; Newsom et al., 2007). The 'two-way symmetrical' forms of public relations advocated by Grunig and others (Grunig and Hunt, 1984; Grunig, 1992) encourage politicians to listen to citizens and act ethically. Indeed, some practitioners have suggested that the application of sound PR practices may help restore certain 'public sphere' ideals (Grunig, 1992; Nessman, 1995). As the Public Relations Society of America declares, PR 'serves to bring private and public policies in harmony.' Newsom and his colleagues (2007: 12) similarly state that one important 'role' of PR practitioners 'is to raise issues and concerns and remind management of ethical responsibilities'.

Third, promotional culture has played an essential part in the rise of independent media and communication, from the printed press to broadcasting and the internet (see chapter 6). In several histories of advertising (e.g., Leiss et al., 2005; Fletcher, 2008), the development of many media formats went hand in hand with the expansion of advertising. Since the 1920s, advertising has provided two-thirds of newspaper and magazine income in the US. Currently, 75 per cent of newspaper income, and between 60 and 100 per cent of that of magazines, comes from advertising (Leiss et al., 2005: 21, 68). In Fletcher's (2008: 2, 27–31) view, most media 'would not exist without advertising'. For him, the rise of ITV and commercial broadcasting in the UK in the 1950s could only have happened with the accompanying boom in total advertising spend, which jumped 43 per cent in ITV's first year (1955). Currently, almost 100 per cent of the income of commercial broadcasters, as well as of free newspapers and online media businesses such as Google, comes from advertising.

A key part of the thesis is that advertising has enabled media generally to be more pluralist and independent from government and political interests. Many media accounts similarly argue that commercially supported, 'free' media are more conducive to democracy than publicly funded media (see, for example, Sola Pool, 1983; Veljanovski, 1989; Waters, 1995; Beesley, 1996; Norris, 2000; Lull, 2001; Lees-Marshment, 2004). Free-market media, they argue, are more efficiently run, innovative and responsive to consumers. The thriving of emerging Web 2.0 online media platforms, involving user-generated content, independent news sites and bloggers, and file-sharing, yet drawing considerable advertising revenues, extends this position (Beckett, 2008; Tuten, 2008; Scott, 2010). Thus, new media, combined with innovative advertising and marketing methods, are enabling a plethora of actors, small and big, traditional and alternative, to find a voice. As Tuten says in her book on advertising (2008: 4): 'Consumers have embraced media democracy, and the industry has responded by creating and encouraging consumers to create and co-create content.' And, for Leiss and his colleagues (2005: 96), 'advertising and the expansion of the commercial media were linked . . . it seems almost inconceivable that we could enjoy the benefits of industrial democracy without the activities of the commercial media.'

Taken together, there is a clear narrative about the positive normative effects of promotional culture on market- and media-dependent democracies. Promotional culture makes markets run efficiently, benefits the economy and creates jobs, ensures freedom of choice for consumers and voters, encourages commercially and politically responsive societies, and supports the independent communication forms necessary for the successful running of both markets and democracy. Thus, for Clifton (2009: 8), 'It is no exaggeration to say that brands have the power to change people's lives, and indeed the world . . . as inspirers and enablers of social change.' According to Wilmshurst and Mackay (1999: 20), 'There is in fact a strong case for arguing that advertising is an essential facility if there is to be freedom of choice . . . The "market economy" way of running things has virtually no rival . . . Advertising is here to stay, virtually unquestioned, for the foreseeable future.'

The rise of promotional culture: critical perspectives

Long-standing criticisms of promotional culture emanate from a mixture of (post-)Marxists, centre-left journalists and conservative traditionalists. In recent decades they have been joined by a range of critics concerned with environmental issues, consumer rights, and gender and racial equality. For critics, the promotional occupations have a rather more problematic history than that revealed by summary industry accounts. The 'professional' status narrative is deceptive, both historically and practically. Promotional culture has not simply enabled markets, democracies and media to advance but has restricted and distorted their evolution in particular ways.

Alternative professional histories

First, the notion that professional promotion has evolved to assist its employers and consumer-citizens alike makes little sense. Promotional intermediaries, as with any other profession, serve primarily those who employ them. This takes on some significance when one returns to the history of the promotional industries. In many of the detailed accounts above (Tulloch, 1993; Marchand, 1998; Cutlip et al., 2000; L'Etang, 2004; Newsom et al., 2007), it is clear that advertising, public relations and marketing have really expanded to fulfil the particular needs of governments and large corporations. Much state and business promotional activity was, and continues to be, directed at influencing rather than serving larger publics.

State uses of wartime propaganda are widely documented (see, for example, Herman and Chomsky, 1988; Miller, 1994, 2004; Knightley, 2000; Snow, 2004). What is less well known is how much state propaganda and commercial promotion have been linked together in history. L'Etang (2004) and Fletcher (2008) both note the UK government's extensive use of advertising and public relations personnel during the First and Second World Wars. The modern foundations of British public relations – the Central Office of Information (1945) and the Institute of Public Relations (1948) – were then established with former government employees. These came from largely redundant government departments used to administer the empire and disseminate wartime information (the Empire Marketing Board and Ministry of Information). Basil Clarke, Sydney Walton and other founding figures of the UK corporate public relations industry in the 1920s and 1930s were former government wartime propagandists. They continued to use such methods against Irish Republicans and striking unionists. Dan Edelman, of Edelman, and Alfred Fleishman, of Fleishman Hillard, leading industry figures in US public relations, also began their careers in US military propaganda and information roles (all examples in Miller and Dinan, 2008). More recently, Hill and Knowlton was employed by the exiled Kuwaiti government to invent fake Iraqi atrocity stories. These helped persuade the US Congress to attack Iraq in the first (1991) Gulf War.

Similarly, several authors (Cutlip et al., 1985; Marchand, 1998; Newsom et al., 2007) note the historical role of PR in managing US public concerns about big corporations. Marchand (1998) records the extensive advertising and PR initiatives employed by expanding corporations from 1890 to 1940 in an effort to allay the fears of small-town Americans. Numerous local initiatives, driven by skilled consultants such as Bruce Barton, transformed public anxieties. By the 1940s, big business had instead come to be viewed as part of 'the nation's strength' and as 'America's representative social institutions'. Such activities proved vital during the 1930s Great Depression and during protests in the 1960s and 1970s. Thus, Cutlip and his colleagues (1985: 23) write: 'it is not mere coincidence that in the past, business interests have taken public relations most seriously when their positions of power were challenged or threatened by the forces of labor, the farmer, the small shopkeeper.'

However, sterner critics argue that, even in everyday commercial and peacetime conditions, the promotional professions work through manipulation, deception and propaganda. Three popular critiques set the early tone for the negative perceptions often attributed to these industries: George Orwell's *1984* (1948), Vance Packard's *The Hidden Persuaders* (1957) and Daniel Boorstin's *The Image* (1962). Orwell's observations of both totalitarian regimes and propaganda-using democracies informed his dystopian future of repressive states maintained by extreme propaganda operations. Packard offered outraged insights on the new 'motivational' techniques of Ernest Dichter, Louis Cheskin and other pioneers of modern advertising methods. These drew on mass psychology research to produce adverts which played on emotions, prejudices, fears and instincts. Boorstin looked on in disgust as public events and individuals were turned into 'pseudo-events' for promotional purposes.

More recent critical accounts (Ewen, 1996; Miller and Dinan, 2008) show that the history of corporate promotion is also dotted with numerous examples of lies and unethical practices. Ewen (1996: 10; 2001) showed how manipulation was a central feature of professional practice, as revealed in historical trade journals and practitioner interviews. One of these featured the elderly Edward Bernays: 'Bernays conveyed his hallucination of democracy: A highly educated class of opinion-moulding tacticians is continuously at work, analyzing the social terrain and adjusting the mental scenery from which the public mind, with its limited intellect, derives its opinions.' Bernays famously engineered a covert campaign for American Tobacco – the 1929 Torches of Freedom March – which presented women smoking as a statement of gender equality. He carried out many such campaigns for American Tobacco and United Fruit (Ewen, 1996; Tye, 1998). Ivy Lee produced an extensive propaganda campaign to cover up the Ludlow Massacre of nineteen miners for John D. Rockefeller. He regularly fabricated stories about union and community group leaders and also advised senior Nazi Party leaders. In 1934 he was investigated and condemned by the House of Un-American Activities Committee (Miller and Dinan, 2008).

Nelson (1989), Miller and Dinan (2008) and Stauber and Rampton (1995, 2003) have also documented some of the questionable practices of contemporary PR companies. Hill and Knowlton, Burson Marsteller and Carl Byoir have pioneered the creation of fake front groups. These pseudo 'research institutes' and bogus grassroots 'astroturf' campaigns are covertly funded by, and used to support the positions of, large corporations. Organizations such as the California Raisin Advisory Board, the Council for Tobacco Research and the Coalition for Health Insurance Choices have been used to undermine legitimate campaigns and government attempts at corporate regulation and reform.

All this suggests that practitioners, past and present, have been able to act in ways quite contrary to the professional image promoted by the industries themselves. They have been able to do so, and with relative impunity, because in many ways they are not 'professions' – not in the same way that medicine, law or accounting are. In most countries, with some notable exceptions, to work in one of the promotional professions an individual does not need to have particular qualifications, be registered or be a member of an association. A practitioner cannot be disbarred, struck off or prosecuted for using unethical or shady practices (unless contravening other laws). Self-regulation is the norm. Public censure or fines of individual members or companies by professional associations are very rare. As L'Etang's (2004: 229) history of UK public relations concludes, PR has failed to establish itself as a bona fide 'profession', having become established only as 'a discrete occupation'. Consequently, without real 'professionalism', compliance or accountability, claims that such occupations usually act ethically and in the public interest are questionable.

Clearly, the history of the promotional professions is far more mixed than that presented in industry accounts. PR, advertising, marketing, lobbying and branding are employed primarily by large corporations and states and are utilized, first and foremost, to achieve the objectives of those employers. There has been no simple transition towards more responsible, ethical and two-way forms of communication. The methods of P. T. Barnum are regularly revived and with increasing sophistication. Professional development has certainly come a long way, but that does not mean these occupations are fully fledged 'professions' with everything that that implies.

Professions and the reshaping of markets, democracies and media

In several respects, critical historical accounts overlap with those produced by industry advocates. They agree about key events, as well as the significance of the promotional professions to the evolution of market-based democracies more generally. However, in their assessments, promotional culture has not simply and neutrally facilitated the emergence of such institutions and social relations. Instead it has diverted them in particular, problematic directions. Consequently, it has encouraged a particular form of mediatized capitalist democracy that is morally, socially and culturally flawed. Promotion has blinded and tainted individuals, encouraged inequality and prejudice, and corrupted institutions and social relations.

First, the promotional industries have not simply enabled the development of large, complex markets that benefit producers and publics equally. They have facilitated an era of advanced marketization which has come to subjugate individuals and society. The works of Marx and Engels offer the most wide-ranging critique of the capitalist mode of production as it emerged in the nineteenth century. Capitalism is a flawed, contradictory and unsustainable system resulting in increasing inequality and exploitation of the many by the few. Within their works are also some of the foundational steps of a critique of promotional culture (Marx, 1974, 1976; Marx and Engels, 1976). Three things that prolong capitalism are control of 'the means of mental production', the 'estrangement' of labour from the means of production, and 'commodity fetishism', each of which is aided by promotional activity. When individuals begin paid work for others rather than for themselves, and use their wages to purchase goods produced by others, production becomes socially and intellectually disconnected from consumption. In the process, the unequal relations of ownership and production become obscured. Consumption becomes detached from personal 'use' or 'need'. At the same time, commodities become endowed with a new form of 'exchange value'. The exchange value of a commodity is no longer just the cumulative total of resources and labour employed in its creation, but now also includes surplus capital, or profit, to be accrued by owners. For commodities to sell at exchange values over and above production costs, they must take on qualities or values that are disassociated from their labour costs and use value. Commodities then become 'fetishized' as something else, or additional, that individuals acquire when they purchase the good. Since owners also come to control the wider means of mental production, so the exploitative and mystifying properties of capitalism remain obscured.

These Marxist positions have come to form the basis of many post-Marxist critiques of promotional culture (Galbraith, 1991 [1958]; Marcuse, 1964; Williamson, 2002 [1978]; Lasch, 1979; Adorno and Horkheimer, 1979 [1947]; Williams, 1980; Jhally, 1987; Goldman, 1992; Klein, 2000). For such critics, promotional culture encourages individuals to fetishize and desire commodities they do not need or which are even harmful to them. Thus, Galbraith (1991 [1958]) argues that many of the 'wants' and 'desires' of consumers are not natural but created by advertisers on behalf of producers. Producers create wants to maintain a 'dependence effect'. At the same time, promotion obfuscates the true relations of, and extreme inequalities generated by, capitalist democracies. For Jhally (1987: 204), modern mass-mediated society covers over real material and social relations with the creation of promotional signs. Advertising subsumes use value to exchange value, and subsumes real relations and the material further, in what he calls a 'double subsumption of use value to exchange value'. For Goldman (1992: 10, 35), advertising offers consumers false images of themselves and everyday social relations. Individuals begin to fetishize about objects, creating and imbuing them with artificial but desirable meanings and qualities. In so doing, advertising acts as 'an "opiate" to transport us from the pains of the present' and 'reproduces the ideological hegemony of the commodity form'. For Klein (2000), the promotion of fashionable brands, often to young consumers in wealthy economies, covers over the harsh exploitative conditions and low pay of workers who produce those goods in poor economies.

More generally, promotional activity helps direct individual behaviours and social systems towards the servicing of markets and to elevate individual values over communal ones. So, non-commodities, such as people, art, education and social welfare, become commodified and forced to operate according to market principles. Socially generated values are replaced with market-generated ones. Thus, for Williams (1980), the 'magic system' of advertising turns minds away from social, communal thought and towards self-interested goals and satisfactions: 'But users ask . . . for the satisfaction of human needs which consumption, as such, can never really supply. Since many of these needs are social – roads, hospitals, schools, quiet – they are not only not covered by the consumer ideal; they are even denied by it, because consumption tends always to materialize as an individual activity' (see also Strasser, 2003; Bauman, 2005; the last part of chapter 3). Online promotional media, with their offering of networked personalized profiles, blogs, wants, likes and 'digital confessions', similarly encourage a sense of 'hyper-individualism' and social polarization (Baltruschat, 2011; Dwyer, 2011). In effect, promotional culture not only sells commodities, it also promotes a set of accompanying values, norms and beliefs about society, markets and human relations. Consumption, markets and individualism are presented as the norm, and communal activities and welfare states as problematic (Bauman, 2005, 2007).

Critics have also been scathing about the influences of promotional culture on democracy and its contribution to the 'refeudalization' of the public sphere (Habermas, 1989 [1962]). Promotional activity has redirected political organizations as much towards secrecy, propaganda and winning power as towards public information, dialogue and good governance. This begins with the reshaping of political parties into 'electoral-professional' entities (Swanson and Mancini, 1996; Crouch, 2004; Wring, 2005; Savigny, 2008). Parties, when developing policies, instead of being guided by ideological principles and core memberships, have come to be guided by pollsters, marketers and media managers. Campaign energies are overly focused on small sets of swing voters and states. Parties and governments use their advertising budgets and 'spin doctors' (Herman and Chomsky, 1988; Franklin, 1994, 1997; Hallin, 1994; Jones, 1995; Kurtz, 1998) to limit journalist access and influence news content. News becomes full of 'pseudo-events', 'soundbites' and 'dumbed-down' content. It is also increasingly made up of 'information subsidies' provided by large corporate and political public relations operations (Gandy, 1982; Davis, 2002; Davies, 2008).

Of great significance is the power that the promotionally aided corporate sector has over democratically elected states and the policy process (Stauber and Rampton, 1995, 2003; Ewen, 1996, 2001; Klein, 2000; Davis, 2002; Dinan and Miller, 2007; Miller and Dinan, 2008). Davis (2002) recorded that two-thirds of UK PR and public affairs professionals were employed by corporations. The cumulative influence of corporate promotional power over the political process has manifested in several ways, most obviously in direct lobbying of government. Hoedeman (2007: 261) has documented how big business maintains over 1,000 lobby groups at the European Parliament, employing some 70 per cent of the 15,000 lobbyists working there. Opensecrets (2012) found that, in 2010, the corporate-dominated US lobby total spend was $3.55 billion and that just under 13,000 individual lobbyists operated around Congress in Washington.

The access and influence of corporate public affairs has been felt over many decades. Miller and Dinan's (2008) history of corporate public relations charts the extensive use of PR and lobbying by businesses and business associations, both national and international. They document how the National Association of Manufacturers produced an elaborate campaign to undermine Franklin D. Roosevelt's New Deal in the 1930s. Associations as diverse as the UK Economic League and Aims of Industry, the US chambers of commerce and the international Mount Pelerin Society have deployed extensive communication resources to attack union movements, undermine social welfare programmes, lower corporate taxation and reduce regulation. Stauber and Rampton (1995, 2003), likewise, have tracked the efforts of the oil, food, tobacco and arms industries in the US. Their well-resourced lobbying and PR campaigns have repeatedly forced the collapse of government environmental and health reform initiatives. They have achieved similar successes in blocking a number of environmental, food and chemical safety regulatory initiatives at the EU level (Hoedeman, 2007).

Of equal significance has been the fact that the promotional industries have tended to ally themselves and work closely with the Conservative and Republican parties, which naturally favour business. Conversely, they have done much to undermine the parties of welfare and labour: the Labour and the Democratic parties. Fletcher (2008) lists several incidents in the UK when the Labour Party and advertising industry were in conflict, as well as several award-winning election campaigns fought by leading advertising agencies on behalf of the Conservative Party. Among these were S. H. Benson's 1959 campaign and Saatchi and Saatchi's 1979 campaign, which was the beginning of a long-term partnership between party and advertiser. Davis (2002) notes the very close relations between the Conservative Party and the expanding public relations industry in the 1980s and 1990s. For most of their time in office the Conservatives were advised, often freely, by the heads of several leading PR companies, including Tim Bell of Lowe-Bell and Peter Gummer of Shandwick. Each of these agencies, in turn, was awarded lucrative communication contracts working on privatizations and for government departments and former nationalized industries.

Any overview of economic and social policy-making in the last three decades suggests that the nexus of corporations, governments and promotional industries has been extremely effective. Since the late 1970s, governments have deregulated industry and lowered higher-level and corporate tax rates, while also scaling back welfare programmes and union and consumer rights. Nothing typifies this more than the responses to the banking crisis (2007–8) and the depression that has followed. The debts of the private banking sector have been nationalized, with the cutting of welfare states being the price paid. At the same time, further corporate tax cuts and deregulation have been implemented (see chapter 10).

Lastly, promotional culture has not simply enabled the development of independent, autonomous media systems, reflective of wider society interests (see chapter 6). It also shapes media and cultural content in problematic ways. One way is through advertising's encouragement of media producers to develop outputs aimed at mainstream or wealthy consumer markets (Curran, 1986; Curran and Seaton, 2003). Working-class papers, as well as general news and entertainment media which cater to poor, radical or minority audiences, have struggled to survive as they fail to gain advertising. Currently, shifts in advertising, away from serious news print and broadcasting and towards entertainment and the web, are jeopardizing many news operations.

Marketing and other promotional activity also encourage the standardization and homogenization of cultural production. This point was first made by the Frankfurt School (see Adorno and Horkheimer, 1979 [1947]; Adorno, 1991) in relation to the transformation of art, music and culture into commodities produced by the 'cultural industry'. Cultural producers, like industrial producers, attempt to standardize production while simultaneously presenting outputs with a 'pseudo-individuality' to maintain sales. Hence promotional culture is necessary to identify where standardization is required and then to promote similar goods as different. Such observations have been made also about modern cultural outputs in music, television, literature and film (Negus, 1992; Gitlin, 1994; Moran, 2000; Wasko, 2003; Lotz, 2007). For Gitlin (1994), market research and ratings machines have come to dictate what programme ideas get commissioned, as well as to encourage the endless recycling of basic characters, plot lines and formats, on US prime-time television. In Wasko's (2003) account of Hollywood film-making, conservative promotional and marketing departments have a strong say over the funding and shaping of new productions.

Promotional culture is also implicated in the dissemination of deeper social prejudices. Views of the 'other' in terms of race, ethnicity, nation or religion are to be found and reinforced in promotional texts, from advertising to music videos. Women are far more likely to be presented in the home, as supportive wives or mothers, than in workplaces, and they are far more likely to be represented by their body parts and in sexually suggestive poses (Goffman, 1979; Berger, 1972; Dyer, 1982; Goldman, 1992). Particular, desired body shapes, family relations and sexual preferences are regularly reinforced. Dominant white and Western views are also woven into promotion (Goodman, 2002; Watts and Orbe, 2002; Frith et al., 2005; Beltran, 2007). Thus, Goodman (2002) finds that even educated, independent white and Latina women struggle against promotional images enforcing 'thinness' as a desirable and empowering state. Chaudhuri (2001) observes that Indian advertising displaces typical gender norms, choosing instead to promote 'globally oriented', 'cosmopolitan' and 'body-conscious' profiles of 'new' Indian men and women. The study of fashion magazine advertising in the US, Singapore and Taiwan by Frith, Show and Chung (2005) reveals how Caucasian models dominate even in Asian countries. They found that, in their sample, 91 per cent of US ads, 65 per cent of Singaporean ads and 47 per cent of Taiwanese ads used white models. This was in spite of the fact that 75 per cent of Singaporeans and 98 per cent of Taiwanese are ethnically Chinese.

Ultimately, promotional culture has contributed to the development and sustenance of a flawed and contradictory system of mediated, capitalist democracy. Such a system, in its current state, reproduces growing inequality, exploitation and the erosion of precious environmental resources. In so doing, it also corrupts individuals, institutions, cultural and social norms, and values.

Conclusion

Clearly, the promotional occupations have become central to the development of contemporary markets, democracies, media and culture. It is hard to think how large, complex societies could function without them. Most people working in these industries are not employed to produce dark propaganda or engage in covert lobbying, advertising and media campaigns. Those involved have done much to turn them into established occupations, even if remaining far from being 'professions' in the manner of other employment sectors.

However, there is no clear-cut case to say that the promotional professions, on balance, have had a strong positive shaping effect on market-based democracies and media. They are employed primarily by large corporations and states, whose needs they service over and above those of their larger consumer-citizen publics. Promotional practices can have a powerful impact in the shorter term, as in times of war or political and economic upheaval. Over longer periods, they are also likely to have distorting effects, favouring certain norms, values, peoples and organizations over others. In these respects, there is certainly rather more that could be done in terms of professionalization, monitoring and regulation.

3
Audiences and Consumers

Introduction

Audience and consumer society perspectives on promotional culture
were established initially in contradistinction to production-centred
approaches. Whether framed by industry or critical thinking, such
'productionist' accounts were deemed to have neglected actual
individuals and everyday social relations. They also privileged
macro-level political and economic trends over micro-level cultural
ones. In response, a range of social historians, cultural theorists,
anthropologists and sociologists have turned their attention to the
experiences of real consumers and audiences. They have sought to
reinsert a sense of individual agency back into industrial history,
modern market relations and material culture. In so doing, they
reject any notion that promotional culture has a strong, direct influence on consumer behaviour. Instead, it is recast as a form of general
culture and as a 'productive interface' between producers and consumers. Consumers reappropriate it as they do material culture more
generally. Material culture is then used by individuals in a variety of
productive ways – for pleasure, for social guidance, for the establishment of individual identity, and in evolving social relations.

The chapter is in four parts. The first three discuss the counter-
thesis and the ways consumer-audiences make use of material and
promotional culture. The fourth part then reappraises the wider
consumer-audience thesis by asking what exactly it means to be 'a
consumer' in the twenty-first-century 'consumer society'.

Countering the productionist thesis and relocating the consumer-audience

Studies of consumers and audiences have often started with a critique of the 'productionist thesis' (Sassatelli, 2007). Douglas and Isherwood (1979: viii) stated that 'the very idea of consumption itself has to be set back into the social process' and regarded as more than a by-product of 'work'. Miller (1987: 3) questioned why in scholarship there had been 'an overwhelming concentration on the area of production as the key generative arena for the emergence of social relations'. In studies of media audiences (Morley, 1980; Hobson, 1982; Radway, 1984), there was a parallel condemnation of work which focused predominantly on media producers and texts. As Hobson (1982: 136) declared: 'A television program is a three part development . . . it is false and elitist criticism to ignore what any member of the audience thinks or feels about a program.' Such authors argued that individuals had to be conceived of as something more than 'rational, utility maximizers' or passive, malleable 'dupes'. Each also stressed the importance of the cultural (or 'superstructural') as well as the material and economic (or 'base').

The reinstatement of the consumer began with revised social and industrial histories. A key point made is that histories framed by production alone are incomplete. Societies did not undergo industrial transformation simply because of emerging new technologies and production techniques. Evolving consumer habits, as well as wider social changes, must have fed into changing forms of production. Thus, Bocock (1993), Slater (1997) and Sassatelli (2007) trace the elements of a widespread consumer society as far back as the mid-eighteenth or even seventeenth century. These draw on several social histories of Britain and Europe (e.g., De Vries, 1975; Braudel, 1981; McKendrick et al., 1982). As international trade expanded, many hitherto 'exotic' and rare goods, such as sugar, coffee and cocoa, came to be widely consumed as everyday items by the many. For Sassatelli (2007: 9), it was the 'small luxuries of the masses' as much as 'the extravagances of the nobility' which fed into the growing evolution of capitalist production in the early modern period. In Bocock's account (1993), by the latter half of the eighteenth century, commodity advertising, in the burgeoning newspaper and periodical industries, followed alongside, not behind, rushed factory expansion. At the end of the nineteenth century, Veblen (1899) and Simmel (1904) recorded the consumption habits of the rich in the United States and France respectively. Separately, Simmel (2002 [1903]) also observed how growing cities across Europe were being shaped around the organization of consumption and leisure. Transport lines developed to bring people into town centres with large department stores, entertainment venues and sports grounds.

All these accounts suggest that consumers did not come at the end of the chain of production. Nor did they simply adapt to production-led socio-economic developments. Instead, consumers, if not driving evolving forms of production, were certainly contributing to their development. For many, this became all the more apparent during the twentieth century with the emergence of the 'consumer society'. First in 1920s America, and then with renewed vigour in the 1950s, in both the US and Europe, clear signs of a more consumer-oriented production appeared. Older, Fordist, mass-production-led industries became more flexible with advances in technology and design. It was in the postwar decades, when economies grew strongly, that a healthy balance between labour and capital, production and consumption, was achieved. By the latter decades of the twentieth century, advanced economies were increasingly driven by the requirements of the 'sovereign consumer'. Thus, as Lee states (2000: ix), 'Historians looking back at the 20th century may well conclude that it was the century of the consumer society . . . we can scarcely begin to conceive of a form of social life which is not organized around the consumption of mass-produced commodities.'

In many of these accounts (Bocock, 1993; Lury, 1996; Braham, 1997; Lee, 2000), promotional culture is one key element facilitating social and industrial transition. Studies of advertising (Lears, 1994; Leiss et al., 2005), public relations (Marchand, 1998) and branding (Lury, 2004; Moor, 2007) all note the links between emerging promotional practices and consumer behaviours from the late nineteenth century onwards. Mass advertising, branded goods manufacturers and sales catalogues, urban shopping centres and well-known retail stores developed together before the First World War. Promotional and consumer shifts were again linked in rapidly growing economies from the 1950s onwards. For Lury (1996), the expansion of advertising and the greater weighting put on packaging, promotion, style and design in this period formed a fundamental part of the transition and enabled 'the stylization of cultural consumption' to take place. For Bocock (1993), Nixon (1996) and Arvidsson (2006), the growing sophistication of consumer-oriented market research and advertising methods was also a significant development. As such, these accounts dovetail nicely with industry-professional descriptions and histories (see chapter 2). At each historical shift, promotional culture has been key to providing the new feedback mechanisms and interactive interfaces linking producers and consumers.

Running through the literature, it also becomes clear that modern promotional culture is not an independent, all-powerful force influencing passive consumers. The pseudo-scientific claims of marketing experts, to be able to classify and target audiences, are readily dismissed as selling devices, designed to win contracts and reduce 'producer anxiety' (see Ang, 1991; Nava, 1997; Lury and Warde, 1997). Powerful industry leaders, when questioned (see also Negus, 1992; Gitlin, 1994), admit that they often prefer 'gut-instinct' over market research. Indeed, many ground-breaking industrialists, from Henry Ford to Steve Jobs, have been notoriously hostile to marketing. Turning to advertising, the consensus of several decades of media effects research in social psychology and political communication (see summaries in, for example, Livingstone, 1998; Norris et al., 1999; McQuail, 2000) suggests that promotional culture, like communications generally, is likely to have only limited effects on consumers. Advertising's main achievement has been to encourage people to change to competitor brands rather than to change their patterns of consumption (Schudson, 1984; Fletcher, 2008). Lastly, as many studies of the cultural industries confirm (Garnham, 1990; Hesmondhalgh, 2007; and chapter 6), the vast majority of cultural products are financial failures, often in spite of having large marketing and promotional budgets. If promotional culture is not an autonomous, deterministic and effective form of communication, what is it?

Promotional culture as co-created culture

As many industry practitioners and cultural theorists explain, promotional texts are part of wider culture (Berger, 1972; Nava, 1992; Fowles, 1996; Twitchell, 1996; Kelly et al., 2005; Leiss et al., 2005; Fletcher, 2008). They draw inspiration from art and popular culture and, in turn, produce texts that are interpreted and evaluated in the same ways art and popular culture are. Thus, Berger (1972) observed that promotional images frequently drew inspiration from, and made explicit references to, classic works of art. The interviews and observations of working advertisers by Kelly and his colleagues (2005) revealed how they drew on a variety of other popular cultural sources for inspiration, including film, books, art and television. Thus advertisers, quite literally, operate as 'cultural intermediaries'. Fletcher's

(2008) UK advertising history noted that many practitioners also had training or parallel careers in art or film-making. Lindsay Anderson, Stephen Frears, Hugh Hudson, Alan Parker, Ken Russell, John Schlesinger and Ridley Scott are some of the well-known film directors who began their careers making commercials. As Myers (1999), Fowles (1996) and Nava (1992) make clear, if advertising did not tie itself to the signs, symbols and tropes of popular culture, audiences would not engage with it. Arvidsson (2006) similarly argues that enduring brands are those that draw on the wider 'general intellect' or 'productive multitude'.

The key notion that promotional texts both draw from wider culture and are themselves a form of culture has important implications. First, promotional texts may contain multiple meanings and references and, second, audiences may view and engage with them in varied ways. Such ideas have come to underpin much work in cultural studies. Hall (1973) initially argued that language and popular culture are encoded with 'dominant' or 'preferred' meanings, but he also stressed that recipients could decode them in 'negotiated' or 'oppositional' ways. Barthes (1968, 1977), drawing more on semiotics, developed a similar analysis, whereby the 'signifier' (the image) and the 'signified' (the mental construct), which combined to produce 'signs', could become detached from each other. Meanings therefore could be far more open, rich and varied. Texts of all kinds, be they visual or linguistic, could be deconstructed in multiple ways.

Such views came to be tested in studies of television audiences. Morley's (1980) early study looked at viewer consumption of the current affairs programme *Nationwide*. He suggested that the 'polysemic' contents of the programmes, coupled with 'extra-textual determinants', meant that viewer engagement and interpretation could vary considerably. Liebes and Katz's (1990) study of demographically diverse audiences in Israel watching the US soap opera *Dallas* found large deviations in consumption and interpretation across social groups. Viewers tended to use the programme 'as a forum for discussing their own lives'. Groups accordingly picked and chose what elements, characters and themes to engage with, often ignoring others entirely. Similarly, Hebdige (1988) described how, from the 1950s onwards, Italian motor scooters came to develop a range of associations for varied groups and with different users in Europe. Coombe (1998) also demonstrated the way fans have engaged with stars' identities and popular culture on their own terms. In one case, middle-class female fan networks rewrote and circulated *Star Trek* episodes and characters. These contained new mixes of submissive and strong women characters, as well as gay romances between the leading male characters. More recently, 'fanfic' (fan fiction) has spread rapidly through fan websites. Thousands of fans now produce their own stories and serials, often in parallel universes containing characters from *Harry Potter, Sherlock Holmes, Twilight* and *Lord of the Rings*.

These same positions, vis-à-vis open texts and active audience engagement, are reproduced in several studies of promotional culture and consumption (Fiske, 1989; Nava, 1992; Livingstone and Lunt, 1992; Fowles, 1996; Crane, 2000; Leiss et al., 2005; Arvidsson, 2006). So Nava (1992, 1997) argues that fourteen- to 24-year-olds consume and evaluate commercials quite independently of the products they are promoting, as if they were autonomous cultural goods. Myers (1999: 14) states that 'Advertising . . . provides a text that audiences may take up and transform, or may ignore entirely.' Fiske (1989) and Livingstone and Lunt (1992) reveal how individuals develop their own means of interacting with shopping spaces, often in ways not intended by retail store owners. The latter observe how shoppers develop their own 'rules', 'guides' and 'strategies' for shopping. In both cases, shoppers negotiate or challenge, consciously and unconsciously, the consumption conventions set by shops and vendors.

Such arguments have been further extended in discussions of digital media, promotion and consumption (Lotz, 2007; Spurgeon, 2008; Tuten, 2008; Scott, 2010). New technologies are fragmenting mass media and, consequently, top-down, mass forms of promotion. In their place, innovative advertising and promotional formats have enabled a far wider range of channels, publications and websites to emerge, catering to numerous niche markets. As Lotz (2007: 15) states about US television, in 'the "post-network" era . . . viewers now increasingly select what, when, and where to view from abundant options.' Most significantly, it is the Web 2.0 sites of the last decade, such as YouTube, Google, Amazon, Twitter, Flickr and Facebook, which have really enabled consumers to engage actively with 'conversational media'. Such sites build on the two-way, interactive and dialogical features of the Web. Search engines, independent fan and comment sites, and social networking spaces allow consumers to look for, assess, review and share, all while they consume. Increasingly, it is consumers, or 'prosumers', who are 'co-creators' and promoters of online content, including videos, pictures, viral buzzes and comments. In Spurgeon's words (2008: 4, 20), 'New media audiences cannot be conceived of as passive consumers of these services. Indeed their active participation, especially as content creators, is crucial . . . the creative participation of individual consumers and bottom-up processes of consumer self-organization are being realized.'

In effect, media audiences and consumers have been reinserted back into social and industrial history. Consumption always influenced production patterns and, during the twentieth century, came to be an equal if not dominant partner in shaping post-industrial economies. Because texts are open and polysemic, and individuals actively and selectively interpret them, promotional culture has a less direct influence over audiences and is instead to be seen as another form of interactive culture. It acts as a productive interface between producers and consumers.

Consumer reappropriation and uses of material and promotional culture

A key theme linking varied studies of consumers and audiences is the reappropriation of material culture for the achievement of personal use. In this respect, individuals *productively use culture and commodities* rather than merely *using them up*. Consumption then, as well as interacting with culture, reappropriates it and draws on it for further personal productive processes. Thus Lury (1996: 1) states: 'the use or appropriation of an object is more often than not both a moment of consumption and production, of undoing and doing, of destruction and construction.' Miller (1987) concludes that the utility of objects and culture relates to the degree to which consumers may 'reappropriate' or 'recontextualize' them. Sassatelli (2007: 196) declares that 'Consumption is a form of value production which realizes the objects as lived culture . . . by appropriating goods in everyday life consumers decommoditize them.'

This reappropriation is to be observed, on a mundane level, in daily actions and habits, both in work and in leisure. De Certeau (1984: 16) looked at the practices of ordinary life, from working to shopping, renting and reading. For de Certeau, individuals adopt particular 'tactics' in their lives. They selectively 'poach' from what they encounter, acting as 'bricoleurs' to create their own forms of ownership and use: 'Everyday life invents itself by poaching in countless ways the property of others.' For Hebdige (1979, 1988) and Miller (1987), individuals 'reappropriate', 'recontextualize' and 'decommodify' everyday commodities for a variety of 'uses', often in ways not conceived by producers. For Hebdige (1979), punks reappropriated the common safety-pin and other ordinary items to create their alternative looks. Miller (1987) observed that rows of council house homes, identical from the outside, were transformed in very diverse ways when viewed within. Fiske (1987) similarly described the varied forms, styles and reappropriations of jeans among different user groups.

What also becomes clear is that, once the products of material culture have been reappropriated, consumer-audiences engage with and make use of them in several ways. The 'uses' identified are varied, but all move beyond the standard 'use value' linked to the production, exchange and consumption of everyday goods.

One of these uses is simple pleasure brought during active engagements with culture. For Barthes (1977), the reading of good texts brings *plaisir*, or pleasure. Those texts which encourage greater reader interaction ('writerly texts') also bring an accompanying sense of *jouissance*, or bliss. Campbell (1989 [1940]) questioned historical accounts of consumers whose needs were either 'instinctive' or 'manipulated'. Instead, he argued that they actively developed needs and gratifications and 'autonomous imaginative hedonism'. Radway's (1984) study of reader responses to romance novels noted that, regardless of the means of cultural production and dominant codes, readers gained real pleasure from their reading. Plot lines and characters strongly reinforced patriarchal dominance in society. However, women readers still gained emotional fulfilment through following the upward mobility and achieved independent self-identity of the female characters. Stacey (1994) found something similar in her study of British women cinema-goers in the 1940s and 1950s. They engaged positively with a mix of female role models, characters and fashions that both reinforced and challenged patriarchal society. At the same time, the whole cinema experience itself brought a mix of satisfactions during a period of war and deprivation.

Second, promotional culture offers social and psychological guidance to individuals. In late or post-modernity, the pace of change increases, people are more transient, and traditional sources of guidance, such as community, religion and family, are less assured. So individuals look elsewhere to identify norms, values, practices and fashions. Simmel (2002 [1903]) identified this issue in his observations of urban dwellers in the sprawling new European metropolises. Consumption was one way that individuals could reassert their psychological autonomy 'in the face of overwhelming social forces'. For both Lears (1994) and Marchand (1998), promotional culture worked to ease and reconcile small-town, traditional populaces to new, modern environments consisting of large corporations, urbanization and new technologies. For Leiss and his colleagues (2005: 89): 'Quite simply, individuals need guidance . . . In the consumer society, marketing and advertising assumed the role once played by cultural traditions and became the privileged forum for the transmission of social cues.' Lury makes a similar point in relation to modern brands. In an ever hastening cycle of new goods and services, brands offer 'continuity over time'. This maintains a sense of security and longevity while also enabling multiple and repeated changes of goods. As Lury states (2004: 9), 'the interface of the brand manages the "response time" of interactivity, the interval between products.'

Third, consumers use material and cultural goods to establish their sense of identity and their social relations with others. Veblen (1899), Simmel (1904), Sombart (1922) and Bourdieu (1984) have each provided an account of how material culture is used to establish identity, class and social distinction. Veblen (1899) wrote in some detail about the 'conspicuous consumption' of the 'leisure class' in the United States. Choices of food, clothing and dwelling, but also of ornaments, amulets, idols and narcotics, each identified 'the mark of the master' and distinguished 'the superior class' at the end of the nineteenth century. Simmel (1904) documented how the wealthy of eighteenth- and nineteenth-century France required a steady stream of new fashionable clothes to maintain their elevated positions in society. The consumption of material culture thus became a means of social distinction, a set of signifiers of wealth and power.

Bourdieu (1984; Bourdieu et al., 1990) offered a more complex and wider-ranging account of the links between consumption, identity and class. In his research framework, all individuals develop their own 'habitus' out of their upbringing and social relations and from their accumulations of social, economic and cultural 'forms of capital'. This then determines their tastes, dispositions, preferences and opinions. Cultural tastes and preferences become a means of 'distinction' which not only determine preferences, but also help to define and classify people to others. Bourdieu applied his concepts in extensive surveys of the French public, recording key social variables such as education, income, profession and parental occupation. These were then correlated with cultural practices and preferences, such as museum attendance, newspaper selection, and musical and literary tastes. Clear patterns between the two emerged.

Douglas and Isherwood (1979) and Miller (1987, 1998, 2008, 2010) have written extensively about individual identity formation and social relations during interactions with material culture. In his ethnographic studies, from South London to Trinidad and India, Miller argues that individuals have a dialectical relationship to all forms of material culture. Goods make people as much as people make goods. Thus the sari, with its pallu end, is involved in 'creating a specificity to being an Indian woman' (2010: 30, 12) – something both 'Indian' and individual. By the same token, an elderly, lonely man's extreme lack of possessions reflects an 'empty' person whose individual identity failed to emerge (2008). For Douglas and Isherwood (1979), material 'goods' consumption has a 'ritual function' that serves to 'make and maintain social relationships'. For Miller (2008), material possessions are no replacement for human relations but do enrich social relationships in a variety of ways. In studies of subcultures (Hebdige, 1979; Thornton, 1995) or 'neo-tribes' (Maffesoli, 1991), social groups cohere as they jointly reappropriate and use spaces and material and cultural goods. Just as high fashion and conspicuous consumption marked out the wealthy groups in centuries past, so now do everyday choices of clothes, music, online forums, modes of transport, and spaces. In studies of television audiences (e.g., Morley, 1980; Ang, 1985; Liebes and Katz, 1990), television viewing is a social practice. Viewers engage with and review media in dialogue with family and social groups. Thus, as Slater (1997: 2) explains: 'the study of consumer culture is not simply the study of texts and textuality, of individual choice and consciousness, of wants and desires, but rather the study of such things in the context of social relations.'

Last of all, culture may be used as a source of resistance and opposition (Hall and Jefferson, 1976; Hebdige, 1979; de Certeau, 1984; Fiske, 1987, 1989; Willis, 1990; Crane, 2000). For de Certeau (1984: 16), the individual reappropriation of everyday goods is also a low-level act of opposition: 'The tactics of consumption . . . lend a political dimension to everyday practices.' Renters make properties their own, in defiance of property owners, by changing the décor, having wild parties, and hiding or ignoring building problems. At work they can steal small items, make use of their facilities for non-work purposes, take long lunches and call in sick when well. Fiske (1987, 1989, 1996), in his studies in the US and Australia, took this sense of oppositional cultural reconfiguration further: 'the distribution of power in society is paralleled by semiotic struggles for meanings. Every text and every reading has a social and therefore political dimension.' Consumers therefore act as 'semiotic guerillas', subverting the apparatus and objects of material culture at every turn. Shopping malls, video arcades and beaches are reappropriated.

Television programmes and clothing are selectively sampled and then redefined. Tabloid newspapers, far from being sources of dominant ideology, are challenges to 'the power-bloc' of elite sources, ideas and institutions which dominate public news discourse.

Thus, the audience-consumer view of commodified and promotional culture in advanced market-oriented societies offers a rather more positive vision. Goods and texts of all varieties are open to reappropriation by active consumers. Reception and consumption are not simply passive occupations that use up things but are also productive and creative activities. The commodities of capitalist production can be decommodified and used in many ways: for pleasure, personal guidance, individual identity formation and social relations, and in resistance and opposition. Both producers and promotional intermediaries have rather less influence over consumers than they would like to think.

Reappraising the consumer-audience position

In this final section the consumer-audience perspective is itself critically re-evaluated. Some objections are long-running, such as the rising influence of the 'cultural turn' or the over-idealistic impression of oppositional audiences. More recent critiques have asked just what it means to be a consumer and have begun deconstructing the notion of the 'consumer society' itself.

One key line of objection concerns the overstated nature of cultural and political resistance. Many leading audience-consumer researchers, although not all, have acknowledged the limits of individual autonomy as well as a background sense of producer power. Miller (1987: 175) explains that only some goods are open to 'reappropriation', under 'certain circumstances' and among particular 'segments of the population'. He also makes clear that consumer 'recontextualization' should not be confused with 'resistance'. Morley (1996: 291) writes, with respect to audience reception: 'The power of viewers to reinterpret meanings is hardly equivalent to the discursive power of centralised media institutions.' Lury (2004) insists that the interactive exchange between producers and consumers is 'asymmetrical', being balanced clearly in favour of producers.

Critics (Williamson, 1986; Curran, 1990; McGuigan, 1997; Slater, 1997) have been rather more forthright in their condemnation of the 'over-romanticized' view of consumers. They argue that demonstrating polysemy does not equate to disproving that texts are full of 'dominant' or 'preferred' meanings. As Williamson remarked (1986: 14): 'Madonna appeals to young girls' desires to be sexy and important but that doesn't mean I think she is revolutionary.' McGuigan (1997) objected to the notion of the all-powerful 'sovereign consumer' inherent in 'cultural populism'. He condemned the excesses of writers such as Willis and Fiske, equating their positions to neo-liberal economist accounts of markets and market participants. Similar counter-claims have been made about digital media's empowerment of individuals (Andrejevic, 2002; Turrow, 2009; Fuchs, 2011; Winseck, 2011; Curran et al., 2012). Large media and promotional conglomerates continue to dominate the structures, content and traffic flows of the Web. Online architectures and user-oriented and interactive sites are still predominantly commercial creations geared to selling. Individual net freedoms in mature democracies are usually exploited for social rather than political activities. They also come at a cost to personal privacy, as movements and activities are tracked and recorded.

More recently, a counter-thesis has emerged that suggests that capitalism has become expert at socially absorbing and neutralizing opposition. All too easily, cultural resistance has been assimilated in the postwar era as capitalism has reinvented itself. Boltanski and Chiapello (2007) returned to a long-running question of (post-) Marxists: How do the majority of the population, who gain unequally from capitalism, put up with it? They sought the answers in a study comparing management texts from the 1960s and the 1990s which documented the evolving 'moral' philosophies of the managerial class in their justification of capitalist production. These directed business behaviours to adapt in ways that marginalized, split and confused critics. So, for example, discourses supporting more autonomy and freedom of choice for worker-consumers have justified increasing casualization of the workforce and the scaling back of the state and labour rights. As such, Boltanski and Chiapello's thesis presents a contemporary advance on Gramsci's previous writing on hegemony (see Gramsci, 1988).

Such a thesis has been developed also in relation to promotional and popular culture in several accounts (Frank, 1997; Klein, 2000; Heath and Potter, 2006; McGuigan, 2009). These record the strategic reappropriation of antagonistic cultures by the advertising and cultural industries. According to Frank (1997), Madison Avenue advertisers knowingly tapped into the 1960s counter-culture. They began to sell goods with appeals to rule-breaking, defiance and mockery of the establishment. This co-optation of oppositional culture has since become a common strategy in contemporary advertising (see Goldman and Papson, 1998; Leiss et al., 2005). For McGuigan (2009: 1), capitalism has rebranded itself as 'cool'. It sells itself and its wares within promotional frames that convey street sense, cynicism and dissent: 'Cool capitalism is the incorporation of dissatisfaction into capitalism itself.' In effect, counter-culture movements have popularized dissent but distracted attention away from more fundamental political and economic criticisms of capitalism. Mocking the system has replaced substantive challenges to it.

A second line of critique highlights the impact of the consumer society on consumers as workers. 'Sovereign consumers', unless born into wealth, must also be subaltern employees. Consumer freedoms and choices often impose considerable restraints on working conditions. As Klein (2000) pointed out, privileged Western consumers get to consume relatively low-priced clothes, but only because workers in developing economies are paid less than a dollar a day to make them. Ehrenreich (2001) made a similar point when personally adopting and documenting the working life of those employed in cafes, supermarkets and cleaning jobs in the US. Such workers, she noted, were poorly treated, had few rights, and rarely had the surplus capital to spend on consumption, even when working two jobs. Ritzer (1998, 2004) confirmed that many Fordist/Taylorist aspects of production and labour control are very much alive in the McDonaldized leisure and fast-food industries of the twenty-first century. Sennett (2006: 2) similarly documents the erosion of employment security and working conditions among middle-class professionals. Employees have to change jobs and careers with greater frequency, and struggle to build up strong social ties and 'craftsmanship' in their occupations: 'The fragmentation of big institutions has left many people's lives in a fragmented state: the places they work more resembling train stations than villages.' As Bauman (2005, 2007) observes, the pay and conditions of developed, consumer-led economies are increasingly seen as a hindrance to competitiveness and profits. Their response is to cut wages and jobs. Ironically, this undermines the same demand-led economic model that drives the consumer society.

Such developments add further support to those who argue that the 'consumer society' is an unsustainable system whose historical zenith has already passed. In Lears's estimation (1994: 11), its high point was probably reached in the 1970s. Thereafter, the balance between production and consumption tilted against consumers as companies began moving their operations abroad in search of cheap labour: 'Without a well-paid working population, mass consumption could no longer serve as the integrative glue of civil society.'

Lears's view, in 1994, has clearly been borne out by developments. Real wages, for a large proportion of the working population, have stagnated in recent decades (see Chang, 2010; CBO, 2011) – a fact hidden by cheaper consumer goods, property bubbles and consumer credit. The creation and distribution of credit, which so encouraged the rise of the consumer society, has also enabled it to be artificially sustained. Total private debt in the UK rose from £570 billion in 1997 to £1,511 billion in 2007. In the US it rose from $5,547 billion in 1997 to $14,374 billion in 2007 (Turner, 2008: 26, 71). Increased personal and 'pleasurable' consumption has also led to a steady rise in obesity, smoking and alcohol-related diseases (Shlosser, 2002; Wilson and Pickett, 2009).

The consumer society has also proved unsustainable at the national and global levels. For some years, environmental campaigners, scientists and heterodox economists have concluded that economies based on growth and consumption are self-destructive in the long term. Fossil fuels and other natural resources are finite. Continued environmental impacts, such as global warming, are a significant threat to both human life and economies (Gore, 2006; Monbiot, 2006; Stern, 2007; Jackson, 2011). Since 2008, it has also become clear that the consumer societies of wealthy Western nations were in fact built on a financial mirage. Financial engineering, clever national accounting and market bubbles all covered over the significant growth of global trade imbalances and national debts (Krugman, 2008; Turner, 2008; Elliott and Atkinson, 2009; Stiglitz, 2010; UNCTAD, 2009). Nations such as China have produced and exported more than they have consumed. Others, such as the US and the UK, have done the reverse. Formerly wealthy countries, such as Iceland, Ireland, Greece and Portugal, have become effectively bankrupted (see chapter 10). The national debts of the US and Japan, the first and third largest economies, as well as of the Eurozone, continue to mount, with no obvious economic solution in sight.

Third, there has developed a body of literature that has asked just how autonomous or rational consumers are. As several authors suggest, the concept of consumption, and all that it implies, is in need of deconstruction (Wernick, 1991; Strasser, 2003; Bauman, 2007; McGuigan, 2009). Strasser (2003) and Hochschild (2003; Hochschild and Machung, 1997) look at how modern cultures of consumption have steadily reclassified women's work in the home as 'non-work'. For Strasser (2003), promotional culture has come to present home appliances as 'convenience' consumer goods which have liberated housewives. In many other ways, leisure and consumption have been consciously separated from work but, increasingly, both involve work. Fast-food restaurants have trained customers to clear their own tables. Utilities companies and banks expect home dwellers to read their own meters, print their own forms, and pay their bills through automated phone and online systems. Consumers have to book and print off their own cinema and airline tickets and locate the answers to their problems through labyrinthine websites and phone systems. 'Crowdsourcing' invites consumers to test products and supply knowledge to producers for free. In effect, consumption, designated as non-work, now often includes elements of unpaid consumer labour to cover what was originally done by producer employees.

Consumption is made productive and profitable for producers in other ways. Jhally and Livant (1986) noted that watching television could also be considered 'work'. Individuals were forced to watch adverts and were paid with entertainment. This notion has been actively extended in the era of digital information and branding. Media companies encourage freely supplied user- or consumer-generated content, fill their space with it, and then charge advertisers and users to access it. To engage fully with reality and talent television shows requires paying to vote for preferred candidates. So much of what individuals do in advanced economies is now logged in cross-referencing databases (Andrejevic, 2002; Lyon, 2007; Bauman, 2007; Turrow, 2011). What began with the recording and analysis of bank transactions has moved to the purchasing habits of consumers as they shop with credit and store cards, in person and online. Such information is collected, aggregated, used in marketing and production decisions, and sold on to others. Marketing activities, which previously were voluntary, and paid consumers are increasingly involuntary, unpaid and a source of additional producer profit.

By the same token, consumers engage in 'immaterial labour' in the way they unconsciously promote goods and services and participate in brand-building (Lury, 2004; Arvidsson, 2006; Bauman, 2007). As Lury (2004) and Moor (2007) explain, trademark and copyright law has enabled corporations to take ownership of brands and commercially exploit them at the expense of consumers. For Arvidsson (2006: 35), both brand producers and consumers contribute to the 'general intellect' which nurtures brands, but 'it is this excess productivity that brand management seeks to appropriate'. Wearing and using branded goods, from Levi's and Louis Vuitton to Apple and Aston Martin, not only signifies something about the user, it also advertises and promotes the brand. Participating in fan websites for television series, film and music managed by entertainment producers spreads brands across multi-media platforms (see Baltruschat, 2011; Gillan, 2011). Consumers thus contribute to the building and sustenance of brands that producers then own and utilize. Indeed, 'brand equity' is now estimated to make up a large proportion of the value of companies such as Coca-Cola and McDonald's (see Lindemann, 2009). Brands are then used to sell new goods, licensed out to multiple franchise operations to sell more goods, and employed in cross-promotional branding to sell other goods (Meehan, 1991; Lury, 2004; Epstein, 2005; Hardy, 2010).

Finally, in work and leisure, the promotional consumer society encourages individuals personally to adopt and internalize the practices of promotion. Some years ago, Hochschild (1983) explored how service companies exploit the 'emotional labour' of their employees. Flight attendants have to adopt certain mannerisms, verbal lines and cognitive cues as well as uniforms and practical procedures. This process works to manage personal employee behaviour while on the job and as part of the service to clients. More recently, Bauman (2007) has argued that the dual acts of consumption and promotion now extend to the individual consumer (see also Wernick, 1991). In order to participate in consumer society it is necessary to turn oneself into a promotional commodity. One selects clothes and other goods not only to establish a sense of identity, but also to promote the 'commodity-self' to others. Social networking sites, online dating and modern CVs sell and circulate the self. They make private emotions, confessions and tastes open to public scrutiny and consumption. 'Commodity fetishism' has been joined by 'subjectivity fetishism'. Thus, as Bauman concludes (2007: 6), individuals are, 'simultaneously, promoters of commodities and the commodities they promote. They are at the same time, the merchandise and their marketing agents . . . recast themselves as commodities.'

Critics pose a series of questions which undermine several key elements of the consumer-audience perspective. Resistance is limited, 'over-romanticized' and easily absorbed by evolving modes of capitalism. Consumer society reshapes the employment conditions of consumers themselves, often in problematic ways. It is a wasteful and unsustainable mode of socio-economic system, reliant on finite resources and financial manipulation. Non-work and leisure activities associated with consumption increasingly involve real work. Personal forms of emotional and immaterial labour are freely exploited. To these ends, promotional culture benefits producers over consumers and promotes not just commodities, but 'false' ways of thinking about work, labour, leisure and consumption.

Conclusion

Ultimately, it was always necessary to reinsert the consumer-audience back into social, industrial and promotional history. Individual needs and wants have always influenced socio-economic systems. Critical assumptions about top-down forms of cultural and communicative control and passive, accepting audiences were too simplistic. Promotional culture cannot work simply through manipulation and propaganda. However, at the same time, consumer-audiences are not as 'free', 'individual' and 'active' as the promotional industries and consumer-audience scholars like to argue. The consumer society has many negative consequences. It is unsustainable at an individual, a society and a global level.

4
Texts: Situating the Text in Promotional Culture

Introduction

This chapter discusses promotional texts and their place in established promotional societies. Such texts provide the communicative links between message producers and audience consumers. In so doing, they also link the linguistic to the social and the symbolic to the material. However, the nature of those links and how to categorize and analyse promotional texts are topics of considerable debate between conflicting camps of scholars.

The chapter is in six parts. The first looks at the alternative methods used for analysing texts. This is important as so many discussions of promotional texts rely on quite different methods of analysis, meaning debates are based as much on method as on conceptual approach. The next four parts sketch out distinct conceptual approaches for situating promotional texts within society. These are industry-applied forms of analysis, which treat texts as autonomous reflections of the social; critical forms of textual analysis, from (post-)Marxist to feminist, which see the symbolic as being in the service of material power; audience and readerly conceptions, which see texts as co-constructions of both producers and audiences; and postmodern accounts, which elevate the symbolic over the material and human social relations. A final, sixth part pushes the case for texts to be situated, once again, within the material conditions of their construction.

Before continuing, it is useful to clarify what exactly constitutes a promotional text. Clearly, almost anything (Barthes, 1973 [1957]; Dyer, 1986; Baudrillard, 1988b; Wernick, 1991; Bauman, 2007) – physical, cultural, virtual or human – can be classed as a text with promotional qualities. Stars and celebrities are presented in multiple public, promotional texts (chapter 7). Ordinary people present themselves outwardly in CVs, social networking sites and in their branded choices of goods (chapter 3). Basic commodities, organizations, ideas and buildings are sold in sign-rich packages (chapter 5). News, 'fact-based' reports, and popular music and culture can all contain promotional information (chapter 6). Thus, everything can be treated as a text with promotional as well as basic communicative qualities.

This point aside, the following discussion is concerned primarily with text-based studies of promotion. The majority of these focus on overtly promotional texts, usually in advert form, and promotionally influenced texts, mainly in the form of PR-influenced news. Such works will provide most of the examples in this chapter. However, it is worth noting that analyses of promotional texts have also been conducted on political posters, manifestos and speeches (Wernick, 1991; Hall Jamieson, 1996; Ansolabehere and Iyengar, 1995; Fairclough, 2000; Krzyzanowski and Oberhuber, 2007). So, too, analyses have deconstructed music videos (Jhally, 1987; Kellner, 1995), business management publications and financial documents (Davis, 2002; Boltanski and Chiapello, 2007) and the promotional materials of charities, NGOs and other non-profit groups (Wernick, 1991; Goddard, 1998; Sireau, 2009).

Methodological differences in analysing promotional texts

Discussions about promotional texts may be as occupied with methodological approaches as about actual content or significance. Thus, how promotional texts are sampled, collected and analysed may also have a strong bearing on the arguments made. A range of methods have been developed, drawing on a mix of linguistic, anthropological and cultural studies disciplines. Three common approaches are discussed here: quantitative content analysis, semiotics and discourse analysis. One point of consensus is that there is no consensus, not even within clearly distinguishable traditions. Thus, semioticians are split between the alternative works of Saussure, Peirce and others. In Chandler's (2002) opinion, 'Semiotics involves no widely agreed theoretical assumptions, models, or empirical methodologies.' Discourse analysis (DA) is similarly divided. Barker (2008: 152) describes the field of discourse analysis as 'a motley domain, made up of scholars who probably cannot agree on any fundamental definitions'.

He outlines seven different broad approaches to DA. Each of these seven is also split. Wodak and Meyer (2009: 5), writing about one of these – critical discourse analysis (CDA) – state: 'CDA has never been and has never attempted to be or to provide one single or specific theory. Neither is one specific methodology characteristic.' Thus the summary descriptions that follow are, of necessity, broad brush.

The least contested but narrowest method used is quantitative content analysis. Large quantities of adverts or news texts are sampled and coded according to defined parameters. Words, images, settings, human characteristics, key phrases, sources, physical placement and other elements are recorded to produce an account of the promotional corpus under investigation. For example, Jhally (1987) sampled 1,000 adverts from US network prime-time and sports-time periods. He recorded percentages of product and person types, lifestyles, values and interpersonal relations. Herman and Chomsky (1988) calculated the percentages of articles covering particular topics in the *New York Times*'s coverage of elections in Central America. Davis (2002) recorded the source types cited and key arguments used in 425 financial news articles during a corporate takeover. Frith and her colleagues (2005) coded and counted eight distinct 'beauty types' in 1,236 adverts in fashion magazines in three countries over a fourteen-month period. Choices of samples, coding frames and what is counted can themselves be quite subjective. However, such work pays greater attention to social science methods, such as sampling and working to clear coding frameworks.

Qualitative approaches tend to be far more complex, jargon-ridden and diverse (Chandler, 2002; Barker, 2008; Wodak and Meyer, 2009). In many classic studies, sampling is unused, as adverts and news texts are chosen strategically or for convenience. There is little adherence to methodological principles, such as representativeness, triangulation and reproducibility. That said, more contemporary qualitative research is likely to pay greater attention to these guidelines, make clearer decisions about the 'corpus' studied, and supplement analysis with quantitative and computer-aided tools (see, for example, Fairclough, 2000; Leiss et al., 2005).

The most common approach, frequently applied to analyses of visual adverts, is semiotics. This linguistic approach builds on the work of Saussure (1974 [1916]) and/or C. S. Peirce (1931–58). Barthes's early creative application of semiotics to adverts, among other forms of culture (1973 [1957], 1970, 1977), is also considered a key step. Semiotics offers a series of conceptual tools with which to discuss the composite images and meanings constructed in advertising. Its breakdown and categorization of language, mental concepts and linguistic relationships has a particular appeal when it comes to deconstructing how adverts operate. Semioticians study 'signs' and 'sign systems'. Signs are made up of 'signifiers' – the form the sign takes, be it visual, aural, written or material – and 'signifieds' – the mental construct.

The signifier of an apple may be the physical apple, a photograph or picture of an apple, the word 'apple' or the sound we hear when 'apple' is pronounced. Any of those signifiers has an associated mental image of an apple. Signification links the two, thus producing meaning. Saussure's original work emphasized the structural relationship between the two parts of the sign, as well as showing little interest in the material object itself. However, it is the fluidity (or 'arbitrariness') of signifier–signified relationships, as well as material–symbolic links, which have drawn more contemporary analysts of advertising to semiotics. Clearly, 'apple' has many signifiers and many signifieds. There is a generic, fairly stable link around forms and mental constructs of apples but, at the same time, there can be infinite variation too.

Within semiotics, sign relationships may be described and analysed in various ways. One useful categorization separates them into 'symbolic' (arbitrary), 'iconic' (bearing close resemblance) and 'indexical' (most 'natural') in relation to their 'referent' (object). If the physical apple is the referent, a photograph of a plain apple is indexical. Simple drawings of apples or their outlines are iconic. The apple logo used by Apple Inc., or an image of Adam and Eve and their forbidden apple, is something more symbolic. Promotional culture, as a process, can be seen to transform the status of signs in ways that make the 'iconic' or 'symbolic' appear more 'indexical'. It is also argued that promotional culture has shifted the balance of signs from a period of 'indexical' predominance to one of 'symbolic' hegemony. Apples probably remain more indexical than symbolic, although, that said, Apple electrical goods are so prevalent now that when the word 'apple' is uttered many people may just as well be referring to the good or the company. Just try Googling 'apple'.

In Peirce's work, all signs can also be classified according to their degree of 'modality' – i.e., their proximity to reality. Signs can never be an exact substitute for things, but there is considerable variation in their approximation to what they represent. Once again, promotional culture has a tendency to create signs with a lower 'truth value' while also presenting the appearance of reality – i.e., creating a sort of mock or pseudo-modality. Apple shampoo or shower gel conjures up notions of nature, thus disguising the unnatural chemicals used to create and package it. Adverts for apple shampoo may well be set in nature. Similarly, texts rely on associational relationships between words or signs. Signs contain meaning that is both 'denotative' ('literal', 'naturalized' or 'common sense') and 'connotative' (of a socio-cultural, emotional or ideological nature). Once again, promotional activity increases the overlap between these two while also making connotation appear as denotation. The naturalness of apple shower gel is connotation presented as denotation. Language more generally relies on 'tropes', 'metaphors', interpretive 'codes' and 'intertextuality', all of which may be altered significantly by the practices of promotional culture. Each of these concepts has been applied in several classic deconstructions of advertising (Williamson, 2002 [1978]; Jhally, 1987; Goldman, 1992; Leiss et al., 2005; Danesi, 2006).

Discourse analysis (DA) is also commonly used to investigate promotional and promotionally influenced texts. The strands and inspirations of DA draw most often from linguistics but also are more diverse. They include conversation analysis (Garfinkel, 1967; Goffman, 1967; Sacks, 1972), discursive psychology (Potter and Wetherell, 1987; Potter, 1996), critical discourse analysis (CDA) (Fairclough, 1991, 1995; van Dijk, 1987, 2008) and Foucauldian theory (Foucault, 1971, 1975, 1980; Said, 1980; Tagg, 1988). Forms of DA are applied most often to language and written texts rather than to visual ones. Its varied adherents are distinguished from traditional linguistics, and push further than semiotics, in emphasizing the social situatedness of language. Language may be the object of study, but it is clear that discourse reflects social relations, interactions and institutional practices. Any analysis of language, its concepts, transformations and omissions, is taken to be representative of the (often unconscious) understandings, behaviours and identities of those producing the texts.

Discourse analysis offers its own conceptual tool-kit and language with which to break down and interrogate texts. Key to much DA is a desire to highlight 'manifest' and 'latent' meanings in texts, to uncover the 'normalizing discourses' or 'mystifying ideologies' of society. In this respect, studies investigate 'rhetorical devices' such as 'metaphors' and 'metonymy', 'mental modalities' or 'interpretive frames'. Particular elements, such as narratives, genres, modes of address and the use of key words, are highlighted. Like semiotics, such concepts appear very useful for deconstructing adverts, speeches, promotional texts and promotionally influenced texts.

Cook (2001, 2004) uses such tools to investigate broadcast adverts and the conflicting promotional discourses around GM crops. Goffman's (1979) study of adverts breaks down and categorizes gender relationships, arguing that the 'frames' of constructed adverts reflect their wider social structure. Dyer (1982), Brierly (1995) and Myers (1999) similarly deconstruct the communicative apparatus of adverts using DA-style tools. More critical users of DA (CDA or Foucauldian) have revealed the dominant, latent discourses of politics and news. Thus, Fairclough (2000) uncovered the wider and not always compatible discourses of Tony Blair's New Labour. Kantola's studies of the *Financial Times* (2006, 2009) revealed the dominant discursive frames of its global economic elite sources.

Texts as autonomous reflections

The next four sections sketch out ways of interpreting promotional texts and situating them in society. The first of these interrogates and evaluates texts on the basis of their being able to reflect, or speak to, the 'innate human condition'. The text itself is given a certain autonomy, to be studied independently as one would a piece of art or a new car design. Comparisons are made, but only with other similar texts, and on the basis of human reflection or technical mastery. Normative judgements, questions of power and wider social processes tend to be absent. Such approaches can be found in several linguistic, literary critical and anthropological studies. They are also common in typical industry case studies of advertising and journalist accounts of 'reflective' news media.

Traditional forms of literary criticism (see Selden and Widdowson, 1993) focused purely on literary texts as discrete entities. Russian Formalists or Anglo-American New Critics assumed that authors were autonomous and that universal human truths existed. High art was that which tapped into and revealed such truths. Such approaches to analysing public texts, from film to music, remain typical of media critics of popular culture.

Anthropologists and sociologists too have sought to observe and record texts as being indicative of social structures and communication in natural settings (e.g., Lévi-Strauss, 1972; Garfinkel, 1967; Goffman, 1967). It is in such a vein that Erving Goffman's (1979) analysis of 508 advertising stills was conducted. Goffman focused on the presentation of gender roles and relations, recording distinct differences, such as in professions depicted, subordinate postures adopted, family compositions and body parts shown. From these he concluded that, 'ritually speaking, females are equivalent to subordinate males and both are equivalent to children' (ibid.: 5). He made it clear that such adverts were 'displays' of a ritual or ceremonial nature, a series of 'make-believe scenes', understood by both posing models and viewing audiences. Scenes were clearly unnatural and models were 'slimmer, younger, taller, blonder' than in real life (1979: 21). However, Goffman also argued that the behaviours depicted were indicative of actual gender relations, only to exaggerated extremes: 'If anything, advertisers conventionalize our conventions, stylize what is already stylization' (ibid.: 84). In effect, his account highlights gender inequality in advertising, but he is not overly critical of such a 'natural' state of affairs. Interestingly, his work has provided evidence and inspiration for more questioning feminist critiques of advertising that have followed since.

Few other studies make such clear social statements. However, many do analyse adverts in terms of their ability to reflect widely recognized human traits and psychological dispositions. Brierly (1995), Goddard (1998), Myers (1999), Cook (2001) and Danesi (2006) approach their discussions of advertising texts and brands in such a way. Each acknowledges the importance of the social and the audience but chooses to dissect adverts technically, as autonomous objects. For Brierly, ads can be categorized by their psychological appeal: 'reason why', 'atmosphere', 'USP' (unique selling point). Danesi talks of a natural 'taxonomy of human needs' and suggests that brands are more successful if they score highly on a 'connotative index' (CI). A high CI has greater 'psychological force'. So, certain letters, such as 'X', geometrical forms, images and words have a greater CI value and thus a greater psychological pull. Myers (1999) and Cook (2001) reveal how commodity promotion appeals to classic human values, such as family, national and local traditions, romance and marriage. Wrigley's gum and Levi's 501s have both exploited such appeals in long-running series of adverts.

Each of these authors (see also Dyer, 1982) offers detailed breakdowns of the components, linguistic tools and structures of adverts on such a basis. These often start with categorizations according to genre, medium, product type or consumer type. Formal promotional strategy also distinguishes adverts – for example, 'hard sell', 'soft sell', 'reason and tickle', 'heritage' or 'constructed ordinariness'. Each reveals how adverts make their appeals by creating associations, symbolism and connotative meanings, which are then re-presented as indexical or denotative meaning. To that end, a number of key rhetorical and visual devices are used: props, settings, modes of address, stereotypes, slogans, metaphors, rhymes, graphic models, and so on. Key words and phrases are routinely drawn upon. By such means, particular desirable human traits, such as wealth, love, power and luxury, come to be coupled with particular products. Brands come to be associated and built around broader sets of human appeals and lifestyles. Such studies and dissections are, in effect, more academic (or abstract) versions of what happens in the advertising industry itself. Annual award ceremonies and industry textbooks offer case studies revealing the hows and whys of successful advertising campaigns.

Reflectionist accounts of news texts follow a similar analytical logic. These see news as presenting a mirror of the world as it really is, in terms of events, people and presentation. Through various means, professional, 'public journalism' (see Gans, 1979; Glasser, 1999; Lichtenberg, 2000; Zelizer, 2004) has developed procedures and values for selecting stories according to 'the public interest'. News itself is made up of topics and sources guided by universal 'news values' (Galtung and Ruge, 1965; Tunstall, 1971; Gans, 1979; Tiffen, 1989). Even though these accounts are written in different time periods and countries, there appears considerable overlap in such values. Many thus conclude that they transcend the preferences and attitudes of individual journalists. 'Professional' news comes to reflect wider society in terms of agendas, information sources and opinions.

Critical analyses of texts and power

Critics, mainly (post-)Marxists and critical discourse analysts, conceptualize texts quite differently. Mass-produced texts do not reflect society or the human condition. Instead, they disseminate versions of reality that reinforce the power of particular classes, dominant groups and institutions. They also subjugate the 'other' – the other being defined variously by class, gender, ethnicity, sexual orientation and nation. Thus, promotional texts and promotionally influenced texts are never entirely independent of their powerful producers and sources. Their function is to persuade, influence, mystify and distract on levels well beyond the mere selling of particular goods. At a symbolic level, they contribute to larger ideologies and discourses which, in turn, support the real, material basis on which power and inequality are maintained.

Marxist forms of literary criticism offer a long tradition of textual analysis along such lines (e.g., Althusser, 1971; Benjamin, 1970; Adorno and Horkheimer, 1979 [1947]; Lukacs, 1972). Debates were often concerned with the question of whether modern literature conveyed or exposed dominant ideology, class inequalities and relations of production. Other critical traditions also drew on literature and historical texts to make their points. Foucault (1971, 1975, 1979) documented the normalizing discourses that developed about madness, sexuality and crime in early modern European nations. Said (1980) did the same in his study of 'Orientalist' Western discourses about Eastern 'others'. Feminist literary criticism (e.g., Millett, 1970; Barrett, 1980; Moi, 1985) similarly interrogated patriarchy and 'phallocentrism' in literature, as well as the total omission of women from literary canons.

These same themes are frequently explored in critical studies of advertising. Starting with (post-)Marxist accounts, it is often revealed how advertising obscures relations of production with tropes of nature. For Williamson (2002 [1978]: 11, 19), advertising is all about the mystification of true relations. Adverts create their own 'ad worlds', 'seemingly separate from the material', but 'clearly ideological systems'. The technologies and manufacturing processes that underpin commodity production are disguised by 'referent systems' based on 'nature' and 'the natural'. Thus 'Ideology functions by misrepresenting our relationships to the means of production: and advertisements . . . show us our "natural" relationship to that revealed' (ibid.: 136). Barthes (1973 [1957]), too, deplores the 'ideological abuse' inherent in presentations of 'naturalness' in mass culture. He deconstructs how the chemical and abrasive condition of the detergents Persil and Omo is disguised with appeals to 'whiteness', 'purity' and 'care' and, at the same time, their manufacture by the multinational company Unilever is covered over.

Adverts also legitimate and disguise real corporate activities and behaviours by an appeal to enduring human values, desires and narratives. For Goldman (1992: 2, 100), adverts reaffirm the 'ideological supremacy of commodity relations' with such associations. So companies such as McDonald's and Kodak explicitly link their products to the maintenance of 'family integrity', or 'continuity' with idealized 'community' or history. The irony is that large corporations are also implicated in the erosion of such social relations. Thus 'McDonald's seizes upon anxieties stimulated by separation and isolation, and implies these can be annulled and overcome through consumption of McDonald's as a commodifying sign.' Goldman and Papson (1998) make a similar point in their analysis of Nike. Nike's adverts and other promotional material have consciously created a 'recognizable philosophy'. This includes both a self-mocking attitude to corporations and an appeal to social issues such as US inner-city deprivation. Such a public promotional philosophy is in direct contradiction to their anti-social corporate practices (see also Klein, 2000).

Gender exploitation is another key theme revealed in critical textual analyses of advertising. Particular female body shapes and roles, at work and at home, are overly emphasized, reinforcing unequal gender relations. Dyer (1982: 109, 124) recorded that women, although accounting for 41 per cent of the workforce, made up only 13 per cent of working characters in UK advertising. Women generally appeared in home settings, particularly in the kitchen and bathroom, while men appeared in business or outdoor settings. Dyer, Berger (1972) and Goldman (1992) each noted that women are often represented by particular body parts or as 'decorative, passive objects'. Berger (1972: 47) contended that adverts, drawing on art tropes, automatically presented women as objects to be observed by men: 'men act and women appear. Men look at women. Women watch themselves being looked at.' Goldman (1992: 113) argues that many adverts link their products to female empowerment, but only through a process of self-objectification: 'A seemingly paradoxical claim, regularly made in consumer adverts, has women enhancing their social and economic power vis-à-vis men by presenting themselves as objects of desire.'

Critical studies of new content suggest that news does not evenly reflect society but is instead a reflection of daily news-gathering practices and powerful promotional source influences. They reveal how certain source types, usually in governments and corporations, have greater access and more beneficial presentations. News agendas, story frames and narratives remain advantageous to them. Such critiques have been applied often to the case of war coverage. Herman and Chomsky's (1988) 'propaganda model' looked at US news coverage of conflicts and elections in war-torn Central America and South-East Asia. Their analysis suggested that US government influence over reporting, even in the *New York Times* and the *Washington Post*, resulted in news agendas and frames that promoted US foreign policy objectives. This supported US military actions abroad, legitimized administrations and elections favoured by the US administration, and de-legitimized those it did not. Lewis's (2004) survey of UK media content in 2003 found that most news reproduced claims of the 'possible' or 'likely' existence of 'weapons of mass destruction' in Iraq: 89 per cent of references to the subject 'assumed their probable existence' (see also Kull et al., 2004). More recently, Herman and Peterson (2011) analysed US coverage of the 2009 election in Iran. They found, contrary to many independent international reports showing a clear victory for Ahmadinejad, that the large majority of coverage framed the story as a 'rigged' or 'fraudulent' election. Once again, this was in line with US foreign policy.

Industry, finance and the economy is another subject area where critical content analysis of news texts has been applied. The early work of the Glasgow University Media Group (GUMG, 1976, 1980, 1982) included an extensive textual analysis of the 'contours' of news coverage of UK industrial relations. The group found that such reporting focused on strikes, often in ways that presented trade unionists as unruly, unreasonable and violent. Conversely, managers and ministers were portrayed as rational, calm and reasonable. In the wider reporting frameworks applied to the British economy, excessive wage claims and union obstructionism were blamed for causing national economic decline. Kumar's (2007) account of the 1997 UPS (Union Parcel Service) workers' strike revealed similar issues around US news coverage of unions. Likewise, analysis of financial and business news has revealed how debates around finance, markets and globalization have been framed by corporate elite sources and interests. Davis (2000b), in his study of business news coverage of a 1995 corporate takeover, found that just 2.8 per cent of the 501 individuals cited came from outside the City. Subsequently, only 7.1 per cent of articles even mentioned the impact of the takeover on the 80,000 employees involved and only 4.2 per cent the impact on the millions of ordinary customers. Kantola's (2006) critical discourse analysis of *Financial Times* content found that its coverage of some thirty-two elections between 2000 and 2005 repeatedly backed candidates which supported pro-market reforms. It was critical of democracies, publics and leaders that did not (see also Durham, 2007; Kantola, 2009).

Fairclough's (2000) critical discourse analysis of New Labour's first years of government (1997–9) dissects the 'inner logic' of the party's 'third way' philosophy on conflict, markets and globalization. It draws on Tony Blair's speeches and a varied corpus of political texts, among them books, pamphlets, published government documents and news coverage. Key words make multiple appearances in the corpus: 'new' (609 times), 'reform' (143), 'business' (195), 'work' (383). These are then linked to frameworks which include such terms as 'justice', 'social', 'fairness' and 'rights'. In so doing,

New Labour drove an economic agenda favourable to free-market economics, free trade and globalization, while couching their presentations in more centre-left forms of rhetoric: 'New Labour . . . seek to achieve rhetorically what they cannot achieve (given their neo-liberal commitments) in reality – a reconciliation of neo-liberal "enterprise" with "social justice"' (2000: 16).

Audiences and open and writerly texts

A third tradition of textual analysis presents itself in clear opposition to the more determinist Marxist and CDA perspectives. This, to be found in strands of literary criticism, media studies and cultural studies, stresses the openness of texts and the potential for audiences to interpret them in multiple ways. As such it offers a direct challenge to structuralist semiotics and notions of dominant ideology or discourse. Instead, the emphasis is on readerly texts, fluid sign systems and negotiated codes.

Barthes, in *Mythologies* (1973 [1957]), was already hinting that signifiers and signifieds may not be so tightly or 'structurally' linked. Then, in his essay 'The Death of the Author' (1967, in Barthes, 1977), texts were presented as interim planes of meaning, reordered from the large stock of language and significations that had gone before. Authorship was diminished as work was reinterpreted by every new reader. Barthes then argued that texts could be more 'readerly', encouraging a passive, unchallenging reading, or more 'writerly', facilitating active readings and individual interpretations. Separately, in the late 1970s there emerged a body of 'reader-oriented theories' in literary criticism (Iser, 1978; Fish, 1980; Culler, 1981). These started with the view that texts do not have fixed, rigid interpretations. Each reader brings their own knowledge and conceptions to what they read, thus imposing their own meanings too.

In cultural studies, related work claimed that mass-produced, popular texts could be open and that audiences could be active interpreters of their contents. Hall (1973) argued that media texts are encoded with meaning during their construction, to be decoded at the point of reception. However, decoding does not reproduce what is encoded exactly. While there are 'dominant' or 'preferred' codes and readings, Hall stressed that recipients could also decode in 'negotiated' or 'oppositional' ways. Meanings in popular culture were thus far more open, rich and varied. Texts of all kinds were now to be thought of as 'polysemic', ever evolving in communication circuits and subject to 'extratextual determinants'. Such a conceptual framework came to be applied to many analyses of popular texts. Fiske and Hartley (1978) offered such readings of dance competitions, game shows, drama and news. Bennett and Woollacott (1987) looked at James Bond films and written texts. Such work became core to audience-oriented research, typified by Morley's work on the current affairs programme *Nationwide* (1980; see chapter 3).

The framework has also informed several studies of advertising texts. These criticize mass society interpretations of advertising as ideological manipulation and instead emphasize polysemy and the decoding skills of active audiences. Nava (1988, 1992, 1997) looked at advertising texts aimed at young people and the responses they stimulated. She argued that advert construction was fairly 'democratized' and 'fragmented', being influenced by multiple types of popular text, including art, cinema and music. Fowles (1996) too emphasized the creative tensions that are present during advertising construction (see also Kelly et al., 2005). Advert producers have to navigate through a number of conflicting actors and objectives. These are between clients and ad agencies, conveying information and being creative, promoting product functions and consumer appeals, words and visuals. They also contend with the uncontrollable associations of other texts. As Fowles concludes (1996: 9), 'All that advertisers can do is recondition the public's symbols and pray that consumers will supply agreeable meanings to the new creation.'

Just as the advertising encoding process is more conflicted and fragmented, so the possibilities for decoding are more open. Nava (1992; 1997: 45) and Crane (2000) argue that the so-called victims of advertising – youth, minorities and women – have become increasingly immune to advertising's commodity fetishism and identity stereotyping. In Nava's studies, advertisers were forced to acknowledge, within their own ads, that their teenage targets were 'knowing' and cynical about advertising itself (see also Leiss et al., 2005). She concluded that 'what emerges is much greater interpretive openness than the textual analyses allow'. Likewise, for Crane (2000), the promotion of contemporary women's clothing lifestyles is subject to 'hyper-segmentation', 'conflicted gender hegemonies' and 'a wider range of social identities'. This enables consumers to be more active interpreters.

Cronin (2000) and, to a lesser extent, Fowles (1996) tread a more mixed line. Both emphasize that dominant gender codes exist within advertising texts, but also that textual openness and actor reflexivity allow for flexible interpretation and change. Adverts do create gender stereotypes but are also subject to alternative readings. Cronin's (2000: 6) nuanced analysis of advertising texts weaves a way between the positions of 'consumer sovereignty' and 'passive victimhood'. Individuality and identity are ever works in progress, operating 'through contradictory frameworks of both identity and difference'. 'Subjects' are produced 'performatively' while engaging with, and interpreting, open texts. Cronin concludes, from her study of 270 French and British adverts (1987–95), that advertisers do conceptualize target audiences from 'imagined ideals' of demographic markets. Accordingly they construct gendered identity codes. However, these can be presented in more or less 'reflexive', 'literal' or 'ironic' coding formats. More ironic or reflexively coded adverts, which are more common in male-targeted ads, in turn, elicit greater consumer engagement and 'self-actualization'.

Poststructuralism, postmodernism and sign-saturated texts

Poststructuralist and postmodern approaches offer another analytical perspective on texts. Many of their advocates acknowledge core points made by critics of capitalism. Similarly, they share the audience-studies notion that textual construction and consumption are fluid processes. However, they also diverge considerably from both critical Marxist and audience positions. Many question both the normative basis of (post-)Marxist criticism and the notion of active, autonomous audiences. The audience is no more alive than the author. Instead they come to re-emphasize the predominance of the symbolic over the material, social norms and conscious actors. Texts, in aggregate, become dominant and autonomous but, at the same time, their individual communicative power is derivative, superficial and fleeting. Promotional culture has clearly contributed to an era of 'sign saturation' but, by repeatedly altering the links between signifiers and signifieds, so too, it has weakened individual signs, meanings and values.

There are several sets of ideas associated with the postmodern thesis (Lyotard, 1979; Foucault, 1980; Baudrillard, 1988b; Lash and Urry, 1987, 1994; Featherstone, 1991). One of these counters the foundations of modernist epistemology. The norms and values of modernity, like truth, equality, religion and progress, are no more than social and cultural constructions (Lyotard, 1979; Foucault, 1971, 1975, 1980). They are born of humanity's 'logocentric' tendencies. Likewise, Marxism, feminism, humanism and liberalism are grand 'meta-narratives' of modernity but have no 'innate' foundation or 'truth' in society. In effect, social and individual existence is without a natural foundation, having only a temporary and specific existence, operating in the service of power/knowledge.

A second set describes society transition from an industrial-material basis to a symbolic one. Advanced post-industrial (or post-Fordist) economies have become more decentralized, 'disorganized' and oriented towards consumption and the service industries (Lash and Urry, 1987; Harvey, 1989). The speed and variety of new communication technologies mean that social experience is subject to more rapid change and sense of 'time/space compression'. Contemporary societies, which have expanded media and promotional industries, are increasingly concerned with 'the production, circulation and consumption of "materials" that are cultural' (Crang, 1997: 4). There is thus a greater emphasis on the production of 'symbolic goods' and the 'aestheticization of everyday life' (Featherstone, 1991). All are increasingly drawn into a 'sign-saturated world' of fleeting significations and symbols. In total, this has resulted in a new 'economy of signs and spaces' (Lash and Urry, 1994).

Baudrillard (1983, 1988b) has written extensively about the symbolic consequences of postmodernity, as well as the part played by media and promotional culture. He strongly emphasized the dominance, over all else, of signs, and that there is no 'authenticity' in anything – identities, values, truths, social relations. In terms of production, he argued that 'symbolic value' and consumer-oriented society had come to subordinate both 'exchange value' and 'use value', as well as production generally (1976). Thus, goods and services of all kinds become desirable, not because they have a real use or financial value but because of what they symbolize. Over time, the emphasis on the symbolic has resulted in a perpetual churning out of temporary, superficial signs, indistinguishable from substantive, anchored signs, norms and values. For Baudrillard, in the postwar period, such an ongoing process has pushed society into the 'third order of simulacrum', whereby it becomes impossible to distinguish the 'real' from a 'hyperreal' world of endless 'simulations'. As he says, 'Disneyland is presented as imaginary in order to make us believe that the rest is real, when in fact all of Los Angeles and the America surrounding it are no longer real, but of the order of the hyperreal and of simulation' (1983: 25).

Baudrillard's work, as well as several parts of the postmodern thesis, has influenced several studies of promotional texts (Wernick, 1991; Kellner, 1995; Goldman and Papson, 1996, 1998; Lash and

Lury, 2007; Odih, 2007). Many of these authors focus on promotional culture's contribution to the transformation of capitalism and social relations. Wernick (1991) and Lash and Lury (2007) both describe the shift from material to cultural ascendancy. As Wernick states (1991: 185, vii), there is 'an alteration in the very relations between culture and economy', characterized by the hegemony of 'pan-promotionalism' over the 'economic base'. He analyses promotional texts in commodity advertising, politics and the university sector in order to trace such a transition. Lash and Lury (2007: 4, 6) similarly describe an industrial evolution towards a globalized, cultural dominance of the economic, an indeterminacy of objects and identities, and a shift from commodity to brands production: 'Culture is so ubiquitous that it, as it were, seeps out of the superstructure and comes to infiltrate, and then take over, the infrastructure itself . . . The commodity is dead; the brand is alive.' Over three years, they gathered a corpus of texts tracing seven 'cultural objects', including *Toy Story*, Nike, Swatch, global football and contemporary British art. They randomly 'followed' their objects, collecting visual and verbal texts to map their moving symbolic 'biographies' within what has become a 'virtual capitalism'. An analysis of advert stills through the twentieth century by Leiss and his colleagues (2005) shows such a trend empirically. Advertising steadily moves away from appeals to functional use value and towards increasingly abstract, symbolic values. Odih (2007) analyses a slightly longer period of advertising, tracing a similar shift. Ads begin with 'reason why', rational appeal frames and simple identity models. They slowly become texts characterized by the 'eclectic', 'parody', 'pastiche', the 'self-reflexive' and the 'inter-textual'.

These studies equally emphasize promotional culture's role in producing a state of sign-saturation and instability. Promotional culture facilitates an ever faster production–consumption cycle of consumer goods, continually attaching and then detaching an array of symbols, signs and associations. For Wernick (1991: 121), 'It is as if we are in a hall of mirrors. Each promotional message refers us to a commodity which is itself the site of another promotion. And so on, in an endless dance whose only point is to circulate the circulation of something else.' As Goldman and Papson (1996: 8) explain: 'Think of it [advertising] as a giant harvesting machine – but, instead of harvesting wheat, it harvests signifiers and signifieds/meaning . . . Advertising contributes in this way to a postmodern condition in which disconnected signs circulate at ever increasing rates, in which signifiers become detached from signifieds and reattached to still

other signifieds.' The texts of promotional culture thus become fragmented, endlessly derivative and referential, shallow, temporary and
meaningless.

Consequently, identity also becomes fragmented and destabilized.
Wernick traces how male gender roles in advertising texts have
shifted over time. As the labour market changed and gender relations
were altered, so adverts came to present multiple competing models
of maleness. Odih (2007) makes similar observations about shifting
female gender roles and identity. Kellner's (1995: 256) deconstruction of MTV videos and adverts observes multiple changing identity models and subject positions being offered to women. Modern
celebrities, from Madonna to Lady Gaga, offer the promise that individuals may always reconstruct themselves if they want. However,
such choices also add to ontological insecurity and instability: 'new
advertising campaigns undermine previously forged identities and
associations . . . and contribute to producing more unstable, fluid,
shifting, and changing identities in the contemporary scene.'

Texts and a return to the material, power and the ideological?

Audience and postmodern conceptions leave a view of promotional
texts as open, fragmented, free-floating, ever changing and superficial. Texts are part of a cultural-symbolic plane that holds sway over
the material but, at the same time, dilutes and erodes that plane. Such
a direction of travel either ignores or denies long-running concerns
with ideological/discursive control, material inequality and power.
Arguably, such issues have become more, not less, evident in our
sign-saturated times. This suggests that promotional texts should not
be so easily divorced from the material conditions in which they are
constructed, communicated and received. Even if they offer multiple,
fragmented codes and frames, and audiences can decode more freely,
texts have not entirely lost their discursive or ideological power.

In this respect, certain authors have attempted to retain elements
of both postmodern and critical thinking in their conceptualizing
of texts. For Harvey (1989) and Jameson (1991), postmodernity is
better reconceived as the 'cultural logic of late capitalism' (see also
Bauman, 2005, 2007). Kellner (1995: 9) agrees that postmodern
theory offers illuminating insights but also states that 'the claim
concerning a new postmodern rupture in society and history is exaggerated'. Goldman and Papson (1996, 1998), in particular, maintain
the links between promotion, the symbolic, power and the mate-

rial. Thus, modern advertising brings 'hypersignification' and 'self-reflexive hyperrealism' but is also part of a 'Hobbesian' 'sign war' between corporations. In their study of Nike's promotional texts, the material conditions in which the firm operates are clearly tied to the symbolic presentation of the company brand. Behind the Nike philosophy and image, there is a huge marketing budget and cynical production machine, exploiting labour conditions in developing economies and maximizing profits at home. As Goldman and Papson conclude (1998: 175): 'In a global cultural economy, economic growth is contingent upon the growth of sign value . . . physical labor is no longer the primary source of value in the consumer commodity.'

While culture may be becoming more fragmented, cultural production, including promotional text production, is more concentrated. In the last decade, just five conglomerates have come to control a majority of all popular media and communication formats in the US (Bagdikian, 2004). By the 1990s, just seven transnational promotional industry conglomerates (Interpublic, Publicis, WPP, Omnicom, Havas, Grey and Aegis) had control of 37.1 per cent of the worldwide market for producing and disseminating promotional texts (Leiss et al., 2005: 379). Similarly, demonstrating that promotional texts have become more symbolic, fragmented and contradictory is not the same as saying they have no coherence and share no common codes or dominant interpretive frames (see Corner, 1991; Kellner, 1995). At any specific time and place, there are strongly overlapping themes, models and associations present across multiple promotional texts. Aggregate sign convergence, even if temporary, can still generate mass responses and material consequences. If enough news texts reported 'weapons of mass destruction' in Iraq in 2003 or cast doubt on the science of human-made global warming, oppositional decodings have not proved particularly effective.

Underneath the symbolic, power and inequality continue to develop in very real material ways (Wilson and Pickett, 2009; Chang, 2010). In 2004, the fifty largest transnational corporations each had revenues greater than the GNPs (Gross National Product) of 133 UN member states (Willetts, 2008: 333). Those at the top of the production tree, owning or managing such conglomerates, have seen their earnings rise out of all proportion to those of the employees in their companies. In the 1950s the average American CEO was paid thirty-five times what the average worker was paid. By 2010 that had increased to 300 to 400 times as much. Between 1979 and 2006, the top 1 per cent of US earners increased their share of national wealth from 10 per cent to 22.9 per cent (figures in Chang, 2010: 144, 257).

According to Whittaker and Savage (2011), since the 1970s, the share of income growth of the bottom half of the UK population has steadily declined, reaching just 12 per cent in 2010 (or 10 per cent if bonuses are included).

Conclusion

There remain strong divides when it comes to deciding how to analyse promotional texts, what they represent, what their function (if any) is in society, and their links (if any) to power and the material. As argued here, promotional texts are not autonomous or neutral reflections of society. The links between mass-produced texts and the material conditions of their production, circulation and consumption cannot simply be bracketed out. As such, any analysis of texts, in isolation and without other data sources, can make only limited general claims about culture, audiences, producers or society. Similarly, thinking about power, be it discursive, symbolic or material, should not be excluded altogether. Promotional texts may have multiple influences in play during their construction. They may be fragmented and conflicted. They may be decoded in multiple, ever changing ways. However, they can still retain considerable discursive and symbolic force, which means they also have an influence on material power.

Part II

Commodities, Media and Celebrity

5
Commodities: Promotional Influences on the Creation of Stuff

Introduction

This chapter looks at the production and promotion of everyday commodities, from clothes and cars to cell phones and computers. By many accounts, the main reason the promotional industries emerged initially was to sell ordinary 'stuff'. Currently, the promotional professions still derive most of their income from (re)packaging and promoting new and old goods to consumers. This means promotional activities mediate between producers and consumers, both selling to consumers and returning feedback to producers (see chapters 2 and 3). A question less discussed in the literature is how promotional culture might influence the creation and manufacture of commodities themselves.

The majority of studies are concerned more with promotion's intermediary role between producers and consumers than they are with its influence on commodity production per se. 'Top-down' accounts of production, promotion and dissemination are juxtaposed with 'bottom-up' or 'collective behavioural' approaches. However, as this chapter argues, there is a third way of looking at promotional intervention in commodities markets. Drawing on work in economic sociology and cultural economy, it argues that promotional practices are also important for the shaping of corporations, industry fields and markets themselves. These influences, in turn, impact upon the production and dissemination of goods. Following the general discussion, the chapter presents more in-depth studies of markets in clothing fashions and hi-tech commodities. The final case study compares Apple and Microsoft.

Top-down and bottom-up perspectives on the creation and promotion of stuff

Where do mass market goods originate? How are their 'uses' established? How do commodity fashions rise and fall? What part, if any, is played by promotional culture in these questions? Broadly speaking, studies tend to take either a 'top-down' or a 'bottom-up' approach to promotion, commodity production and fashions. Both centre on producer–consumer relations and communication and tend to privilege one or the other. Promotion either persuades consumers or it feeds back their responses to producers.

Starting with top-down accounts, it is the wealthy who first attain new fashions, luxury items and the latest technological goods. They can afford these things before mass production lowers costs and expands distribution. In industrial history, trade and emerging technologies created new markets and commodity lines that initially serviced businesses and wealthy individuals. These outputs then would trickle down to larger consumer bases. Thus, in the seventeenth and eighteenth centuries, international traders brought back exotic new materials, foods and crafted products. At first these were only for the rich, but eventually, as trade expanded, they came to be part of everyday consumption (Bocock, 1993; Sassatelli, 2007). In the nineteenth and early twentieth centuries, specialist producers began producing more complex, manufactured goods. These slowly became more accessible to the emerging middle classes as large corporations used mass-production methods to lower costs (Lears, 1995; Marchand, 1998; Leiss et al., 2005). Henry Ford's top-selling Model T is the prime example. Car use was transformed, over a few decades, from being an elite hobby into a more widely used mode of transport.

Socio-historical accounts similarly recorded that new fashions and trends in clothing began with the wealthy. Veblen (1899) and Simmel (1904) both observed that it was they who became the patrons, arbiters and consumers of luxury goods, high culture and new fashions. Simmel (1904) observed high fashion as it emerged in eighteenth- and nineteenth-century France. Here, the rich, aided by sumptuary laws and independent couturiers, used new fashions to distinguish themselves from those of lower status. Even so, fashions trickled down. New lines of apparel became more widely recognized and affordable, and so came to be adopted by those lower down the social scale.

In many ways, modern commodity production is still a top-down affair, albeit for different reasons. The newest and most advanced commodity lines are bought first by the commercial sector or the wealthy, before eventually being made more widely available. In addition, market concentration and conglomeration, with many top-down centralizing features, are common in most product markets. The fashion industry provides one of many examples (Braham, 1997; McRobbie, 1998; Agins, 1999; Tungate, 2005). The largest fashion conglomerates and designer brands, such as LVMH and Ralph Lauren, have multi-billion dollar turnovers and controlling stakes in multiple brand-name companies. In 2010, LVMH had a turnover of €20 billion and employed over 83,000 people. Its holdings include Louis Vuitton, Givenchy, Loewe, Marc Jacobs, Donna Karan, Acqua di Parma, Tag Heuer, Le Bon Marché, Emilio Pucci and Fendi, among many others. The Arcadia Group in the UK owns Burton, Dorothy Perkins, Evans, Miss Selfridge, Topman, Topshop, Wallis and BHS, as well as having interests in Debenhams, Selfridges and House of Fraser. A relatively small number of multinational fashion houses and designers take up an estimated 80 per cent of the floor space of big stores and 80 per cent of the advertising and editorial space in the fashion press (Tungate, 2005: 64). Small, select groups of big-store buyers, editors and designers make all the important decisions each season. Their choices are then emulated by large producers, catering to mass consumer markets and supplying cheaper, more practical versions of what has recently appeared on the catwalks.

Promotional intermediaries have multiple roles in this top-down dissemination process. Promotion is employed by large producers to inform and/or manipulate consumers to buy goods. It also links networks of celebrities, elites, producers and journalists, who join forces to promote goods, one another and media to large groups of consumers. In effect, producers, cultural intermediaries and promotional professionals combine to reinforce a top-down system of commodity-sign production, promotion and distribution.

This top-down perspective is countered on several grounds. First, notions of top-down influence are harder to substantiate in the contemporary world (see chapter 3). Through the twentieth century, many of the foundations of capitalist production became less centred and more disorganized (Hall and Jacques, 1989; Harvey, 1989; Lash and Urry, 1987, 1994). The earlier class distinctions, which once strongly defined consumption patterns, are now negligible in most goods markets in wealthy economies (Blumer, 1969; Crane, 2000). Modern consumers are extremely media savvy and resistant to the content of advertising (Nava, 1992; Myers, 1999; Crane, 2000). There are multiple cultural and social influences on fashions and tastes from popular culture, social media, rival industries and nations (Nava, 1992; Fowles, 1996; Kelly et al., 2005; Fletcher, 2008). In fact, the vast majority of new commodities and fashions fail to make a profit and are usually abandoned (Blumer, 1969; Garnham, 1990; Hesmondhalgh, 2007). In effect, we have moved to a state of cultural anarchy, making corporate and centralized attempts to predict and dominate trends very difficult.

Second, there is much to indicate that bottom-up influences have become increasingly influential in the commodity production process. Everyday clothes and objects are de-commodified and refashioned by ordinary consumers and subcultures, with alternative uses and symbols identified (Hebdige, 1979; Miller, 1987, 2010; Fiske, 1989). These can then feed back upwards and influence larger, commercial producers. Sophisticated marketing methods, coupled with new information and communication technologies, have made customer-to-producer feedback a systematic process (Murray, 1989; Braham, 1997; Slater, 1997). EPOS (electronic point of sale) data are immediately fed back from stores to producer centres. Short-run production lines and JIT (just-in-time) delivery make sales highly responsive to public demands. In effect, instead of 'one-way' promotion and dissemination lines, running top-down from producers to consumers, there are two-way or 'horizontal' lines. For others the relationship is best conceived of as one of 'interlocking cycles of production and consumption' (Lury, 1996) or a 'circuit of culture' (du Gay, 1997).

Returning to the case of clothing fashion, for many during the course of the twentieth century, 'bottom-up' influences have led to 'fashion pluralism' and the 'democratization of fashion' (Blumer, 1969; Agins, 1999; Jackson and Shaw, 2009). Fashion designers, editors and other arbiters instinctively look to popular cultures and trends, realizing that success requires a correspondence with 'the incipient taste of the fashion-consuming public'. It is 'collective tastes' and 'collective moods' that matter (Blumer, 1969). For Agins (1999), 'the end of fashion' means the end of elitist Paris-based fashion houses dictating and the rise of market-oriented designers. For Tungate (2005: 40), democratization is epitomized by companies such as Zara, which shamelessly turn out cheap, mass-produced lines within two to three weeks of a well-received catwalk show: 'the era of slavish brand worship is over ... we are also our own stylists'. For Fiske (1989) and Davis (1992), it is typified by the constant adaptation of jeans. Jeans have come to mean all things to all consumers, from builders and ranchers, to youth subcultures and 'deviant counter-cultures', to high-cost designer wear.

In all of these accounts, promotional culture has little power to persuade consumers. Its most prominent roles are in gaining media exposure for commodities and providing sensitive and quick market feedback. New stuff exists because enterprising entrepreneurs exploit new technologies and industrial processes to create commodities that consumers want. People then accept these, find their own uses for and adapt them, often feeding back to or even inspiring producers on the way.

Both the top-down and bottom-up positions offer quite conflicting accounts of the role of promotional culture in commodities markets. Both, however, engage with the issue via debates about the nature of producer–consumer relations. For this reason, neither says much about how promotional culture may influence the creation of new commodities themselves.

Promotional culture and the reshaping of commodity uses, firms and markets

The following section moves away from the previous two positions to present an alternative but equally significant third means of promotional influence. This suggests that the impact of promotional culture on commodity production has been less direct, being guided by the diverse promotional needs of corporations and markets themselves. Such things as firm branding or investor relations strategies, business-to-business relations, and competition to set industry standards all influence commodity production decisions. Such a perspective draws on work from across economic sociology and cultural economy. Studies here look more closely at meso-level commercial networks, firm organization and the construction of markets.

Promotional influences on the construction of commodities and the retail experience

One obvious way that promotional culture has influenced commodity production is in the way promotional considerations themselves have become part of the manufacturing process. For both (post-) Marxist and postmodern thinkers, contemporary forms of capitalism automatically produce sign-rich commodities or 'commodity-signs'

(Baudrillard, 1988a [1972]; Jhally, 1990; Wernick, 1991; Lash and Urry, 1994). As Lash and Urry state (1994: 15), 'goods often take on the properties of sign-value through the process of "branding", in which marketers and advertisers attach images to goods.' Consequently, promotional 'uses' are now also incorporated into manufacturing decisions.

Wernick (1991) illustrates this point with his account of the English potter Josiah Wedgwood, who did much to industrialize the UK ceramic industry in the eighteenth century. Wedgwood devoted a great deal of his personal time to constructing earthenware purely for promotional purposes. Many of his well-known creations, such as his copy of the Portland (or Barbarini) Vase, were loss-making ventures. He persevered with them because they acted as promotional devices for publicizing his company and his rather cheaper, mass-produced ranges. These, in their construction and presentation, contained references to his showpiece works. Lash and Lury's (2007) account of the twentieth-century emergence of Swatch watches is also informative. By the early 1980s, Asian corporations had come to dominate the market with cheap, digital, multi-function watches. The Swiss watch-making industry was dying out. Its response was the creation of the Swatch line, which remade watches into fashion accessories rather than useful objects. Marketing, design, colour, cheap materials, unreplaceable batteries with limited lifespans, and the choice of retail sites all replaced Swiss technical expertise in production considerations. A series of fashionable, season-linked products, connected by a global brand, followed.

Goods production, in recent decades, has been shifted more generally towards servicing larger brands. Brand names such as Pears or Heinz were once built up by companies and associated with basic products such as soap or foodstuffs. As Lury (2004) describes, a transition took place in the latter part of the twentieth century. Brands developed from being associated with single products to being conceptual centres for ranges of products and services. Brands have become recognized as having value, or 'brand equity', in themselves (Tungate, 2005; Moor, 2007; Clifton, 2009). They can be used to create and sell new product lines, franchised out to retailers, or licensed out to other goods producers for cross-promotional purposes (Lury, 2004; Hardy, 2010). In effect, certain everyday goods are no longer manufactured with any overt 'use value'; use is taken for granted. Instead, production is for building the brand. In many cases, perfumes, shirts and tracksuits, cups, fast-food packaging and toys are not produced to smell nice, wear, consume food in or play with. They are constructed because they are most simply transformed in the service of the wider brand; they are easily brandable.

Promotional requirements have also shaped and reshaped the shopping experience itself. At the end of the nineteenth century, Simmel (2002 [1903]) recorded how the layouts of emerging cities, across Europe and the US, came to be oriented around shopping and leisure. Others (Tomlinson, 1990; Lury, 2004; Sassatelli, 2007) note how large, retail stores and chains began reorganizing and branding their premises to distinguish themselves from large, urban markets and individually branded goods. Alongside Campbell's and Uncle Ben food varieties came Woolworths and JCPenney as one-stop shop lines. So too emerged mail order catalogues (Montgomery Ward and Co., Sears, Roebuck and Co.), shopping malls and shopping centres, store cards and credit cards, and high-brand streets (Savile Row, the Champs-Elysées, Madison Avenue) and stores (Harrods, Fortnum and Mason, Bloomingdales). Others (Agins, 1999; Lash and Lury, 2007; Isaacson, 2011) have observed how brand-name producers now put great emphasis on the placement and design of their stores. Thus, the shopping experience, in turn, becomes influenced subtly by promotional factors. These have already pre-directed multiple decisions and choices by retailers and buyers in advance of any shopping experience (see also D. Miller, 1998; Bowlby, 2000).

Promotional influences on the firm

The choices corporations make about whole product lines and markets can also be significantly affected by promotion-based industrial strategies. As new product markets develop, so promotional imperatives push firms to reposition themselves and alter their products relative to others. Merger and takeover calculations look at potential promotional and market synergies. The need to look good to financial investors can also impact on market and industrial decision-making.

Thus, companies frequently enter into mergers to exploit potential cross-promotional opportunities. At the end of the 1980s, Sony, the highly successful Japanese electrical goods corporation, made a huge investment in software and content-producing companies, buying up the likes of Columbia and CBS (Negus, 1997). The move was driven, in part, by potential 'synergies' to be derived from the hardware and software parts of the company, enabling combined promotion. This took huge investment and corporate restructuring but, as Negus documented, resulted in a costly clash of production cultures.

More recently, Karmak (2010) recorded Lego's attempts to exploit its model-building blocks by moving into associated markets, such as electronic games and children's entertainment. This spreading of the brand – which again involved considerable restructuring and investment – failed, leaving large financial problems.

The need for large, publicly quoted companies to reshape themselves in order to please financial investors has also been documented (Zorn et al., 2005; Froud et al., 2006; Sennett, 2006; Davis, 2007). Sennett (2006: 40) noted that, at the start of this century, US pension funds held a company's stock for an average of only 3.8 months. As he concluded, 'Enormous pressure was put on companies to look beautiful . . . demonstrating signs of internal change and flexibility . . . even if the once-stable company had worked perfectly well.' Froud and her colleagues (2006) detailed how firms such as General Motors have changed their corporate strategies, promoting a set of 'narratives and numbers' to financial investors in order to boost share prices. Agins (1999) offered a similar account of how the financial sector had influenced fashion designers who chose to float themselves in the 1990s on the New York Stock Exchange. Ultimately, financial investment cycles were forcibly imposed on incompatible fashion cycles. Designers such as Donna Karan, who could not adapt, failed. Others who did, such as Liz Claiborne, proved far more resilient (see also Brands, 1999). In effect, the need of companies to promote themselves to large shareholders has resulted in significant restructuring.

Such firm restructuring, according to promotional requirements, has been present at many points in the history of General Electric (GE). Until the 1920s, the company's varied divisions were all geared to supplying other companies with component parts such as engines and transformers. Bruce Barton, who led the developing promotional strategy, turned the 'soulless company' into a corporate 'family', promoting 'electrical consciousness' in contemporary US society (Marchand, 1998). This pulled together the disparate parts of the company while also redirecting its manufacturing activities towards consumer markets. GE began producing everyday electrical appliances for the public and soon dominated markets in washing machines and vacuum cleaners. Many decades later, under Jack Welch, the company was reshaped by promotional strategies once again. In the 1980s, its focus was switched to financial products and capital markets as part of a strategy sold to big investors. For twenty years shares rose and Welch's management was deemed hugely successful. However, Froud and her colleagues (2006) demonstrate that the actual core industrial business remained relatively stagnant. The appearance of growth came from GE Capital, a financial services division, which grew through borrowing and takeovers. The two parts of the company offered a mutually reinforcing model of success, but, in effect, the expansion into financial products and markets disguised the problems of its industrial division.

Promotion and the shaping of markets

In recent decades, work in new economic sociology and cultural economy (e.g., Granovetter and Swedberg, 1992; Callon, 1998a; du Gay and Pryke, 2002; Amin and Thrift, 2003; MacKenzie, 2004) has devoted attention to the social construction of markets themselves. This work varies in the way it conceptualizes economic actors, networks and technologies but shares a common social relations focus. Economic sociologists reveal how social influences shape market institutions, networks, and the rules and regulations by which markets are structured (Granovetter and Swedberg, 1992; Swedberg, 2003). Elsewhere, it is argued that the profession of economics and its associated disciplines, such as marketing, accounting and advertising, 'perform' markets (Callon, 1998b; du Gay and Pryke, 2002). That is to say, such professions observe markets and, in the process, configure them too. As such, individuals calculate and act within the localized logics of their markets, which are themselves informed by economics, marketing and linked professions (see also chapter 10).

Such a logic can also be applied to commodities markets. Indeed, several authors have suggested that economics and the promotional professions have been influential in such ways (see Cochoy, 1998; Slater, 2002; McFall, 2004). Cochoy (1998) traces the history of the marketing profession as it emerged to fill the gaps between economic theory and business practice. In so doing, he contended, it also had a strong shaping effect on real-world goods markets. McFall (2004) argues along similar lines but with respect to advertising at the end of the nineteenth and start of the twentieth century. From another vantage point, so do Peterson (1994) and Negus (1999) when discussing the music industry. Peterson suggests that producers of radio shows construct imagined listener markets in order to categorize music. In so doing, they impose market conventions and styles on what is produced and presented. Negus (1999) describes a similar process in relation to the way large music corporations select and promote new acts.

Slater (2002) takes this line further. He argues that firms also

compete within industries to set the norms, regulations, and accounting and technical standards which define an industry sector. Success
here becomes a source of competitive advantage. Promotional activity
is then directed towards related businesses (B2B), professional associations, regulators and law-makers. In Slater's words (2002: 247),
'Marketing is not only about competition within markets, within
given structures. It is a competition over the structures of markets
and market relations themselves ... every firm wants to redefine
the boundaries of markets by reframing goods.' In effect, companies
both compete within established commodities markets and define the
terms of competition itself (Molotch, 2003). Promotional activity is
an integral part of this.

Granovetter and Swedberg (1992) demonstrate the importance
of setting industry standards with the example of the QWERTY
keyboard. Its design is unlikely to be the most efficient layout available now, but it made sense when first used in printing machines in
the 1860s. Despite the invention of more effective keyboard systems
since, it is QWERTY that continues to set the standard a century
and a half later. The point is also made in relation to the 1970s promotional conflict that developed between JVC's VHS and Sony's
Betamax video formats, which competed to become the established
norm to be adopted by manufacturers, film studios and consumers
(Liebowitz and Margolis, 1999; Greenberg, 2008). Considerable
expense was devoted to winning these promotional battles directed at
technology companies and film producers. Eventually, despite public
polls and press accounts favouring Betamax, it was VHS that came
to dominate the market. In the crucial initial period, more businesses
came to believe that the longer recording time and cheaper models of
the latter would make the VHS format more appealing. DVDs later
surpassed both as technology moved on.

To sum up, promotional culture has had a number of indirect
influences on the construction of mass-produced products. This
impact goes far beyond the mere selling of goods. Increasingly, it is
there during the initial design and manufacturing stages, often direct-
ing decisions towards the fulfilment of wider promotional goals. It
also has a hand in reshaping firms and their corporate strategies as
well as in determining the shapes of markets. As an influencing factor
it can be as significant as new technologies and evolving consumer
demographics. The next two sections, on clothing fashion and hi-
tech goods, illustrate this third perspective in greater detail.

Promotion, clothes and fashion: from haute couture to the high street

Clothes, fashion and promotion appear interconnected in multiple ways. For centuries, clothes have acted as a visual means of distinction, separating individuals and groups (Simmel, 1904; Breward, 1995; Wilson, 2003). In the latter part of the twentieth century, fashion producers created multiple public forums with which to promote their wares: catwalks, trade shows, specific fashion media, retail spaces. Promotion is personified in the shape of the supermodel, celebrity designer and celebrity-turned-designer. For McRobbie (1998) and Tungate (2005), it is hard to see where design and promotion end and independent fashion journalism and criticism begin. In today's unpredictable and fast-changing clothing industry, marketing is considered a central component of fashion education and everyday operations (Tungate, 2005; Jackson and Shaw, 2009; Posner, 2011). Despite all this, there are few social science-based studies of fashion promotion itself. Indeed, as several scholars note (Phizacklea, 1991; Davis, 1992; McRobbie, 1998), there are few studies of fashion as an industry per se.

The main discursive paradigm for discussing promotional influences in fashion remains the 'top-down' versus 'bottom-up' debate, as best summed up by Davis (1992) and Braham (1997; and see above). Simmel's (1904) top-down emulation model, whereby elite fashions permeate or 'trickle down' to the larger masses below, is countered by Blumer's (1969) account of top designers and buyers responding to wider 'collective tastes' when setting new fashions. Evidence for both positions is evident in many contemporary accounts. However, much in them also reveals how promotional activity has had more subtle influences on the industry and its participants.

First, promotion has transformed clothing into 'fashion' (Davis, 1992; Wilson, 2003; Tungate, 2005). Historically, clothes had a simple 'use value'. They suited one's everyday occupation and marked it out to others. Bakers, tailors and soldiers were all distinguished by clothing. Then, from the nineteenth century, clothes became converted into fashion, with new 'use values'. These included 'uses' for social distinction and for social relations outside of one's occupation. Promotional culture facilitated that transformation. In Wilson's words (2003: 3), 'What is added to dress as we ourselves know it in the West is *fashion* . . . something qualitatively new and different. Fashion is dress in which the key feature is rapid and continual changing of styles.' For Tungate (2005: 1), 'When clothes leave the factories where they are made, they are merely "garments" or "apparel". Only when the marketers get hold of them do they magically become "fashion".' Jeans form a prime example. What was once working apparel is now also leisure wear and a mark of distinction, designed and sold to multiple classes of consumer (Davis, 1992).

Fashion promotion also turns clothing consumption into an ever faster moving cycle of demand for the new. As Davis (1992) notes, in centuries past, fashion cycles were very slow, often changing over several decades. He argues that the independent couturiers of mid-nineteenth-century France, such as Charles Frederick Worth, began pushing fashion cycles to move faster. He concluded that the pace of the fashion cycle increased through the twentieth century, especially in the postwar period. That pace appears to have hastened even more in the last two decades. Braham (1997: 150) cites a 1992 survey which showed that 80 per cent of US clothes had 'in-shop lives' of twenty weeks or less, with 35 per cent having ten weeks or less. More recently, Jackson and Shaw (2009: 122) observed that many fashion chains had lines lasting only three to four weeks. Zara changed its lines seventeen times per year (every three weeks on average). The authors concluded that: 'In some respects fast fashion is educating consumers to expect change ever more frequently.'

Second, the promotional professions have shaped the fashion industry itself in various ways. For Davis (1992: 114), the fashion industry has developed a 'complex of institutional, organizational and market structures that channel and, at the very least, mediate the fashion process'. This includes the creation of fashion 'seasons' and 'micro-seasons', recognized fashion centres (Paris, Milan, London, New York), an annual round of more than 1,500 catwalk and trade shows, an established fashion press, and a conveyor belt of celebrity models and designers (Tungate, 2005; Jackson and Shaw, 2009; Posner, 2011). Each of these has their own promotional element as well as organizing the institutional structures, market formats and timetables of the fashion industry.

Over time, branding imperatives have increasingly come to influence those structures, markets and timetables. The fashion house, the designer, the catwalk and the retailer have all been reinvented to service the brand. Once, fashion houses promoted themselves and used catwalk shows to present their lines to retailers and the outside world. Now promotion revolves around the big-name designer who is 'the face' of the fashion house. The catwalk show, which offers little direct commercial gain, now sells designers as much as their lines (Agins, 1999; Khan, 2000; Arnold, 2001). The designer-linked brand is then used to sell the cheaper fashion line and ranges of easily branded commodities. These include leather goods, perfume, cosmetics, watches, jewellery, furnishings, china and even paint. For Agins (1999: 14), it is those designers which have embraced the new model who have succeeded. Pure, original designers, such as Isaac Mizrahi, and high-art Paris fashion houses have declined: 'today, a designer's creativity expresses itself more than ever in the marketing rather than in the actual clothes . . . The top designers use their images to turn themselves into mighty brands.' For Khan (2000: 126), 'given the current fascination with designers as cult figures, those who are best able to maximise the potential of this revered institution [the catwalk] will find themselves much in demand.'

Third, fashion industry competition is enacted frequently through elite business-to-business promotional activities. Several studies (Blumer, 1969; Davis, 1992; Braham, 1997; McRobbie, 1998; Tungate, 2005) discuss the central power of key groups of networked elites in the fashion world. These include large fabric producers, retail chain buyers and fashion houses, as well as top fashion editors, 'style bureaux' and financial investors. As McRobbie (1998) records, there is a considerable degree of movement between such occupational groups. Fashion careers often criss-cross between design, retail buying, editorial and public relations. What also becomes clear in these accounts is how much time is spent closely monitoring competitors and in self-promotion to linked elite groups.

Thus, Tungate (2005: 82) observes the 'formidable marketing skills' of the 'fabric merchants' who promote their new ranges to top designers and buyers. Braham (1997) notes how designers, while presenting their newsworthy catwalk creations, simultaneously push the cheaper, more practical versions to big-store buyers behind the scenes. McRobbie (1998: 126) records how designers produce to gain fashion media exposure: 'designers are creating clothes and collections not so much for real sales as for imagined consumption . . . It is the national and international press, as well as *Vogue*, *Elle*, *Marie Claire* or *Just Seventeen*, which they have in mind when they see their clothes go down the runway.' The outcome of such promotional efforts, at a B2B level, very often has a defining influence on the wider, more dominant lines each season. Relatively few select materials and colours provided by victorious fabric suppliers become widely adopted for a season (Tungate, 2005). Hundreds of designs from a show are narrowed down to some six to eight chosen models, to be bought by one or two hundred store buyers (Blumer, 1969). Ultimately, consumers may still have a wide choice of clothes, but what is on offer can be relatively restricted in terms of colours, fabrics and other standardized season elements.

Fourth, marketing imperatives not only observe, but also define and direct, consumer retail experiences. Fashion marketing books (e.g., Jackson and Shaw, 2009; Posner, 2011) offer detailed guidance on the means by which consumers and 'taste groups' are identified, categorized, segmented and targeted. Classification methods include demographic profiles (class, age, etc.), purchasing behaviours ('big spenders', 'label seekers', 'early adopters', 'laggards', etc.), lifestyles and psychographics (attitudes, beliefs, opinions, values). Designers and retailers use such information both to identify and to produce for such imagined markets. Thus, Topshop and Arcadia target thirteen- to 25-year-old women, Dorothy Perkins looks to 25- to 43-year-old women, and Evans appeals to 'larger females' of all ages in the 14 to 24 size range. As Agins (1999) explains, successful US fashion designer labels, such as Tommy Hilfiger, Ralph Lauren and Donna Karan, built their empires on identified demand from key consumer markets. They also enforced strict control over the choice of retail sites and store presentation. This is the same whether in a boutique area of a large department store, in a stand-alone shop, or licensed out to a local owner. Department stores have adapted accordingly. Jackson and Shaw (2009) describe how, during the 1990s, large shops such as Selfridges were extensively redesigned and positioned as a 'House of Brands'. Tungate (2005: 77) declares that such large department stores have become 'nothing less than brand theme parks'. In effect, consumers are channelled towards particular sites, stores and brands which have themselves been established on the basis of marketing and branding considerations.

Promotion in fashion may or may not directly influence consumer choices. However, it does have a strong effect on the shaping and reshaping of the fashion industry itself. It makes ordinary apparel into 'fashion' that changes in increasingly rapid cycles. It affects many of the institutional and structural elements that organize the industry, its markets and retail spaces. It influences top-level decision-making in a competitive business environment and determines the retail experience. In all these regards, promotional culture may not succeed in telling consumers what to buy or which fashions to copy. But it does tell them, indirectly, that clothes have other uses and increasingly limited lifespans and that designer labels bestow status. Similarly, it tells them what shops they should patronize and the limited range of colours and fabrics that they may choose from in any particular season.

Promotion and hi-tech goods: from the printing press to the Microsoft–Apple computer wars

When it comes to new hi-tech products, it is natural to assume that emerging technologies are the principal driving force behind their creation and production. A modernist discourse suggests that scientific progress and industrial evolution drive epochal changes in society. Entrepreneurs from Thomas Edison and Henry Ford to Bill Gates and Steve Jobs (Brands, 1999) have succeeded by developing and packaging new technologies into commodities that consumers want. Such accounts leave little space for the social, cultural or promotional. However, as argued here, these elements have been as significant to the emergence of technological goods markets as scientific discovery and entrepreneurial push.

Typical of many industrial accounts is a propensity towards technological determinism. Sola Pool (1983) describes the advent of the printing press in Europe in 1450 as nothing less than a revolution. It was essential for the growth of Protestantism, the codification of law, the evolution of science and agriculture, increased literacy and education. Daniel Bell (1973) posits that new technologies were responsible for changing society from an industrial-based to a service-based economy (see also Toffler, 1971, 1980; Meyrowitz, 1985). Piore and Sabel (1984) argued that information and communication technologies transformed old and inflexible, Fordist production methods into the 'post-industrial society' (see also Harvey, 1989). More recently, similar claims have been made about the socio-economic impacts of the 'computer revolution', the 'digital economy' and the 'network society' (Negroponte, 1996; Gates, 1996; Castells, 1996, 2001).

Such technological determinism runs the risk of demoting the importance of socio-economic, political and cultural factors, as well as the role of human agency (Giddens, 1991). The mode of production, the nuclear family, language, bureaucracy, the state, religion and the codification of law are comparable driving forces of social development. Such factors can affect whether technology develops, how it develops and whether it becomes disseminated across society. Indeed, many technologies and technological commodities are never widely adopted or are adopted in different ways and at different times (Winston, 1998; Webster, 2006; Curran, 2010; Curran et al., 2012). As Winston records, the typewriter was originally patented in 1714, the fax machine in 1847 and the television in 1884, while the World Wide Web was conceived in 1945 – all well before they became available on a mass scale.

In some industrial histories, the issue of standardization is one key determining factor. In Molotch's (2003) study of the origins of everyday stuff, even simple objects, such as toasters and toilets, are constructed according to a whole set of technical, regulatory, economic and social standards. The ability to influence these standards, as well as the political and other networks that set them, can be very significant. Thus, Granovetter and McGuire (1998) argue that standardization, in the early years of the US electrical industry (1880–1925), did not necessarily produce the most efficient or technically best standards. Instead, a few large electricity supply companies came to dominate the key industrial associations and certifying boards which set the initial technical standards and regulatory regimes. Other local, smaller companies and authorities then found themselves forced to comply with these new industry norms. Their competitive disadvantage increased.

Such studies suggest that social relations have a significant influence on whether or not new technologies and hi-tech commodities are adopted, and in what shapes and ways. Accordingly, alternative research on new media and in science and technology studies (see MacKenzie and Wajcman, 1999; Lievrouw, 2004; Livingstone, 2005; Lievrouw and Livingstone, 2006) stresses the utility of 'recombinant' and 'social shaping' approaches for investigating how new technologies are adopted. If the social is more significant, so, it might be argued, is promotional culture.

The following case, on the rivalry between Bill Gates's Microsoft and Steve Jobs's Apple, illustrates the alternative ways promotional culture has influenced hi-tech goods production. The industrial conflict between the two men goes back to the mid-1970s, when the young Gates and Jobs first set up companies to exploit the fledgling home-computer market. Jobs's famed product launches apart, many popular accounts and mythologies do not dwell on the role of promotion. Instead, the history focuses on new technologies, networks, hot-housing and rivalries in what came to be known as Silicon Valley. Both CEOs and companies took advantage of inspired individuals and larger technology companies (IBM, Xerox, MITS, SCP) around them. It is also a story of two fiercely driven entrepreneurs who were socially awkward and often impossible to work with, but who were bestowed with visionary genius. For Gates, his technical knowledge, combined with his business and legal acumen, were key. For Jobs, an ability to combine and package the technical and design skills of others and an innate instinct for consumer demand were fundamental. Promotion seems secondary. Gates is a notoriously poor public presenter. Jobs was known to be scathing of conventional market research.

However, as one reads through the personal biographies and histories of these CEOs and their companies (e.g., Wallace and Erickson, 1992; Brands, 1999; Moritz, 2009; Isaacson, 2011), the words 'salesman' and 'marketer' come up frequently. Brands (1999) often talks of Gates's 'aggressive marketing' as crucial to Microsoft. Wallace and Erickson (1992) refer to him as a 'ruthless salesman' and document his 'tireless salesmanship'. Moritz (2009) calls Jobs a 'mesmerizing salesman', and Spanier (2011) refers to him as Apple's 'marketer-in-chief'. What is also clear in these accounts is that, more often than not, the marketing and salesmanship referred to is that being directed at the industry itself. The ability of Gates and Jobs to convince skilled engineers and investors to join them, journalists to promote them and dealers to stock their products was very important. Most significant was their respective abilities to persuade other companies to work with them and on their terms. This, in effect, allowed them to set the standards and parameters of the computer and other digital industries.

In the 1980s and 1990s it was Microsoft that prevailed because of Gates's earlier dealings with other computer companies (see Wallace and Erickson, 1992; Brands, 1999; Liebowitz and Margolis, 1999). This enabled Microsoft to become the *de facto* standard setter in the industry and ultimately to become indispensable to rivals and partners alike. Microsoft took and developed the BASIC programming language and DOS (Disk Operating System, originally QDOS from SCP) to produce MS DOS. Gates's key move was to woo IBM with this: to offer a cheap system, to get it on every new IBM machine, but also to retain the ability to license it to other companies. He went to great lengths to get this poorly paid deal because he guessed that many rivals would produce IBM clones. They would then need the same software to operate them. Hardware producers and software application writers alike would become dependent on it. Some years later, Gates completed the same trick with his Windows operating system. He persuaded hardware companies to preinstall his software – operating system and applications – within all their computers, thus offering all-in-one packages to consumers. By the late 1990s, 90 per cent of PCs sold worldwide contained Microsoft software. For Wallace and Erickson (1999: 182), Microsoft's success owed much to how Gates 'haggled, cajoled, browbeat, and harangued the hardware makers of the emerging personal computer industry, convincing them to buy Microsoft's services and sales'.

During this time, Jobs did the opposite (Moritz, 2009; Isaacson, 2011). He insisted on maintaining control of the complete computer package, organizing both hardware and software development. Neither the hardware nor the software was compatible with other producers. Nor were new Apples compatible with earlier models. This approach resulted in higher unit costs and far fewer developers willing to produce software applications for Apple. Regardless of its superiority in design, user-friendliness and originality, Apple failed to compete. In 1982, sales of Apples and PCs were roughly equal, but by 1983 PCs were outselling Apples by three to one (Isaacson, 2011: 160). From then on, Apple declined, and two years later Jobs was fired by the company he had started.

In 1997, twelve years after he left, Jobs returned to an impoverished Apple. By 2011, before his death, Apple had leap-frogged Microsoft to become the world's leading technology company (at the time of writing it is the largest company quoted on the New York Stock Exchange). Apple computer sales were restored and the company had produced best-selling new products in three markets: mp3 players, cell phones and tablet computers (the iPod, iPhone and iPad). In each of these cases, Jobs placed Apple in the position of market standard setter, just as Gates had done previously with PC computer operating systems. This began with his re-envisioning a future for home computers as 'digital hubs' that linked new hardware and content in adjacent sectors. iPods offered technical and user-friendly advances on previous mp3 player designs. More importantly, they linked to Apple computers both for file management purposes and to make music purchases via Apple's iTunes website. To do so, Jobs had to persuade the competing CEOs of the top five music companies to sell via iTunes. Apple was now placed centrally, and seen as indispensable, in two industries. Jobs conjured the same trick with iPhones and iPads in relation to apps. These were not simply stylish, sophisticated new products designed for existing markets. They also offered key platforms for other application producers to work with.

Jobs also succeeded because, as in clothing, cars and other commodity lines, he made hi-tech goods have value beyond 'use value'. Computers, mp3 players and cell phones were turned into fashionable objects. From Apple's early years, Jobs always emphasized design and user-friendliness in his products. However, on his return to the company in 1997, he increasingly emphasized elements of fashion and branding in all aspects of the company. This came from his experiences running NeXT and Pixar, as well as sitting on the board of the clothes retailer Gap. He began having weekly three-hour marketing meetings and developed his own worldwide advertising agency (Spanier, 2011). This employed 200 staff just to promote Apple. The iMac, launched in 1998, offered little technical advance but was promoted on its colourful and translucent design. For Isaacson (2011: 356), it became 'an iconic new product', and 32 per cent of its sales were to first-time computer users. In 2001, Jobs began setting up a chain of Apple stores. Unlike most computer shops, these were placed in prestige shopping areas and were arranged like designer fashion stores. Jobs personally pushed their development and design, using Gap and Ralph Lauren for inspiration. By 2011, everything Apple produced had its brand centrally positioned and was promoted as much on non-technical qualities as technical ones. According to Moritz (2009), Jobs had succeeded in turning new technological commodities into 'objects of desire'.

Conclusion

Promotional culture is not particularly associated with the construction of commodities or markets per se. Generally, its influence is considered more secondary in terms of its informing or persuading consumers about new products, or in feeding consumer responses to existing products back to producers. However, as argued here, promotional activity has had a rather stronger shaping effect on both manufacturing processes and markets. That effect is less overt but no less significant in nature. Promotional objectives influence design and construction decisions. Promotional activity guides larger corporate strategies and restructuring. It is also part of business-to-business competition that seeks to gain market share, to define market rules and standards, and to shape the retail experience.

6
News Media and Popular Culture: Promotion and Creative Autonomy

Introduction

This chapter investigates the multiple influences of promotional intermediaries on the production of news media and popular culture. Advertising has tended to be a crucial form of finance for most forms of mass communication. Public relations has emerged as a hidden form of 'information subsidy' for news and parts of the entertainment media. Marketing research on media audiences now plays a significant part in key financing and production decision-making. In addition, personal agents and publicists, working in support of the 'star system' (see chapter 7), add a further layer of promotional input. As each industry has developed, so they have become more centrally positioned in media and cultural production. Their shaping of outputs has become more systematic.

The central issue discussed here is one of creative autonomy for those who work in the news and cultural industries. Journalists, writers, directors, musicians and others all attempt to maintain a degree of independent control. However, they often find themselves constrained by organizational, economic and market pressures. These are frequently exerted through promotional intermediaries. The core question is: To what extent do promotional needs impose on the autonomy of employees and therefore shape media and cultural content?

In terms of news media, autonomy is important to journalists who try to produce objective, informed and balanced news stories. However, because news is also a business, commercial concerns can restrict reporter independence. The sensitivities of large advertisers, as well as the need to produce saleable news copy, can influence their decision-making. Public relations, either as a form of subsidy or as a means of managing journalists, also impacts on outputs. The issue of autonomy is just as significant in the cultural industries but the promotional challenges are different. Producing popular culture is highly risky, requiring substantial up-front investments in unpredictable consumer markets. Large media conglomerates have responded by using promotional intermediaries to reduce risks and exploit hits. The result, some argue, is that mainstream culture is increasingly industrialized, homogenized and standardized. Thus, as with reporters, organizational pressures can end up using promotional intermediaries to constrain creative employees.

The chapter is in three parts. The first discusses news production and journalist autonomy. The second, drawing on the work of the Frankfurt School, explores the debates around cultural autonomy in the music and television sectors. The final part documents the ways and means promotional culture has influenced and shaped creativity in the Hollywood film industry.

Promotional culture and independent news journalism

The notion of professional autonomy is fundamental to several classic accounts of how fourth-estate journalism operates best in democracies (Alexander, 1981; Harrison, 1985; Schudson, 1996, 2003; McNair, 2003; Zelizer, 2004). Independent journalists have greater objectivity and can report a plurality of competing interests and opinions. Most significantly, they are free to act as a check on powerful institutions and individuals. The 'occupational ideology' of professional journalism, with its organizational and cultural norms (public service, accuracy, impartiality), helps guide reporter practices (see Schudson, 2001; Deuze, 2005). Market-oriented pragmatism (Koss, 1984; Veljanovski, 1989; Sola Pool, 1990) ensures that news is broadly reflective of the concerns of the mass of citizens. Through such means, 'public journalism' (see Glasser, 1999) has developed to service the interests of the mass of citizens. Ultimately, these ideals and practices have their flaws but, on balance, shape journalism in positive ways (Lichtenberg, 2000; McNair, 2003; Zelizer, 2004; Schudson, 2003). Through all these accounts, reporter independence remains a given.

However, at the same time, market and organizational constraints can erode journalist autonomy. Because most news is produced by private corporations, it must operate as a business as well as providing a public service. Consequently, news production has always been more vulnerable to the influences of promotional culture than most professional accounts would acknowledge. This has become very significant in recent decades as news has steadily become less profitable.

Promotional influences begin with advertising. In practice, commercial news is financially dependent on a combination of sales and advertising. This can affect news production in both overt and structural ways. For example, big corporate advertisers are known to apply direct pressure to media owners on certain news topics deemed sensitive to their interests (see also Herman and Chomsky, 1988; Curran, 2002). More significantly, advertiser needs can systematically shape long-term news agendas and news values. Curran (1986, 2002; Curran and Seaton, 2003) has shown how advertising needs have influenced UK newspaper content in order to accommodate particular audiences. Radical working-class papers, such as the *Daily Herald*, which were once best-sellers, failed through the twentieth century because advertisers were not interested in either poor or radical consumers. By the same token, poor or ethnic minority audiences are less likely to find coverage of issues important to them. Similarly, the need to appeal to and entice fickle audiences and advertisers leads news gatherers to focus more on stories of conflict, human interest, celebrity and scandal (Sparks and Tulloch, 2000; Thompson, 2000; Delli Carpini and Williams, 2001; Thussu, 2008). Such story selection may end up being *of* public interest rather than *in* the public interest, as complex or long-term stories may be ignored or minimally covered.

Public relations, working on behalf of news sources, has also come to impinge on news production and reporter autonomy in varied ways. Some of these are quite strategic and overt. For instance, PR intermediaries attempt to control journalist access to newsworthy information, public figures and restricted areas. This includes access to prominent politicians and legislative spaces (Kurtz, 1998; Barnett and Gaber, 2001) and military leaders and zones (Thussu and Freedman, 2003; Tumber and Palmer, 2004). Promotional practitioners, working in the interests of their employees, may 'spin' stories, initiate 'pseudo-events' (Boorstin, 1962), apply public pressure ('flak') to journalists, or undermine their news accounts. Of increasing concern is the rise of 'astro-turf' or 'third-party' campaign organizations. In these cases, campaigns are supported by seemingly independent public and scientific bodies, which are actually directed and funded by powerful corporate and political organizations (see, variously, Stauber and Rampton, 1995, 2003; Ewen, 1996; Monbiot,

2006; CMD and Spinwatch). Thus the 'propaganda model' (Herman and Chomsky, 1988) has a powerful case to make – especially so in times of war or international crisis and during the current global 'war on terror' (Miller, 1994, 2004; Knightley, 2000; Philo and Berry, 2004; Snow, 2004).

Equally important is the way many forms of daily news production have become highly dependent on source supply which, itself, is produced or shaped by public relations. All news organizations are driven by the need to fill set amounts of news space with great regularity. To construct stories, journalists, as perennial non-experts, are forced each day to rely on sources for information, explanation, quotes and other content. Accordingly, they gravitate towards those beats and sources which are more likely to offer good copy or story information (see Gans, 1979; Hallin, 1994; Patterson, 1994; Schlesinger and Tumber, 1994; Franklin, 1997). Several past studies have observed that, as journalist resources become stretched, so dependency on external source supplies, or 'information subsidies', rises (Sigal, 1973; Fishman, 1980; Gandy, 1982). Sigal's study of the *Wall Street Journal* and *New York Times*, for example, found a direct correlation between staffing and resource levels, on the one hand, and the number of stories based on source supply, on the other.

Such a correlation is now extremely significant because, in the globalized, digital age, the standard industry business model is breaking down. In several established democracies (not all) news has been struggling to be profitable for some decades. Since the 1970s, the following trends can be observed with some consistency in the US, the UK and elsewhere: more news outlets but fewer consumers per outlet; pressure to fill 24-hour rolling news; the need to repackage news for multiple media platforms, including the internet, mobiles and tablet computers; price wars and global market competition, brought by the internet and global news channels; the flourishing of cheap web-based news companies and news aggregators, such as Yahoo and Google; and the steady migration of audiences and advertising to entertainment media and online sites. In 2011, newspapers gained $207 million in online advertising but lost $2.1 billion in print advertising. By 2012, many parts of the print and broadcast news industry in the US and Europe were struggling to survive. Since 2000, an average of fifteen newspapers have gone bankrupt each year in the US (Pew, 2012).

In an effort to remain profitable, news organizations have raised prices above inflation, increased output and cut staff relative to outputs (see Franklin, 1997; Davis, 2002; Kovatch et al., 2004;

Davies, 2008; Pew, 2009b; Freedman, 2009). The end result is that journalists are expected to produce more and more with fewer and fewer resources. In the UK, Tunstall (1996) estimated that, between the 1960s and 1990s, individual output had at least doubled. Franklin (2005) concluded that modern news production had become almost factory-like in its practices, to the extent of becoming 'McDonaldized' (Franklin, 2005). Davies (2008) concluded that journalists are now having to fill three times as much news space as they did in 1985, turning journalism into 'churnalism' (see also Lee-Wright et al., 2012). In the US, Kovatch and his colleagues (2004: 28) recorded that, between 1985 and 2004, network news correspondents were cut by 35 per cent while story output per reporter increased by 30 per cent. Pew (2012) calculated that the US newspaper industry had shrunk 43 per cent and lost 28 per cent of journalist jobs since 2000.

Consequently, many established news producers have encouraged a systematic dependency on 'information subsidy' supply. There are now a variety of types of such subsidy. These include the use of news wire material, plagiarized copy already published by rivals, and unpaid pieces by public figures, experts and 'citizen journalists'. Most importantly, it consists of a range of materials supplied by public relations practitioners and other promotional professionals, often working through these same wire services and public figures. Indeed, in recent decades, the public relations profession has expanded impressively to supply such demand. In the US, PR practitioner numbers rose from 19,000 in 1950 to an estimated 258,000 in 2010; a rise to 316,000 by 2020 is projected (Cutlip et al., 2000: 31; US Bureau of Labor Statistics, 2010). According to McChesney and Nichols (2010), there are now four times as many PR specialists as media editorial staff employed in the US. In the UK (Miller and Dinan, 2000), the sector grew elevenfold in real terms in just over two decades between 1979 and 1998. Importantly, as most industry surveys reveal (e.g., PR Week surveys, 1993, 1999; CIPR, 2011), 'media relations' is the most common activity of its practitioners. Surveys also show that an increasing number of PR practitioners have prior experience of working in journalism (Davis, 2002). In 1994 (NUJ, 1994), 7.3 per cent of the UK National Union of Journalists worked in 'Press/PR'. In 2006 (NUJ, 2006), 28 per cent did so.

It is difficult to determine exactly what percentage of news comes from PR materials, but a few key studies are quite revealing. An Australian electoral commission study of Queensland news in 1993 found that 200 out of 279 government news releases were taken up in reported stories, and 140 of them were reproduced 'virtually verbatim'. Another study, by Clara Zawawi, found that between 53 per cent and 65 per cent of news stories in three Australian newspapers emanated from PR material (reported in Turner et al., 2000: 42). In the UK, a study of 2,207 newsprint items and 402 broadcasts by Lewis, Williams and Franklin (2008) found that 19 per cent of press stories and 17 per cent of broadcasts were entirely or mainly reproduced PR material; 49 per cent of press stories were either entirely or mainly dependent on news wire agency copy, much of which itself had come from press releases. In the US, McChesney and Nichols (2010) estimated that 40 to 50 per cent of newspaper stories began life as press releases, while only 14 per cent originated from reporters.

In many ways the scandal in the UK surrounding phone hacking at News Corporation's *News of the World* illustrates many of the points made. News Corporation is a major international media conglomerate, owned and run primarily by Rupert Murdoch, with extensive interests in news and entertainment in many countries. Murdoch's *The Sun*, the *News of the World* (*NoW*), *The Times* and the *Sunday Times* in recent decades have become some of the most profitable national newspapers in the UK, bucking the downward industry trend (see Currah, 2009). However, in mid-2011, after five years of rumours, secret court settlements and stalled police investigations, it became clear that the best-selling *NoW* had run an industrial-scale phone-hacking operation. To date, over 4,000 victims have been identified. The scandal led to several senior resignations at News Corporation and the Metropolitan Police, the closing of the paper, the Leveson Inquiry into press behaviour, and several criminal investigations.

One way of analysing what happened at the *NoW* is through its particular business model. Profitability was built on finding more cost-effective ways of producing news. Some of these, such as the adoption of new technologies, were legitimate. Others were less so. Among the latter, systematic phone hacking of public figures was a far cheaper way of finding regular news scoops than traditional, time-consuming and costly forms of investigative news-gathering. Other ways included cutting staff while expanding output, extensive use of PR materials, cross-media promotion and use of content across News Corporation's multiple media platforms (see Davis, 2002; Hardy, 2013; Lee-Wright et al., 2012). Another aspect of this case was the extensive and close relations that had built up between news media and powerful sources and institutions. As leader of the opposition from 2005 to 2010, David Cameron had 1,404 meetings with journalists (*Daily Telegraph*, 2012). *NoW*'s editor, Andy Coulson, became the Conservative Party's head of communication, while Neil Wallis, a deputy editor, became a PR consultant for the Metropolitan Police. In the fifteen months following the 2010 election, David Cameron had seventy-six meetings with news executives and editors, a third of which were with News Corporation. In the same period Ed Miliband had forty-eight meetings, fifteen of which were with News Corporation (BBC news broadcast, 25 July 2011).

In truth, journalism has never been as autonomous as it would like. Reporters do not have the necessary resources of time, money and knowledge required to fulfil professional expectations. The presentation of professional autonomy is, in part, a promotional confidence trick of the industry itself. However, the autonomy that did exist has been steadily eroded by market forces in recent years. Just as the advertising-based business model of news production appears to be failing, the resources of promotional culture are strengthening. This has forced a growing dependency on the information subsidies supplied by promotional intermediaries and media-trained news sources. It has also made news into a more promotional format. To the public it is presented in the same way, but what is left is a pale imitation of what it once was (see Nichols and McChesney, 2009; McChesney and Pickard, 2011; Pew, 2011, 2012; Lee-Wright et al., 2012). What exists is increasingly watered-down, under-researched and checked, cannibalistic, rehashed, and highly dependent on PR materials. Rather like a fake Rolex watch, it is not all that it seems.

Promotion and entertainment media: music and television

Promotional constraints on creative autonomy and cultural outputs

Many of the working conditions and organizational constraints that influence journalist autonomy are also present in the entertainment industries. Both types of worker are employed predominantly in large multinational media conglomerates which compete for direct sales and advertising in competitive consumer markets. However, in other ways, the organizational and promotional influences and pressures are quite different. Mass entertainment production has a less recognized public role and fewer regulatory pressures. Instead, it is a high-risk occupation, at the mercy of short-term trends and consumer fashions. As such, creative autonomy is challenged less by external PR and media management and more by advertiser and internal marketing demands.

The increasing centrality of promotion to the production of popular culture is linked to the specific risks and unpredictability of the cultural industries themselves (see Miege, 1989; Garnham, 1990; Gitlin, 1994; Hesmondhalgh, 2007; Murdock and Wasko, 2007; Mosco, 2009). Financial unpredictability is the norm, as the vast majority of cultural products, from films to music and books, are loss-making failures. These are usually balanced by a very small number of big hits which take in large profits. Thus, in the 1980s, only one in nine music singles and one in sixteen albums made an actual profit (Garnham, 1990: 161). In 1997, 80 per cent of the 50,000 book titles published made a loss (Moran, 2000: 38). Hesmondhalgh (2007: 19) notes that, in 1999, just eighty-eight recordings, or 0.03 per cent of the total released that year, were responsible for some 25 per cent of sales overall.

The risks and precariousness of many cultural industries are exacerbated by certain key factors. CDs, films, books and television series are 'prototypes' that are expensive to develop and relatively cheap to mass reproduce. That means that costs are front-loaded into the initial development of a product which may well be a failure. Profits are made in mass reproduction and sales where reproduction costs are tiny. At the same time, there is an extremely high turnover of cultural products, with each one having a very limited time slot with which to make an impact. Books, films, CDs and television series are each given just a few weeks to sell or are discarded rapidly to make space for new products. This also means that expensive marketing and distribution operations are required to promote and disseminate each new cultural product, which has either to create a new audience from scratch or lure a temporary, fickle one back. Lastly, producers are reliant on a relatively small number of distributors or networks to take and disseminate their products, be it in film, music or television. They, like mass audiences, have to be persuaded and may be equally capricious.

The companies best equipped to cope with these extreme financial risks and market unpredictability are large conglomerates (see Bagdikian, 2004; Murdock and Wasko, 2007; McChesney, 2008; Mosco, 2009). In the last decade, just five (Bagdikian, 2004) or six (McChesney, 2008) conglomerates, crossing television, music, publishing, the internet, video/DVD distribution, and hardware production, have come to control a majority of all popular media and communication formats in the US. These large corporations have integrated their operations horizontally and vertically, enabling greater control of all parts of the creation, production and distribution process. Such moves mean they benefit from economies of scale, spread economic risks and exploit synergies across media platforms, thus capitalizing on hit products (Gray, 2010; Hardy, 2010). Such powerful producers can also push risk onto smaller suppliers and producers and, if it suits, take over small, profitable companies.

These conglomerates have also come to deal with industry risks by employing a range of promotional professionals who, in various ways, constrain creative autonomy. Public relations staff and personal agents work alongside 'creatives' to build audience awareness ahead of distribution (see, for example, Negus, 1992; McDonald, 2000; Moran, 2000; Wasko, 2003; chapter 7). Associated promotional requirements are then enforced on 'stars' after production. However, it is during the production process itself that promotional intermediaries, primarily marketing experts, have had most impact on the autonomy of cultural producers. Because of the high up-front costs, market research and knowledge of the potential consumer base is vital before committing investment. In Hesmondhalgh's (2007: 193) estimation, 'marketing' indeed represents 'the most important change in organizational control in the cultural industries'. Marketing experts have an increasing say over what gets selected and how it is modified during production by 'creatives'. According to Gitlin (1994), in the era of the large TV networks in the US (now fading), thousands of programme ideas would be whittled down to just a couple of new series a year. Marketing and promotional considerations were key to persuading network managers, investors and distributors of the merits of a new TV show. In the music industry (see Negus, 1992, 1999), artist and repertoire staff select artists according to perceived audience trends. Writers, stylists, technicians and marketing people all contribute to the creation of band images, the chosen musical style and individual music releases.

All these factors create a series of organizational tensions between cultural producers and creative artists. The desire to create something new and original is set against producing something that is regular, predictable and recognizable to audiences. The wish to develop something unique and authentic that might gain a large new audience also increases the commercial risk of consumer rejection. Promotional staff sometimes mediate between the two but also act as the company's enforcement agents. Promotional intermediaries think about the commercial while artists think about the creative. Intermediaries think about what is predictable and reliable, based on their research of past work, while artists focus on the new and original and look to future fashions. Intermediaries think about mass markets while artists think about their peers, critics and industry awards.

One critical way of interpreting the influence of promotion on the cultural industries is offered by the work of the Frankfurt School (Adorno and Horkheimer, 1979 [1947]; Adorno, 1991). In their postwar critique, they argued that mass-produced popular culture contributed considerably to the maintenance of the capitalist system. It dulled the minds of the masses and offered them an unchallenging diversion from the real conditions of working life. This was because cultural production was driven by corporate imperatives rather than artistic ones, and thus created increasingly mechanized and industrialized outputs. Like other industries, popular culture came to be 'standardized' and 'interchangeable' as a means of increasing efficiency during production. Plots, story lines, character types and music genres all developed standard formats which came to be repeated again and again. Characters, particular kinds of scenes and musical bar sequences can all be picked out of one product and, with minimal adaption, be used in another. These tendencies encouraged cultural 'homogenization'. At the same time, to keep consumers purchasing, producers had to pretend their products were new and different. So, they promoted their differences and the individuality of their products, thus manufacturing a sense of 'pseudo-individuality' for each new creation. Since then, promotional intermediaries have come to play a central part in all of these functions. They aid in identifying and standardizing new outputs during the marketing process. They then artificially promote the pseudo-individuality of those products through advertising and public relations. Creative autonomy is constrained accordingly.

Frankfurt School-style perspectives have been applied to more recent studies of the cultural industries. Burston's work (2000), for example, looked at 'mega-musicals', of the kind reproduced in cities worldwide. He found that no scope for artistic interpretation was allowed for dancers, set designers or directors, as branded shows had to be reproduced identically, regardless of country. Studies of the dominant television networks in the US, by Gitlin (1994) and D'Acci (1994), offered detailed accounts of how multiple levels of bureaucrats and market researchers come to dominate programme-making. They observed how network pressures always encouraged programme-making according to established formats, using regular plot lines and recognized and attractive actors. Market-testing, screen-testing, focus groups and Nielson ratings were the tools used to encourage and constrain. Such restraints continue to be applied in prime-time network television (Kubey, 2004; Lotz, 2007; Gray, 2008: 25; Kelso, 2008).

Gray, while arguing that things are not as constrained as in Gitlin's research period, still records the continuing propensity to go for the tried and tested, remakes, spin-offs, sequels and prequels: 'Television, then, can fail abysmally to do anything other than copy itself at times.' CBS's multiple CSI and other crime-based dramas typify such a programming approach. Even non-network channels regarded as innovative and challenging, such as HBO ('It's Not TV'), have restrictive and conformist elements in their organizational culture (see Santo, 2008; Kelso, 2008). HBO developed a reputation for producing 'challenging' and 'edgy' shows, such as *The Sopranos*, *Sex and the City*, *Six Feet Under* and *Deadwood*. But, at the same time, it is highly brand conscious in its development strategy and is still part of Time Warner, a vertically integrated, centralized conglomerate. It tends to engage already proven talent, has many network practices, and still fills most of its schedule with sports coverage, mainstream and populist fare, such as *Real Sex* and *G String Divas*.

Most recently, multimedia and promotion have been combined in media conglomerate strategies to produce contemporary forms of standardization, homogenization and pseudo-individuality. Big budget prime-time series, such as *Lost*, *24* and *Heros*, have become multimedia events, re-presented across media platforms in alternative formats and geared towards maximizing revenue streams (Lotz, 2007; Baltruschat, 2011; Gillan, 2011). In Gillan's (2011: 2) account, such series have become transformed 'into a multiplatform series of networked texts (e.g., 24, the broadcast series, the interactive website, the mobisode and mobile game, the playstation game, the interactive DVD-Rom, the DVD box set . . . the board game, the companion volume, the novelization, the tie-in books, the fanzine, the trading card game)'. Reality television talent competitions, such as *The Apprentice*, *The X Factor* and *American Idol*, also exploit multiple promotional possibilities and revenue sources. According to Baltruschat (2011: 48), such shows are franchised formats, reproduced globally, which make extensive use of multimedia platforms to generate extended brand awareness. They are the main utilizers of product placement promotion. In 2007, *American Idol* alone had 4,349 product placements. In addition, these shows rely less on professional creatives as amateurs provide the content. Audience participation then becomes a live marketing device for selecting future content, deciding which vote-winning individuals return. Such acts have then already gained lengthy television public exposure before record companies take them up and promote them (see Murray and Ouellette, 2009; Turner, 2009).

In effect, the commercial and promotional needs of the cultural industries have increasingly encroached on the practices of their creatives. Ratings, external advertisers and sponsors have always had a direct or indirect influence on content. However, as marketing practices have advanced, so promotional intermediaries have come to play a more central role in cultural production. Such promotional professions help to reduce risk, make the unpredictable predictable, make production more standardized and efficient, minimize the costs of failures, and maximize successful outputs and synergies. But, at the same time, creative autonomy becomes more restricted, innovation and artistry are reduced, and homogenization and standardization become the mainstream norm.

Creativity and autonomy retained

Alternative accounts of the cultural industries and creative autonomy begin with direct critiques of the Frankfurt School position itself. For some time, many in cultural studies have condemned what they see as an elitist, establishment defence of 'high culture' that is dismissive of popular culture and 'the masses' (Gendron, 1986; Fiske, 1989; Morley, 1992; Nava, 1992; Fowles, 1996). It is also far too determinist and pessimistic in its assumptions about audience malleability. Promotional intermediaries, in turn, make inflated claims about what they do, as the high rate of market failures, regardless of promotional budgets, demonstrate (see also Ang, 1991; Lury and Warde, 1997; chapter 3).

In terms of the production process, the signs are that organizational and promotional control are rather more difficult in practice than critical theorists assume. Cultural production is a messy, fragmented business, not easily determined by economic and organizational factors. It cannot simply be compared to other forms of factory-line, industrial production. In music (Frith, 1988; Garofalo, 1992; Negus, 1999; Toynbee, 2000), production, of necessity, is dispersed and decentralized. Even in large majors and conglomerates, production is made up of a number of specialist groups, self-contained tasks and decision-making points. This leaves plenty of space for creative autonomy. For those looking at 'cultures of production' (du Gay, 1997; Negus, 1997, 1999), creatives are themselves influenced by their external social and cultural interactions, as well as by 'genre cultures', outside the site of production. Such influences are then imported into a company's 'culture of production'. They cannot simply be redirected or bracketed out by organizational or marketing factors.

Negus (1997) demonstrates just how complex cultural production can be in his case study of Sony's takeover of Columbia and CBS at the end of the 1980s. Sony, a very successful Japanese consumer electronics company, bought up US producers of cultural content and attempted to take advantage of the potential synergies between the two. Ultimately, the company lost billions of dollars on failed products and went through several expensive and protracted legal battles with its contracted artists. The reason for such a failure, according to Negus, was that Sony had tried to impose alien working practices, technological and economic logics, and different 'cultures of production' on the companies they had taken over. What was successful for a Japanese hardware production company failed when imposed on creative musicians and film producers in the United States.

There is another strong line of reasoning which also casts doubt on the Frankfurt School's position. As Hesmondhalgh (1998) argues with respect to popular music, independent producers provide a vital source of cheap research and development for the industry. Toynbee (2000) too argues that music production, over the decades, has become steadily decentralized in nature, with innovation often occurring within relatively autonomous 'proto-markets'. Both make the point that consumers expect new, evolving trends and ultimately reject over-repeated mainstream fare. If successful, new acts and musical styles come to be taken up by bigger producers, thus perpetuating an interdependency between large music conglomerates and smaller independents. By such means, multiple new popular musical styles and genres have been adopted (see also Negus, 1999). A similar relationship has been observed in the way smaller cable channels, such as HBO, FX and Showtime, have come to interact with the large US networks and media conglomerate funders (Gray, 2008; Kelso, 2008; McCabe and Akass, 2008). Personnel move between the two. Innovative programme and production models, when proving successful, are picked up by larger networks and inspire new shows and formats.

Such developments have been encouraged all the more by new technologies and organizational structures (see Christopherson and Storper, 1986; Murray, 1989; Robbins and Cornford, 1992; Hesmondhalgh, 2000; Wasko, 2001; Lotz, 2007). Much cheaper entry and production costs, as well as the growth of multiple channels and alternative means of distribution, have enabled a whole range of autonomous, creative producers to emerge. They have also severely weakened the power and profits of major corporations. Indeed, many major corporations, in the television and music industries, have seen a sharp decline in their fortunes in the digital era. In the case of US television, at the start of the 1980s the three networks (ABC, NBC, CBS) accounted for 90 per cent of the TV audience. By 2004–5, that had dropped to 46 per cent (Lotz, 2007: 10). Ultimately, smaller producers still have less power over distribution and remain economically insecure. However, it is also in the interests of all in the industries that spaces for independent production, innovation and creativity are maintained.

Promotional culture and creative autonomy in the Hollywood film industry

This section looks at the long-term impact of promotional culture on the autonomy of creative artists involved in Hollywood film production. It offers two contrasting accounts. The first presents a history in which the power of the major studios has been eroded, thus enabling creative autonomy to flourish. The second suggests that, although film-making has been transformed in many ways, the major studios are as dominant as ever. In both accounts, promotional culture and promotional intermediaries have played a significant part in reshaping the wider film industry.

Central to the history of Hollywood is the long-term relationship between a handful of major, all-powerful studios and the creative independence of its artistic and technical workforce. In most historical accounts of Hollywood's evolution (McDonald, 2000; Epstein, 2005; King, 2005; Mann, 2008), a key turning point in relations was the 1948 anti-trust case against Paramount. Until this point seven major studios (MGM, Warner Brothers, Paramount, 20th Century-Fox, Columbia, Universal and RKO) dominated the production process. These seven, which received 95 per cent of ticket sale revenue, either owned the viewing theatres or were able to dictate the terms of sale to independents. Each studio developed its own vast lots on which several films were churned out rapidly and simultaneously. Stars of the day were tightly contracted to the studios, which managed their publicity and dictated which films they made. A handful of producers would 'green-light' a film, monitor daily director progress, and supervise the editing. In effect, between the 1920s

and 1940s, the studios dominated in every way. Artistic autonomy
remained fairly restricted for writers, directors and actors.

After 1948 all that changed. The Paramount ruling forced the
studios to sell their theatre chains and limited their ability to dictate
the terms of film rental. Television also began providing competition as theatre attendances dropped steadily. Guaranteed profits
disappeared, and the industry was forced to restructure itself over
the next three decades. As the centralized control of the studios fell
apart, so the scope for greater autonomy and creativity emerged.
Creative artists, including actors, directors and writers, established
more contractual freedom. An emerging array of promotional intermediaries, among them talent agencies, business managers, publicists and entertainment attorneys, came to represent their interests
to the studios (see McDonald, 2000, 2008; Wasko, 2003; Schatz,
2008). Successful artists could dictate both their choice of projects
and much higher salaries. In Mann's (2008) account, the conditions
encouraged a 'postwar talent takeover', as the likes of Jimmy Stewart,
Bette Davis and Billy Wilder became free to develop creative new
film projects. Newcomers, such as Burt Lancaster, Kirk Douglas and
Elia Kazan, set up their own production companies. A 'new wave' of
films, drawing on European art-house inspirations, socially and politically challenging subjects, and non-mainstream, niche genres, were
rolled out. So were sown the 'seeds of the more truly groundbreaking
work of the Hollywood Renaissance of the 1960s and 1970s' (Mann,
2008: 243). Several decades later, Wasko (2003: 29) revealed that
star actors and directors, such as Woody Allen, Mel Gibson, James
Cameron, Ridley Scott, Wes Craven, Will Smith, Tom Cruise, Nora
Ephron (now deceased), Tom Hanks, Clint Eastwood and George
Clooney, continued to thrive with their own production companies.

At the same time, there was a general shift towards film-making
by independent producers as the majors began to make fewer large-
budget productions. Christopherson and Storper (1986) describe
the vertical disintegration of the studio majors from the 1950s
onwards. Post-Fordist networks of small, flexible, specialist companies emerged to supply the big studios with expert services, equipment, and independent production companies (see also Levy, 1999;
King, 2005; Mann, 2008). These operated on much smaller budgets,
produced films for non-mainstream markets, and were given greater
scope for artistic risk-taking. They were serviced by new independent
distributors, such as Miramax and New Line, and a growing number
of film festivals, such as Sundance. New technologies, especially
cheap, digital video and home computer editing software, enabled

more players to participate in film production. Cable, pay TV and video (then DVD and, most recently, online suppliers) all took off. These offered alternative markets for showing cheaper and specialist films. They also offered a training ground for film-makers as television and film production increasingly overlapped (King, 2005; Christopherson, 2008). By the 1980s, independent film production, including new subsidiaries financed by majors, surpassed that of the big studios themselves. A series of no-budget or micro-budget productions appeared, such as *El Mariachi* (1992, $7,000), *Clerks* (1991, £27,000), *She's Gotta Have It* (1986, $80,000) and *The Blair Witch Project* (1999, $60,000) (King, 2005: 12). Each of these was eventually picked up by larger distributors and went on to make tens of millions at the box office. By 2010, independent productions far outnumbered studio ones. In that year, the studios made 104 films, their subsidiaries 37, and independents 419, or three-quarters of all films (MPAA, 2010).

There is, however, a contrasting narrative of Hollywood history. This alternative, which is not entirely incompatible with the first account, reveals that, in many ways, a handful of major studios remain dominant in terms of creative control, power and financing. The film-making industry has indeed been transformed but artistic autonomy remains constricted. Promotional culture has played a central part in the reshaping of the sector and is responsible for many of the creative restrictions that have developed.

The first way promotional culture changed the industry was in the creation of a new, large additional cost: that of film promotion itself. In 1947 the average cost of making a studio film was $732,000. The distribution and promotional costs combined were $90,000, or 12 per cent of the overall budget. In 2003, the average cost of a studio film was $63.8 million and its distribution and promotional costs $39 million (figures in Epstein, 2005: 7–9, 18–19). Not only had promotional costs spiralled, they now made up 38 per cent of a film's budget. Even low-budget distribution and promotion run into many millions of dollars. *Clerks* (1991) may have cost $27,000 to make, but almost $2 million was spent making it theatre ready and promoting it. *The Blair Witch Project* cost $4.8 million in transfer and promotional fees and, once it had taken off, another $20 million was spent on its promotion. Such expenditure both increases financial risk and can be covered only by larger studios and distributors. Promotional intermediaries, working on behalf of actors, writers and directors, have also added significantly to the costs of production. As McDonald (2008) explains, just a handful of firms have come to dominate each promotional agency sector in the Hollywood market. Such companies, in aggregate, can take up to a third of a star's income and have pushed up the salaries of leading artists significantly. At the turn of the twenty-first century, leading actors such as Tom Cruise, Tom Hanks, Julia Roberts and Arnold Schwarzenegger were claiming $20 to $30 million for each studio-financed picture they did.

The large increase in film-making costs for mainstream studio productions has had several consequences. It has widened the budget gap between studio films and independents. It has also added considerably to the financial risks of an industry where the majority of pictures fail to generate a profit at the box office. This has turned the majors more towards risk-reduction strategies, such as the use of promotional intermediaries at all stages of production (Wyatt, 1994; Wasko, 2003; Epstein, 2005; Drake, 2008). This begins with the decision to proceed with a screenplay. Thousands of ideas and scripts are rejected at the earlier levels, even after considerable investment. Projects, in order to be 'green-lighted', have to present a package that will include an enticing 'high concept', 'bankable stars' and recognized audience markets. As Drake (2008: 69) explains, film projects undergo initial 'concept testing', 'positioning studies', and focus group and test screenings before release. Post release, there are tracking studies, exit surveys and advertising response studies. Peter Guber, CEO of Sony Pictures, states: 'The importance of marketing, in terms of success of a film, is like air to all of us. It is a crucial resource that you must be breathing from the beginning.' Risk management through marketing results in an emphasis on mainstream themes, established stars, and the adaptation and repetition of already recognized 'brands': adaptations, remakes, franchises, sequels and prequels. Such known brands not only have existing records of success, they have a large head start when it comes to generating an audience for a new film.

The most recent promotional influence on studio film content, and possibly now the most significant, is the issue of cross-media promotion (see Meehan, 1991, 2005; Hardy, 2010). As Epstein (2005) and Schatz (2008) argue, Hollywood was transformed, once again, in the 1990s and 2000s. In this period there was a series of major studio takeovers by larger media conglomerates with extensive interests across other entertainment media. 'Synergy' was the key justification. In 'conglomerate Hollywood', films could now be promoted and distributed across multiple media platforms, all owned by the same media empires. In Epstein's (2005: figs 17–20) historical analysis of the industry, it is Walt Disney's early business model that has prevailed. What has become clear is that films recoup more of their costs in media other than the cinema. In 2003, the six major studios and their subsidiaries spent $18 billion making 185 films, but these films took only $6.4 billion in home ticket sales. Their takings overall were $41.1 billion. The additional $34.7 billion came from home video, television viewing (network, cable, pay), overseas markets, linked merchandise, and licensing contracts to other companies. As Epstein concludes (2005: 20), 'Theatrical releases now serve essentially as launching platforms for licensing rights, much like the runways at haute couture fashion shows.' As an extreme example, *The Phantom Menace* was produced by Fox at a cost of $115 million but sold the merchandising rights to toy-maker Hasbro for more than twice that amount. It also gained roughly $2 billion-worth of cross-promotion from Pepsi (Drake, 2008: 70). As Drake explains, the crucial opening weekend box-office figures are then used by television and DVD rental companies as indications of market take-up and, accordingly, dictate orders and contracts all through the release chain. This, in turn, means marketing, release and promotion are all 'front-loaded' towards the opening.

In other words, a big studio film is no longer just a film. It is a 'commercial intertext' that is conceived and made because of its potential to be distributed and to make profits across a range of media, audiences and related commodities markets. Consequently, the need to produce films that can fulfil these related market require-ments severely restricts the choice of subjects and themes. Films target youth and children's markets, make extensive use of special effects and/or animation, often involve 'bloodless violence' and 'sexless romance', and feature victorious heroes and defeated villains and, of course, happy endings. Hardly any of the top grossing films of the last two decades have strayed far from many of these winning ele-ments. Series of *Harry Potter*, *Lord of the Rings*, *Spiderman*, *Star Wars* and Disney/Pixar animations have regularly led the annual aggregate grossing figures.

Returning to independent producers, it also appears that their creative freedoms continue to be restricted by market forces and the majors. Independent producers may currently make the majority of films in the US, but power remains with the larger, studio-owning conglomerates. The majors control financing and distribution and have international deal-making clout. In 2005, the majors and their subsidiaries released 190 (a third) of films but took in 85.7 per cent of the domestic box office. The top five major films earned more than the entire 345 independent films released (Drake, 2008: 31). The big six media conglomerates (Viacom, Fox, NBC Universal, Time Warner, Sony and Disney) owned 96 per cent of US film distribution and took in 98 per cent of prime-time television and 75 per cent of non-prime-time advertising revenues (Epstein, 2005: 83). This means that independents continue to have a precarious financial existence and to depend on the majors. Consequently, independent producers tend towards ultimate failure or takeover by the majors, or else move towards producing cross-over, mainstream fare (see King, 2005).

As King (2005) and Christopherson (2008) make clear, employment in the sector has become much more insecure. Greater numbers of creative artists, producing more outputs, are chasing smaller budgets and limited distribution opportunities. In 1991 Sundance had 200 applications to its festival, but by 2004 that number had risen to 2,426 applications, most of which had to be rejected (King, 2005: 37). Christopherson (2008) shows that, over the last two decades, the numbers of workers in television and film have increased, but that they are less unionized, work more part time, earn lower wages, and are employed less by independents and subcontracted more to the network/majors. In effect, the conditions which brought a surge in creative, independent film-making have changed once again and in ways that advantage the majors.

To conclude, Hollywood has clearly gone through many changes since its pre-1948 heyday. Many organizational structures which severely constrained creative autonomy have changed. Successful actors, directors, writers and producers have considerably more freedom than they once had. The emergence of a range of independent producers, developing alternative films, genres and formats, is clear. Observers are right to talk of two (or even three) parallel Hollywood film sectors. However, at the same time, other creative freedoms are constrained, perhaps as much as they ever have been. Mainstream film projects and budgets are more restricted and formulaic, produced with promotional business plans in mind. Top stars earn more, but the vast majority of actors and creative workers earn relatively less, have a more precarious existence and work with tinier budgets. Promotional industries and intermediaries, from marketing and advertising to talent agencies and publicists, have had a strong part to play in the reshaping of Hollywood in all its guises.

Conclusion

The news and cultural industries are ever changing as their environments evolve. New technologies develop, audience demographics alter and fashions rapidly shift. This allows new spaces for innovative forms of journalism and independent entertainment production to open up. Alternative news platforms appear, making it difficult for mainstream media organizations or powerful sources to control and restrict the news agenda. Television production companies, film-makers and musical acts emerge and develop all the time. They continually shake up and refresh their markets. Established media conglomerates depend on them for new sources of inspiration. For these reasons, any Frankfurt School-style critique of media production, promotion and restricted creative autonomy seems to be both simplistic and overly pessimistic.

However, at the same time, it is also clear that promotional culture does have a critical influence on these industries and those who work in them. Large organizations are driven by business models that are risk averse and directed to what seems most cost-efficient and synergistic. They are always ready to exploit as much as possible a popular news story, information subsidy, or film or television format. Promotional intermediaries and practices have become the *de facto* means by which these goals are achieved. Thus, creative autonomy, whether operating in large or small companies, always has to swim against the tide.

7

Celebrity Culture and Symbolic Power

Introduction

This chapter looks at the rise of celebrity culture and its relationship to promotion. Celebrities both promote themselves and are part of elaborate promotional nexuses developed by other industries. Assisted by promotional intermediaries, they cultivate their own public images. They also represent and promote their organizations, the cultural products to which they contribute, and goods produced by other companies. As such, they are human 'commercial intertexts' (Meehan, 1991) who generate 'personal brand equity' across a range of cultural planes, and therefore are a key feature of promotional culture. Consequently, 'celebrities' emerge and circulate in texts in ever greater numbers. As the first part of the chapter argues, celebrity generation has become a promotional industry in its own right.

The next two parts of the chapter discuss the significance of this development, focusing on the theme of symbolic power. The question is one of whether celebrity culture has had substantive consequences for wider society. In much of the 'fame' literature, celebrity in itself is seen as fairly unimportant. Celebrities are regarded as superficial and 'powerless', to be juxtaposed with those public figures who are 'well known' for their achievements. In contrast, the chapter suggests that celebrity is something more substantial. Celebrity generates a form of symbolic capital that is exchangeable for economic and political capital, as well as bringing forms of symbolic power. Celebrity therefore becomes a means of attaining power both within particular fields and across wider society. However, because symbolic capital is a relatively unstable capital form, so its elevation has had a variety of destabilizing effects on these fields. The ideas discussed are applied in three case studies, of David Cameron, Jennifer Lopez and Tiger Woods.

The growth of celebrity culture and the celebrity industry

Societies have always had prominent public figures. Many of these stood out through a combination of 'innate' or 'natural' talents and 'charismatic authority' (Weber, 1948). Many, be they political or religious leaders or from popular culture, also consciously promoted themselves and exploited their reputations. George Washington, Andrew Jackson and Ulysses S. Grant all used their fame to make successful entries into the political arena (West and Orman, 2003). Mark Twain, Oscar Wilde and Charles Dickens each made use of nineteenth-century promotional mechanisms such as lecture tours and the popular press (Demoor, 2004; Moran, 2000). 'Film stars' and a 'star' promotional discourse developed in the early twentieth century (deCordova, 1990).

Their acceptance by larger publics, according to accounts past (Michels, 1967 [1911]; Pareto, 1935; Alberoni, 2007 [1960]) and present (Rojek, 2001; Turner, 2004), was linked to wider social and psychological needs. Public figures, whether powerful leaders or 'famous celebrities', are deemed to have a necessary social function. Social organizations need leadership. Large, urbanized, secular democracies need new forms of social and moral guidance to replace that previously provided by religion, close-knit families and communities. Celebrity offers alternative forms of intimacy and guidance, albeit of a 'para-social', distanced kind. It is through celebrity that social and ethical norms and values are played out and understood. Thus, individuals construct their own identities, in part, through engaging with celebrity texts (Dyer, 1986; Stacey, 1994; Marshall, 1997). For Dyer (1979, 1986), film stars are to be seen as complex ideological representations, indicative of their time and place. They 'articulate what it is to be a human being' – the good and the bad – to the audience. Stacey (1994) analysed accounts of British women movie-goers in the 1940s and 1950s. These revealed an attachment to star actresses and identities that reinforced certain male-dominant norms, such as the need to become desirable and get a husband. However, the images also offered foreign 'competing cultural discourses of femininity' which challenged UK female stereotypes.

It is also through public figures that abstract, complex issues are humanized and made sense of. Ordinary citizens may engage with formal politics and news through reporting that focuses on celebrities and public figures (Lumby, 1999; Bird, 2000; Pels, 2003). For Bird (2000) and Myra MacDonald (2000), celebrity news stories are one form of 'human interest' story, of the type that better draws in ordinary citizens. In MacDonald's view, serious news privileges abstraction and rationality, whereas personalization contextualizes stories properly. As such, she says they become 'knowledge-enabling'. For Corner and Pels (2003), the merger of popular culture, personalities and politics enables the public to deploy 'visual and emotional literacy' when weighing up complex issues and political leaders.

Regardless of whether or not society naturally produces or needs celebrities, the creation and maintenance of public personalities has become more than a natural occurrence. Celebrity culture is far more prevalent and widespread. It contains certain 'generic celebrity' elements (Ommundsen, 2007). It is no longer a thing of chance, reliant on the ad hoc emergence of talented individuals. Processes of celebrity cultivation and maintenance have become institutionalized, systematized and commercialized. In effect, celebrity itself has become an industry.

Arguably, its unfettered rise is linked to the fact that a variety of promotional occupations and industries have collectively propelled it in the same direction. At one level, celebrities promote themselves and directly employ promotional intermediaries to help them in this task. Public visibility brings greater opportunities and status as well as greater financial rewards. This is most obvious in film and television. DeCordova (1990) describes how Mary 'Little Mary' Pickford, Roscoe 'Fatty' Arbuckle, Charlie Chaplin, Douglas Fairbanks and others developed their own film-star images a century ago. Mary Pickford began exploiting her popular image in order to raise her salary of $175 per week in 1910, through several leaps, to $10,000 per week in 1916 (McDonald, 2000: 34–5, 100). Since the 1940s, a range of talent agencies, personal managers, publicists and entertainment attorneys have emerged to manage clients' images and commercial interests directly. As Coombe (1998) explains, over time celebrities have gained legal ownership over the use of their image, body parts, stock phrases, mannerisms, performance styles, nicknames and signatures. Ownership and 'image rights' accordingly feature in contracts drawn up by organizations that employ a celebrity. According to McDonald (2008; see also Gamson, 1992), the powerful Hollywood agency sector, which commands up to a third of any star's income, has pushed up star fees considerably. By the 1990s, top Hollywood stars were commanding $20 to $30 million per picture (see also Turner et al., 2000). Personal agents and attorneys are also prevalent in sports, music, politics, business and other parts of the entertainment industry.

At a second promotional level, organizations publicize their stars and the leaders they employ in order to promote themselves and their products. Since the 1980s, film promotion had been commonly built around leading cast members, who are contractually obliged to undertake multiple rounds of interviews and red-carpet appearances (Wasko, 2003; McDonald, 2008). Negus (1992) records the way music corporations routinely invest in extensive publicity and promotional circuits, using the music press, particular venues and festivals to promote their artists as well as their music. Promotional experts have become so influential they can even create new musical acts themselves out of raw, unknown musicians (Marshall, 1997; Cashmore, 2006). Moran (2000) similarly observes the promotional means and intermediaries used to present authors alongside their work. These include book-signing tours, lecture circuits, media interviews, critical arts programmes, literary festivals and award ceremonies. Beyond the entertainment industries, leading politicians are now customarily packaged by their parties (Franklin, 1994; Swanson and Mancini, 1996; Corner and Pels, 2003). PR consultants, pollsters, speech writers, media trainers and image consultants now groom and present senior party figures alongside the parties they represent. In the corporate world, public relations consultants similarly sell CEOs to investors and other businesses as a means of promoting the business (Khurana, 2002; Davis, 2007; Littler, 2007).

At a third promotional level, news and entertainment media promote celebrities as a means of gaining viewers and readers (Rojek, 2001; Turner, 2004; Evans and Hesmondhalgh, 2005). For Turner, Bonner and Marshall (2000: 20–1), celebrity coverage is central to the entertainment and women's magazine sector in Australia. There, in the 1990s, celebrity stories made up 46 per cent of content in entertainment magazines and between 25 and 32 per cent in individual women's magazines. They made up 26 per cent of *Australian Women's Weekly* and 9 per cent of TV news. Such percentages were several times higher when compared to those in the 1970s. In the UK, according to McLachlan and Golding (2000), celebrity stories made up 6 per cent of UK tabloid news in 1952 but had risen to 17 per cent in 1997 (see also Sparks and Tulloch, 2000). The focus on individual figures has also become more important to serious news sectors. For Hayward et al. (2004) the business press in general is overly focused on celebrity CEOs. For Hallin (1994), US news devotes more coverage to presidents than to the activities of US political parties, the administration and Congress put together. According to Deacon and his colleagues (2005: 18), in the 2005 UK general election, the three main party leaders accounted for 39 per cent of all political appearances and 60 per cent of political quotations. Perhaps more significant is the broadcast media's ability to create and then eject its own range of television-made celebrities. Horton and Wohl (1993) first noticed television's attempts to manufacture 'personas' for public consumption in the 1950s (see also Boorstin, 1962). Several decades later, a range of new television formats, such as reality television (*Big Brother*), confessional shows (*Jerry Springer*) and talent contests (*Pop Idol*), have begun creating and then disposing of their own, formerly unknown celebrities or 'celetoids' (Rojek, 2001; Turner, 2009).

A fourth promotional level comes from organizations employing celebrities to endorse their products. Film and sports stars are given free equipment, sportswear and dresses to wear when they perform on the sports field or red carpet (Andrews and Jackson, 2001; Cashmore, 2006). They are also awarded lucrative contracts to appear in advertisements for all sorts of everyday goods, from cars and razors to perfumes and clothes. Their images, or the images of film characters they have created, are used in intensive cross-media promotional campaigns, from videos and theme parks to fast food and toys (Epstein, 2005; Hardy, 2010). Voluntarily, they offer their images in support of interest group campaigns (Sireau, 2009) and political parties (West and Orman, 2003).

In effect, a range of promotional intermediaries, working directly for celebrities and for media and other organizations, cumulatively produce and reinforce celebrity images across a range of texts. In turn these images are used to promote organizations, media texts and commodities. Over several decades, and across several employment sectors, such means of celebrity creation and promotion have become professionalized, systematized, institutionalized and commercialized. Celebrity production is no longer accidental or dependent on charismatic, able individuals. It is a promotional industry in itself.

Celebrities as a powerless elite

Celebrity promotion is an industry deploying considerable resources and generating widespread coverage across multiple media and promotional texts. The question is: Does that symbolic presence equate to something more substantive?

In many accounts, celebrity, in itself, is treated as a relatively insignificant phenomenon. 'Celebrities', as opposed to substantive individuals or real 'heroes', are a 'powerless elite' (Alberoni, 2007 [1960]). They do no more than profit personally from their fame. In Alberoni's early account, they were 'stars, idols, "divas"', as opposed to the 'men of power', who were traditionally comprised of royalty, nobility and religious leaders. Celebrities such as Gina Lollobrigida, Sophia Loren and Marilyn Monroe offered 'escape' and drew 'admiration' rather than 'envy'. Boorstin (1962) was similarly dismissive. They were persons known for their 'well known-ness' and were the opposite of 'heroes' or 'leaders'. They were manufactured 'human pseudo-events'. A key point made by Alberoni is that 'observability' and power may be inversely correlated. Powerful people stay invisible. It is a point that makes sense now. Visible government ministers may have considerably less power than the invisible senior civil servants, corporate leaders and credit-rating agencies upon which they depend.

Contemporary writers on celebrity now offer more multifaceted accounts of fame. They have also broadened its definition to include well-known figures from a range of professions. However, for many of them, there still remains a sense of 'celebrity' being relatively superficial and powerless. It is something ephemeral, temporary, inauthentic and full of contradictions, to be juxtaposed with that which is substantive and meaningful (Turner et al., 2000; Turner, 2004). Several typographies of celebrity are offered in which the authentic and deserving public figure is part of a diminishing minority. For Rojek (2001: 20), 'achieved' celebrity, attained by success in competition, is squeezed between those whose celebrity is 'ascribed', by birth or accident, and those who have it 'attributed' by journalists and other promotional intermediaries. Increasingly dominant is this last group, particularly those who are 'celetoids'. These are ordinary people given 'a form of compressed, concentrated, attributed celebrity'. West and Orman (2003) offer a fivefold categorization of political celebrity. Only the first of these – 'political newsworthies' – have bona fide status. The rest, including 'legacies' (Rojek's 'ascribed'), 'famed non-politicos' and 'event celebrities' (close to 'celetoids'), are not. Each of these authors recognizes that 'celebrity' also bestows a form of symbolic power. Nevertheless that power is neither concentrated nor wielded by capable, innately talented individuals.

The notion of celebrity symbolic power being diluted and dispersed is a common theme. Alberoni (2007 [1960]), Rojek (2001) and Turner (2004) all suggest that the rise of celebrity culture is linked to the equalizing tendencies of democracies. In centuries past, celebrity was restricted to those who had it bestowed on them by virtue of authoritarian, unequal systems. It was 'ascribed' to royalty and nobility without challenge. Modern celebrity represents a levelling out of power. It demonstrates an emerging meritocracy and the possibility of upward social mobility. The more 'ordinary' people can achieve their 15 minutes of fame, as 'celetoids' and 'accidental celebrities', the more symbolic power is dispersed. In mature democracies with digital media environments, audiences too have a greater power to bestow attention on celebrities or to turn that interest elsewhere (Hartley, 1996; Marshall, 1997; Turner, 2004). Fame, by definition, is reliant on an extended audience and interested media. Modern celebrities, be they in business, politics or entertainment, are subject more than ever to the fickle opinions and tastes of audiences.

In some cases celebrity culture is itself seen as indicative of a more critical response to powerful elites and established institutions (Connell, 1992; Fiske, 1996; Simmons, 2003). Fiske (1996) regards such personal, tabloid forms of news as a challenge to traditional, 'high-brow' news. Such 'serious' news is presented as neutral, objective and in the public interest but is dominated by 'the power-bloc' of elite sources, ideas and institutions. Alternatively, tabloid news is about ordinary or working-class people made good and/or becoming celebrities. It therefore legitimizes the public expression of non-elites and non-experts. For Connell (1992), celebrity news, which he prefers to call 'fantastical reportage', is mostly about focusing on the 'deviancy' and the problems of those in power. Celebrity news builds them up and then casts judgement on them and knocks them down. 'The have-nots' can get their revenge on 'the haves'. In effect, it is a 'populist challenge on privilege' that highlights social differences rather than making them unintelligible, remote and abstract.

In each of these discussions of the symbolic significance of celebrity, fame, in itself, does not tend to equate to a substantive form of power. Where it does, that power is not concentrated within individuals or institutions. Instead, it is associated with visible but 'powerless' public figures who usually possess few or no innate abilities. Celebrity symbolic power, in practice, is a great counter to elite power, being more easily achievable, widely dispersed and democratizing in nature.

Celebrities, accumulating symbolic capital and forms of power

Alternatively, celebrity may also be seen as a type of symbolic capital that is transferable to other forms of capital and professional fields. Following Bourdieu's conceptualization of professional 'fields' and 'forms of capital' (1984, 1986, 1993), symbolic capital may be exchanged for political, economic and social forms of capital. It also brings a type of symbolic power which influences wider social discourse and practice (see also discussions in Moran, 2000; Davis, 2010). Whether those forms of capital, and their associated power, are wielded by individuals or organizations, it is a concentrated and substantial form of power. That said, celebrity symbolic capital is also a less stable capital form that produces less manageable forms of power. Its deployment is uncertain and its rise has had unintended longer-term consequences.

That celebrity symbolic capital translates to economic capital is made clear in a variety of accounts. In the first instance, as celebrities build their 'personal brand equity', so they can command greater remuneration for their labour power as well as exploit their image rights. Mary Pickford did just this a century ago. Celebrities and their promotional intermediaries have been doing it with ever greater sophistication since. In 1999, Forbes began producing a list of the 100 most powerful worldwide celebrities, combining data on incomes and media visibility. In 2011, Oprah Winfrey topped the pay list, having earned $290 million over the previous year. The top ten celebrities, who also included Lady Gaga, Simon Cowell and Jerry Bruckheimer, in aggregate earned $1.32 billion from their varied interests (Forbes, 2011). The economic value of celebrity, in turn, is clearly recognized by those that employ them. For example, Nike sold $5.2 billion-worth of its Air Jordan sports shoes and paid Michael Jordan $130 million for endorsing them. In McDonald's (2008) account (see also Wasko, 2003; Epstein, 2005), top stars are packaged to film financiers and producers as part of 'high-concept' pitches. Attracting those with strong box-office track records increases the likelihood of projects getting 'green-lighted', as financial risks are considered to be lower (see Hesmondhalgh, 2005). Indeed, the film records of each film star, as well as their salaries and the ratios between the two, are kept and analysed in the industry. As of 2011, Julia Roberts's thirty-five pictures have earned an average of $71.5 million each. Tom Cruise has chalked up an average of $95.7 million for each of his thirty films. They are both outshone by Daniel Radcliffe, who has made an average of $250 million for each of his eight films, seven of which were in the *Harry Potter* series (boxofficemojo).

Celebrity symbolic capital also translates into economic capital within corporate and financial fields. Wade and his colleagues (2006) found that, on average, CEOs who won an industry award (the 'Financial Worlds' annual CEO award) were employed on contracts worth 10 per cent more than their peers. Davis (2002, 2006) documented just how important the reputation of CEOs and senior managers was for attracting institutional investors, thereby boosting share prices. He cited several polls showing that 'quality of management' was considered 'the most important factor' when investors and analysts were asked how they judged companies. In one well-publicized takeover battle in the 1990s, between Granada and Forte, a comparison of CEOs played a large part in the final decision-making of large investors. Khurana (2002) also found that the share prices of companies shot up on the announcement that a new 'celebrity CEO' was to be appointed. Froud and her colleagues (2006) suggest that the ability of top CEOs to cultivate and play on their 'business icon' status with shareholders has resulted in inflated share prices and escalating levels of CEO pay.

Celebrity symbolic capital is also a means of acquiring political capital within a field. Such acquisitions are of course fundamental in the political field. Party selection of candidates and leaders is increasingly linked to a politician's stock of symbolic capital and estimates of their ability to accumulate it with future voters (West and Orman, 2003; Corner and Pels, 2003; Stanyer, 2007; Davis, 2010; see chapter 8). Just as film-star box-office records can be tracked, so can individual politicians' poll ratings. Such calculations influence both party support for leaders and leader selections of senior party and government appointments. As West and Orman (2003) point out, many successful US politicians have built profiles based on political family links, such as the Bushes and the Kennedys. Such individuals have a head start, having accumulated symbolic capital within powerful, established political, media and corporate donor networks. Their media exposure and public recognition is considerably higher than that of new political entrants.

By the same logic, celebrity symbolic capital generated in other fields is transferable, by dint of voter recognition and appeal, to the political field. As popular culture and politics increasingly overlap (Delli Carpini and Williams, 2001; West and Orman, 2003; Street, 2003), so that exchange becomes more fluid. Celebrities from entertainment, sport and business are recruited to offer endorsements for parties and candidates. Vaclav Havel, Arnold Schwarzenegger, Jesse Ventura and Ronald Reagan all switched from entertainment to politics. Similarly, from the 1980s onwards, successful prime ministers and presidents have increasingly appeared on chat shows, done interviews with entertainment magazines, and made public personal disclosures (see also Parry-Giles and Parry-Giles, 2002; Pels, 2003; Stanyer, 2007). Thus, politicians, and endorsing celebrities, generate 'generic' celebrity symbolic capital, to be transformed into political symbolic capital in the political field. In effect, political celebrity produces a form of symbolic capital which helps politicians rise to, and then maintain, positions of political authority and power.

Celebrity symbolic capital may also bring symbolic power. Although less concentrated in individuals, forms of symbolic power influence wider social behaviours and practices. These, in turn, contribute to more substantive forms of political, economic and social power. Just as several accounts (Alberoni, 2007 [1960]; Marshall, 1997; Rojek, 2001; Turner, 2004) link celebrity to democratic developments, they also link it to ideological strands which sustain capitalism. Three particular celebrity-linked discursive strands stand out: 'individualism', 'consumption' and 'equality'. Starting with 'individualism', for Adorno and Horkheimer (1979 [1947]), as with commodities, the cultural industries create 'pseudo-individuality' where little actually exists. Celebrity normalizes a discourse which commodifies individuals, quite simply because consumption is promoted by single celebrities. Clothing fashions, perfume lines and sporting goods are all directly linked to individual celebrity use in films, advertisements and public appearances (Turner, 2004; Cashmore, 2006). As Rojek (2001: 14) explains, celebrity helps transform abstract desires in order to 'humanize the process of commodity consumption'.

Celebrity culture also presents a strong but false sense of equality in modern democratic society. In Alberoni's estimation (2007 [1960]), stars present a 'narcotizing illusion' of 'social mobility'. For Gamson (1992), celebrity covers over a great contradiction. Public personalities represent the elevation of the everyperson as representative of an egalitarian society. The problem is that very few ordinary people ever do rise to such positions. A parallel position is outlined by Turner (2009) in his account of the 'demotic turn' in media, where public visibility is falsely equated with democratic participation. Similar arguments can be made about gender and racial equality as represented by celebrity figures. For Stacey (1994) and Kellner (1995), prominent women celebrities, from Lauren Bacall to Madonna, may represent powerful autonomous female role models. However, they also present certain gender roles that reproduce male patriarchy and the commodification of female bodies. Jhally and Lewis (1992), Cole and Andrews (2001) and Cashmore (2006) argue that public presentations of ethnic minority celebrities, from Bill Cosby to Beyoncé, succeed on the basis that they present white-friendly images. Their presentation of success covers up the deep racial inequalities that still exist in the US.

The growing importance of celebrity symbolic capital in adjacent professional fields also has significant consequences for those fields. First, the greater emphasis on accumulating celebrity symbolic capital means that otherwise able individuals are disadvantaged and field-specific skill-sets are downgraded. Ommundsen (2007) suggests that, in the literary field, professional achievements may be eclipsed by an emphasis on 'celebrity status'. She and Moran (2000) concur that authors who are more personally marketable for publishers are far more likely to have their work fully promoted. In business, a celebrity CEO may raise their profile in the short term with investors, but may do so by enforcing changes that are not in the long-term interests of the business (Khurana, 2002; Froud et al., 2006). In politics, a politician's ability to attract media coverage can become more important than their command of policy matters or negotiation skills (Meyer, 2002; Corner and Pels, 2003; West and Orman, 2003; Davis, 2010). Citizens, in turn, end up voting for political leaders who do not represent their personal policy preferences (see chapter 8).

Second, celebrity symbolic capital can destabilize the fields in which it operates. Celebrity symbolic capital tends to be rather more volatile and unmanageable than other capital forms because it is reliant on the shifting interests and fashions of others (media and publics). This means the increased weighting given to it within a professional field also has a destabilizing effect on that field. There is an expectation that political and business leaders will keep delivering symbolically, as well as substantively, or be quickly moved on. Wade and his colleagues (2006) found that CEO pay and company share value rose when a celebrity CEO was first appointed but then, within a year, both had usually dropped more than the initial rise. The ability of celebrity politicians to accrue symbolic capital in excess of their actual political and economic power sets up a series of public expectations of politicians and institutions which they cannot possibly fulfil (Dalton, 2004; Hay, 2007). During their tenures, George W. Bush and Tony Blair recorded both the highest and the lowest postwar approval ratings for leaders in the US and UK respectively.

As argued here, celebrity is not simply an insignificant phenomenon. Celebrity brings symbolic capital, which is transferable to economic, political and other capital forms. These bring forms of power, within fields and wider society. Symbolic capital can also have a destabilizing effect on the fields in which it is used. These points are all illustrated in greater detail in three case studies, focusing on David Cameron, Jennifer Lopez and Tiger Woods.

Celebrity, symbolic capital and political capital: the case of David Cameron

This case* looks at how the ability to generate celebrity symbolic capital, among the wider voting public, has become a key source of political capital, and therefore power, inside the political field. The focus is on David Cameron's victory in the UK Conservative Party leadership election in 2005. Some years later, as prime minister, Cameron appears as an established public figure. But in 2005 he was a young, barely known MP, with little public exposure either inside or outside Parliament. Under such circumstances, his rise was astounding. A closer investigation shows that his ability to accumulate symbolic capital through his media skills, contacts and knowledge proved vital to his elevation.

Following the 2005 general election loss, the then leader of the Conservative Party, Michael Howard, announced his resignation on 5 May. A delayed leadership election was announced. To win the contest candidates had first to gain support among the 198 Conservative MPs, whose two ballots would decide the two final candidates. Party members would then cast the final vote. David Davis, the shadow home secretary, was recognized as the clear favourite. David Cameron was one of three other candidates who put themselves forward in late September, when the official contest began.

At this point, it seemed that Cameron's hopes of winning were remote. He was relatively unknown to MPs, having been elected only in 2001 and appointed to his first shadow cabinet position in May 2005. In contrast, his three rivals had had lengthy political careers. They had accumulated significant levels of symbolic capital, being widely recognized both within the UK Parliament (political field) and among voters outside it. Table 7.1 shows the media mentions of the candidates for the three years before the election period. Cameron's

---

* This case is drawn from a larger study (see Davis and Seymour, 2010).

coverage was by far the lowest. Accordingly, most journalists and MPs at the time concluded that Cameron would be last and Davis was the most likely winner. Davis had the most media exposure and a clear lead among MPs, and was deemed ideologically closest to ordinary party members who cast the final ballot. In early September, Cameron was supported by just 3 per cent of party members and less than 5 per cent of Conservative MPs (*Sunday Times*/YouGov, 4 September 2005; *The Times*/Populus, 6 September 2005).

Table 7.1   Media exposure, in eight news titles, of the four lead candidates three years before and during the campaign period (6 May 2002 to 21 October 2005)

	David Cameron	David Davis	Ken Clarke	Liam Fox
6.5.02–5.11.02	17	327	170	132
6.11.02–5.5.03	14	181	215	149
6.5.03–5.11.03	21	213	183	211
6.11.03–5.5.04	26	343	91	124
6.5.04–5.11.04	49	290	56	183
6.11.04–5.5.05	64	444	90	258
Total	**191**	**1,798**	**805**	**1,057**
6.5.05–21.10.05	524	561	424	279

However, everything appeared to change dramatically during the few days of the party conference when the candidates were due to give speeches. After a very well-received speech by Cameron on 4 October, and a poorly received one by David Davis the next day, Cameron was suddenly catapulted out of obscurity to become the front-runner. Media coverage enthusiastically backed Cameron while criticizing Davis. By the time of the second ballot, on 20 October, Cameron had gained a strong lead among Conservative MPs and was clearly ahead in all opinion polls. Little changed before the final membership vote in December, when Cameron won with a two-thirds majority. Why and how did Cameron succeed?

Cameron's success is down to a number of factors. Key among these is his ability to generate symbolic capital. He was not well known in the wider party but he was well connected to several senior politicians and political lobby journalists. After leaving university in 1988 he spent six years working closely as an advisor to the then prime minister, John Major, as well as in the Treasury and the Home Office (see Elliott and Hanning, 2007). His work included media relations with reporters at Westminster. He then left the party and worked for seven years as head of communications at Carlton, a large UK television company. In effect, although little known in the wider party or by the public, he was well known across Parliament's senior political and journalist networks. He had also accumulated wide experience and knowledge of the media and its reporting practices.

Such networks and experiences proved instrumental to Cameron's advance. His core campaign team included several campaign strategists, former journalists and PR specialists with whom he had worked in previous positions. Through the summer period, Cameron and his team proved to be more adept and active than any of his rivals in courting the media. Looking back at table 7.1, Davis received more mentions overall, but Cameron came a strong second. His level of coverage was nine times what it had been. A detailed analysis of news coverage (see Davis and Seymour, 2010) shows that, whether cited directly or indirectly, he was personally quoted more than all the other candidates, including Davis. He also wrote more articles and was the subject of an interview feature more than anyone else.

Davis's ability to generate symbolic capital was modest compared to Cameron's. He had had a long pre-politics business career, then eighteen years as an MP, including several years in senior roles. He was well known across the party and among the public but had few of Cameron's media skills and contacts. He distanced himself from journalists. His campaign was focused on maintaining his strong support among back-bench MPs and appealing to traditional party members. In contrast, Cameron's individual presentation attempted to appeal to the wider electorate beyond the Conservative Party. He made several approaches to left-leaning journalists and publications and consciously positioned himself as the 'heir to Blair'. Some seventy articles drew comparisons between David Cameron and Tony Blair. Cameron's coverage was far more likely to refer to general voters than Davis's.

Leading up to the September vote, three key events occurred, each enabling Cameron to generate symbolic capital with different audiences. The first of these was his official campaign launch to journalists, on 29 September. This was well received. William Rees-Mogg (2005), for example, wrote in the *Mail on Sunday* that 'Most journalists thought that David Cameron had a much better launch than David Davis. David Cameron has some of Blair's skills.' The second, significant event was a BBC *Newsnight* piece, broadcast on 3 October, the eve of Cameron's speech. This showed that Cameron generated the most favourable responses from the general public in focus-group research. The third event was the conference speech, where coverage was very favourable. By then, the reporting journalists had already been positively primed in Cameron's direction. Their verdicts were then passed on to the public.

Over a five-month period Cameron had drawn on both his senior political and journalistic networks and his significant campaign and media experience to move from last to first place among the candidates. He represented the new breed of political leader, with a network of senior political and journalist connections and an ideal skill-set for accumulating celebrity-style symbolic capital. His well-managed media events demonstrated that Cameron was far more capable than Davis of generating positive media coverage and gaining the support of centre-ground, swing voters. Journalists and MPs picked this up and relayed it to watching party members and the public. Cameron then went on to lead the Conservative Party to a muted victory in the 2010 general election. At the time of writing, he is still considered his party's best electoral asset.

Celebrity, symbolic capital and ideological power: the case of Jennifer 'J. Lo' Lopez

This case looks at the career of Jennifer Lopez, who can be seen as both a talented 'star' and a product of the celebrity industry. She has achieved star status across multiple media and commodities markets that include dance, television, film, music, fashion and cosmetics. Between 1995 and 2011 she had significant parts in twenty films which cumulatively made $757 million at the US box office. She also recorded seven albums, the top three of which achieved 21 million sales worldwide. She has gained many awards and nominations in television, film and music. In eight of the last ten years she has made the Forbes annual list of the 100 most powerful world celebrities, reaching number 5 in 2003 and the number 1 spot in 2012. In 2011 she had 3.5 million Facebook friends and 1.6 million Twitter followers (Forbes, 2011). Her celebrity symbolic capital, whether recorded in sales, industry awards, media visibility or social media followers, is indisputable.

Lopez's considerable symbolic capital also brings with it a form of ideological or discursive power in relation to her audiences. Her celebrity 'persona' offers a complex mix of images and character traits which both challenge and sustain dominant social and cultural norms. In some accounts, she is presented as the rare case of a Latina woman succeeding in the white, male-dominated entertainment industries of the US. Her advance has come while emphasizing her Puerto Rican roots, her poor inner-city upbringing and her unfashionably curvy figure. However, in other accounts, Lopez downplays these elements of her public self when it suits, and her success is based equally on her 'collaboration' with dominant cultural norms.

On the one hand, Lopez is held up as someone who challenges the status quo and is a positive role model for women and poor ethnic minorities in the United States. There is a clear narrative running through many of her biographies (e.g., Parish, 2006; Tracy, 2008; Woog, 2008). She came from a modest Puerto Rican family and grew up in the working-class, ethnic neighbourhoods of the South Bronx borough of New York. Through hard work, and against the odds, she worked her way up to become an international star and an inspiration to many. Thus Woog (2008: 6, 8) writes of her 'remarkable determination and concentration'. She quotes Lopez: 'My mom always told me that if you work hard, you can achieve anything. And it's true.'

Lopez's significance to the Hispanic community, and Latina women in particular, has been regularly acknowledged. She was widely praised for her 1997 film portrayal of Selena Quintanilla-Perez, an iconic Mexican-American singer. She has won several ALMAs (American Latino Media Arts), two Latin Grammy awards and several Latin Billboard music awards, and led *People en Espanol*'s 2007 '100 most influential Hispanics' list. Her active presentation of her 'curves and butt' is considered to be a direct cultural and ideological challenge to white, mainstream assumptions of beauty. In this she has come to represent the strengths of natural, Latina female bodies (Negran-Muntaner, 1997; Lim, 2005; Beltran, 2007). In Lim's words (2005: 19), 'she has single-handedly brought back to fashion the look of the full-figured woman.' For Negran-Muntaner (1997: 189), her actions confronted long-established, Euro-American colonial and cultural attitudes towards ethnic women. She contests 'American image gatekeepers . . . and hegemonic (white) notions of beauty and good taste'. She has managed therefore to achieve wider public success while also retaining her Hispanic and Bronx identity, thus becoming a role model for those who are marginalized on account of their race, gender or class.

However, in other ways, Lopez also reasserts many dominant ideological norms in American society. Her rise is linked as much to a well-tuned publicity machine and her 'generic celebrity' qualities. At last count, she was represented by two managers, two agents, two publicists and one attorney. From 2001 she and all her products were widely promoted through her 'J. Lo' brand (Lim, 2005). In 2008 she sold exclusive pictures of her twin babies to *People* magazine, and in 2010 she became a celebrity judge on *American Idol*. All this suggests that her 'star status' and 'public persona' are tightly interconnected. As several argue, many aspects of the persona have been consciously cultivated and managed for commercial purposes. In so doing, Lopez has also reinforced traditional social and cultural values. Along the way she has courted media interest and controversy in her relationships, song lyrics and dress at public events, and through her 'diva-like' antics and 'celebrity entourage' (Holmes, 2005).

In critical accounts (Beltran, 2007; Lockhart, 2007), Lopez's continuing appeal to her poor and ethnic roots is rather overplayed. She has continued to present herself as 'Jenny from the block', a Latina with modest means, while earning large sums annually. In more in-depth studies of her life, her parents have professional occupations and they live in a two-storey house in a middle-class neighbourhood. She is a second-generation American who grew up not speaking Spanish in her home. As her success grew she consciously sought out mainstream film parts (e.g., *Out of Sight*, 1998; *The Cell*, 1999; *The Wedding Planner*, 2001; *Monster-In-Law*, 2005) which were 'ethnic-neutral' (Parish, 2006). Just as her ethnicity is made clear in Spanish-language media in the US, so it is downplayed in the mainstream, English-language press (Beltran, 2007). In effect, Lopez's public identity is malleable and altered according to her audience. Cashmore (2006: 138) quotes survey research which finds that: 'among white teens . . . crossover stars such as Jennifer Lopez . . . are not perceived so much as minorities but as a "different kind of white person"'. Her ethnicity and class thus become 'deactivated' or 'neutralized'.

The same is true when it comes to gender. Much has been made of Lopez's success as both an 'empowered and empowering' artist and a businesswoman in male-dominated industries. However, at the same time she still takes on stereotypical film roles that reduce female power and autonomy. Rios and Reyes (2007) are scathing of her part in *Maid in Manhattan* (2002). Here she plays a poor maid from the Bronx who is swept away by a white male prince (Ralph Fiennes). This panders to Cinderella-style fantasies of beautiful women finding love at first sight and being saved by powerful males. As Lockhart (2007) also notes, her 'strong female' character has been 'saved' by similar such males (Mathew McConaghy, George Clooney, Jim Caviezel) in other films too. The promotion of her Latina body also serves to promote her as a 'sexualized commodity' for the male gaze. In Lambiase's (2003: 70) study of thirty-five celebrity websites,

Lopez's is one of the four most suggestive and revealing, being among 'the most explicitly sexualised official identities'. As an international picture licensing manager admits in interview with Lim (2005: 161), 'If I see a picture where she is half-naked, I know I'm going to get money . . . I made a ton of money off J. Lo's ass!'

In effect, Lopez's story and public persona promote several conflicting elements. A poor, disadvantaged, ethnic minority woman who, with hard work and against the odds, won through to become a powerful and wealthy star. She did so by asserting her individuality and core identity, and thus became an inspirational symbol of the 'American dream'. However, it is also clear that such a dream is, in reality, just a dream for the vast majority of her audience. Their consumption of her varied products, from music to perfume, sells them such a dream. Lopez's race and class are stretched and reshaped according to audience and commercial needs. Her gendered image is connected as much to female submissiveness, personal commodification and sexualized objectification as it is to challenges to patriarchy and the male gaze.

Celebrity, symbolic capital and economic capital: the case of Tiger Woods

This final brief case looks at the links between celebrity symbolic capital and economic capital by focusing on the career of Tiger Woods. Woods is both an impressive athlete and a public star, beloved by golf fans, advertisers and media. He is regarded as one of the greatest golfers and sportsmen of all time. By September 2012 he had won 101 pro tournaments, including seventy-four PGA competitions and fourteen major championships. Between 1997 and 2010 he was world number 1 for more than ten years and was PGA player of the year ten times. During that period he was also consistently listed in the top five of the Forbes annual list of the 100 most powerful celebrities, usually being the highest rated athlete (Forbes, 2012). This was based on a combination of his earnings and his digital and traditional media presence. Throughout, his celebrity status has been packaged and monetized consistently, bringing wealth to himself and the companies he endorses. In his case, symbolic capital has been readily transformed into economic capital. Likewise, his economic capital has declined following his public infidelities and loss of symbolic status.

From an early age, Woods's golfing ability and media interest have gone hand in hand (Cole and Andrews, 2001; Starn, 2011). As a two-year-old, in 1978, he appeared on the *Mike Douglas Show*, playing golf in front of Bob Hope and James Stewart. Other TV appearances followed. His many junior and amateur tournament victories were widely reported. Within two days of turning pro he was signed to the IMG agency (International Management Group) and did his first press conference. He immediately entered into a five-year, $40 million sponsorship deal with Nike and a $20 million deal with Titleist. For advertisers, he was regarded as an endorser's dream. His appeal drew on a combination of his sporting ability, personality and race. From the start, he was presented as a likeable athlete, as opposed to many of his 'trash-talking' contemporaries in the NBA and other sports. 'Virtue', 'clean cut', 'moral', and 'family man' were the terms often attributed to him. His marriage to a former Swedish model in 2004, and the arrival of two children, solidified his public persona. Early on, on the *Oprah Winfrey Show*, he described himself racially as 'Cablinasian' – a combination of *Ca*ucasian, *b*lack, American *In*dian and *Asian*, reflecting his diverse, international heritage. For Cole and Andrews (2001), 'Woods is represented as the embodiment of normal, immigrant, familial America . . . this national-multicultural icon's agency is figured through his squeaky clean image.' Expensive Woods-centred promotional campaigns played on each of these elements.

Further endorsement contracts followed with General Motors, General Mills, American Express, AT&T, Accenture, Buick, Tag Heuer, Gillette, Gatorade and Electronic Arts. Nike signed him to further five-year, $100 million deals in 2000 and 2005. In turn, Nike's golf business turnover grew from $120 million to $500 million between 1996 and 2006. Looking at his career, it is clear that Woods's earnings from advertising and endorsement have been far larger than those gained from his golfing career. In 2007, he earned $23 million from tournaments and $100 million from endorsements (all figures in Chung et al., 2011). In 2012, the top ten sportsmen on Forbes's list earned 53 per cent of their $543.1 million from endorsements. For Woods, the proportion from endorsements was 92.6 per cent (figures calculated from Forbes, 2012).

However, a sudden loss of symbolic capital has also meant a decline in Woods's ability to accumulate economic capital. In November 2009, while still at the peak of his career, his wholesome public image was torn apart. Over a dozen women went to journalists with stories of his affairs. After two weeks of extensive media coverage, Woods declared he was taking an indefinite break from golf.

Immediately, several large firms either ended their sponsorship deals or dropped advertising campaigns using his image. Divorce soon followed. Although Woods returned to the tour in April 2010, his form faltered and he dropped to number 58 in the rankings, though he moved back up to number 2 during 2012.

Such a dramatic loss in symbolic capital was reflected in the loss of economic capital. According to Knittel and Stango (2010), Woods's endorsing companies, collectively, lost between $5 and $12 billion in share price in the weeks following the scandal. Nike, which stuck with Woods, registered the largest losses. Chung and his colleagues (2011) estimated that the firm lost 136,000 customers. Woods's endorsement income has halved since 2010, as sponsors have pulled out or not renewed their contracts. In 2011 he dropped to number 14 on the Forbes money rankings. Despite his improved sporting form in 2012 he continued to decline, to number 20. His significant, sudden loss of symbolic capital, being linked to his 'squeaky clean' and 'familial' image, is unlikely to return to its previous levels – so neither will his endorsement earnings.

Part III

Politics, Markets and Society

8

Politics and Political Representation

Introduction

Institutional politics in mature, complex democracies, of necessity, is representative and, therefore, communicative in nature. Parties develop policies through communication with their members, electorates and other representative organizations. States inform citizens. Publics communicate their views and responses back to their political and institutional representatives. Over the course of the twentieth century, the nature of both representation and communication has shifted in response to changing media, economic and social environments. One key political development has been increasing party professionalization, which has included the widespread adoption of promotional professionals and practices. The questions addressed in this chapter are: How has such promotional professionalization affected political representation? Has professional promotion meant improved or deteriorating communicative links between citizens and political leaders?

For their advocates, political marketing, advertising and public relations have made parties more responsive and stronger communicators. For their critics, promotional practices have contributed to managed communication and more removed politicians and political institutions. Indeed, promotional culture is one reason given for a growing crisis of representative democracy as voting and levels of trust in politics steadily decline. Both positions are discussed and then further explored in three sections: on promotion, media management and citizenship; on the impact of political marketing and professional campaigning in the US; and on the ways promotional parties in the UK have contributed to a more mediatized type of politician and form of politics.

Democracies, promotional politics and the crisis of representation

A crisis of representation in democracies

Citizen representation is a core element of modern large democracies of all varieties (for overviews, see Held, 1989, 1996; Hague and Harrop, 2007). Democracies vary considerably in theory and practice but share some basic components, most of which can be linked to representation. Among these are (see Dahl's original definition, 1971) free and fair elections, the right to vote, freedom of association and to join or lead a political organization, and an independent media. Contemporary political scientists document and evaluate these components, institutions and practices with a view to judging their representativeness and legitimacy. Thus, the electoral system (majoritarian, proportional representation or other) can be assessed in terms of how well it represents a citizenry (Lijphart, 1999; Hague and Harrop, 2007). Elections both enable voters to select representatives and legitimize governments. The formation and organization of political parties, and their relationships to members and voters, is another important element (Dalton and Wattenberg, 2000; Gunther et al., 2002; Childs et al., 2005). Parties provide the organizational hub for representing particular interests in society and developing publicly linked policy and legislation. The role of the media in linking electorates and political representatives is also important (see Keane, 1991; Curran, 2002; Schudson, 2003). The media should debate issues of public concern, relay opinion between citizens and politicians, and act as a check on the powerful. The 'ideal-type' model of democracy and democratic 'public sphere' (Habermas, 1989 [1962]) should link elite decision-making to the mass of consumer citizenry through each of these institutions and practices.

However, in recent decades, a crisis of representative democracy has seemed to be gathering pace. The signs of this appeared long before the current world economic depression and accompanying political paralysis (see Norris, 2000; Dalton and Wattenberg, 2000; Pharr and Putnam, 2000; Putnam, 2002; Dalton, 2004; Hay, 2007). The most overt indicator of this is in the long-term decline in voting since the 1960s. Dalton and Wattenberg (2000: 263) calculated that the median change in voter turnout from the 1950s to the 1990s was 10 per cent across the nineteen OECD democracies for which time-series data existed. New turnout lows were reached in Japan in 1995 (44.9 per cent), in the US in 1996 (49 per cent) and in Canada in 2000 (54.6 per cent). Measures of crisis go further than voter turnout. Putnam (2002: 406) noted that membership of political parties in those same nineteen OECD countries had dropped from 14 per cent in the 1970s to less than 6 per cent in the 1990s. Dalton and Wattenberg (2000: 264) found that only 38 per cent of their publics, on average, had confidence in their national governments, 38 per cent had confidence in their parliament, 32 per cent in their press and just 22 per cent in their political parties. Polls in 2004 showed that 'trust' in political parties was minus 69 in the US and minus 63 in the EU (Hay, 2007: 34).

In the UK, by 2002 only 1.5 per cent of the public were members of parties and only 16 per cent stated that they felt strongly affiliated to a party (Heffernan, 2003). New postwar electoral lows were reached in 2001 and 2005, as turnout dropped from a 76 per cent average to just under 60 per cent, and did not recover much in 2010. Hansard's (2009: 3–4) audit of political engagement found that only 9 per cent said they had contacted a politician and only 3 per cent had donated to or joined a political party in the last '2–3 years'. In September 2009, following the MPs' expenses scandal and the economic slump, only 13 per cent of the public said they 'trusted' politicians to tell the truth (Ipsos-MORI, 2009). Levels of trust in journalists were also extremely low. Between 1983 and 2010, Ipsos-MORI found that trust in journalists 'to tell the truth' moved between just 10 and 22 per cent.

There are a wide range of explanations for this breakdown of trust and faith in mature representative democracies. Indeed the literature is fairly wide-ranging (see, variously, Habermas, 1989 [1962]; Pharr and Putnam, 2000; Crouch, 2004; Dalton, 2004; Hay, 2007). A mixture of socio-economic population shifts, increased mobility, and changes in religion and ethnicity has eroded the traditional ideological and regional links between parties and voters. Citizens have instead joined single-issue interest groups, viewing them as a positive alternative to party politics. The power of global trends and institutions suggests that voting for national governments is futile. Mass media have changed the organization of parties themselves and eroded the direct and local links between politicians and voters. Each or any combination of these causes provide a plausible explanation.

However, there is an additional possible cause which focuses on the actions of parties and governments themselves. Political institutions and organizations have adapted to changing conditions by professionalizing their personnel and restructuring themselves and their practices. A key element of this change has been promotional professionalization. Arguably, this too may have contributed to the crisis of representation.

The rise of promotional culture in politics

As many studies have noted (Blumler and Gurevitch, 1995; Swanson and Mancini, 1996; Webb, 2000; Heffernan, 2003; Lilleker and Lees-Marshment, 2005; Hay, 2007; Negrine, 2008; Maarek, 2011), political parties across the globe have become transformed into 'electoral-professional' parties. Professionalization has involved changing organizational structures, new campaign methods and the employment of external experts, including many from the promotional professions. Initially it was just advertising people who were brought in to help sell politicians and their policies. But this extended to public relations consultants, pollsters, marketing specialists and image consultants, as well as journalists, television producers, writers and film directors.

In the UK, several scholars recorded the manifestations of this promotionally oriented shift from the late 1970s onwards (Kavanagh, 1995; Scammell, 1995; Franklin, 2004; Wring, 2005; Lees-Marshment, 2008). For example, in 1978 the Conservative Party opened their first full-time account with a professional advertising agency – Saatchi and Saatchi. During all their campaigns of the 1980s and 1990s they were advised by the heads of several top-ten PR companies, including Lowe-Bell and Shandwick. During the period of Conservative government, state communication expenditure and personnel also increased significantly. In 1979, the Central Office of Information (COI) budget was £27 million and advertising expenditure was £44 million. By 1988 these figures had risen to £150 million and £85 million respectively (Scammell, 1995: 204–6). The rapid growth in communication personnel and expenditure, documented in the Thatcher years, continued apace during New Labour's period of office (Rawnsley, 2001; Jones, 2002; Franklin, 2004; Wring, 2005). Table 8.1, showing changes in the number of 'information officers' employed in government departments, illustrates this rise.

Greater professionalization and promotion have also meant that funders and outside experts have become all the more important and central to party hierarchies. Similarly, the budgets for running parties and electoral campaigns in the US, the UK and elsewhere have soared. In the UK between 1983 and 1997, Conservative Party spending increased more than fourfold and Labour Party spending rose more than sixfold, both in real terms (Neill, 1998). Spending

Table 8.1   Changes in numbers of information officers employed in government departments, 1979–2012

	MoD	FCO	Home Office	Cabinet Office	PM's Office	Treasury	Total
1979	58	19	27	–	6	12	122
1987	34	13	33	11	6	13	110
1997	47	30	50	14	12	6	169
2001	87	51	80	28	7	30	293
2006	230	41	145	35	24	31	506
2012	237	54	86	108 (merged)		22	507

Source: Figures compiled from 'The White Book', previously known as 'The IPO Directory – Information and Press Officers in Government Departments and Public Corporations', and compiled from COI directories, 1979–2012.

has continued to increase rather faster than inflation. In 2001 the parties combined raised £32.1 million in public funds and donations. In 2010 the figure was £67.3 million (UK Electoral Commission, 2012). In the US, where campaign advertising and fund-raising are more deregulated, politics is oriented rather more around promotional expenditure, professionalization and big donors. In 1974, total campaign expenditure for all candidates to the Senate and House of Representatives was $72.4 million; by 2010 it had reached $1.5 billion. In 1976, presidential candidates spent a total of $66.9 million; by 2008 it had reached $1.32 billion (Ferguson, 2012: 296–7). Combined campaign expenditure, by candidates, party national committees and political action groups, was $5.98 billion in 2008 – an increase of 183 per cent, in real terms, over the 2000 election (Magleby, 2011: 18–19).

While most observers are in agreement about the rise and institutionalization of political promotional culture, there is considerable debate as to whether it has strengthened or weakened representative democracy overall. For practitioners (Grunig, 1992; Nessman, 1995; Wilmshurst and Mackay, 1999; Newman, 1999) such developments have, of course, been beneficial in terms of improving dialogue and communication between citizens, politicians and institutions. There are also several academic observers who have concluded that changes, in the larger scope, have been broadly positive (Scammell, 1995, 1999; Norris, 2000, 2004; Lees-Marshment, 2008). They suggest that using modern political marketing techniques has made parties more representative because they are more consultative and citizen-oriented in policy development. Politics is less dogmatic and ideological and has become more managerial, expert-led and responsive. Similarly positive arguments are put forward for the use of advertising and public relations. Government communication, instead of being a crude top-down affair, has come to be more multi-directional and user-friendly in nature (Grunig and Hunt, 1984; Scammell, 1995; Nessman, 1995). Thus, professionalization of promotion in politics has strengthened the representative nature of the public sphere.

In stark contrast to this line, there has been a steady series of critiques of promotional politics by journalists (Jones, 1995, 2002; Kurtz, 1998; Lloyd, 2004; Woodward, 2006) and critical scholars (Herman and Chomsky, 1988; Habermas, 1989 [1962]; Hall Jamieson, 1996; Franklin, 2004; Crouch, 2004; Wring, 2005; Hay, 2007). They argue that the use of political promotion has never been about two-way communication, dialogue with citizens or an enhanced public sphere. Instead, in spite of practitioner claims, it is about managing public opinion during elections or during difficult periods for the state. During elections, marketing pushes mainstream parties to focus on 'centre-ground' politics, undecided voters and swing states. Media management of elections and political affairs generally has resulted in distorted, partial and confusing coverage for ordinary citizens. In effect, promotional politics has 'refeudalized' the 'public sphere' (Habermas, 1989 [1962]), delivering an elite-managed 'propaganda model' (Herman and Chomsky, 1988). As such, citizen representation has been eroded rather than strengthened. Indeed, if one takes the US example, there seems to be a strong case that increased political promotion has had an alienating effect on the public. In the US, professional promotion was adopted earliest and is now most developed, campaign spending far outstrips other democracies, and voter turnout levels are among the lowest of any mature democracy.

Whichever position one takes, all sides agree that promotional culture has become more central to democracies and political representation. The next three sections extend the discussion. They focus on the topics of media management, political marketing, and the mediatization of promotional politics.

Promotional politics, managed media and citizenship

One concern is with how political promotion impacts on news and public information. For their advocates (Grunig and Hunt, 1984;

Scammell, 1995; Nessman, 1995), political advertising, marketing and public relations have improved 'two-way symmetrical' communication between citizens and their representatives. As the Public Relations Society of America (PRSA) declares, public relations contributes 'to mutual understanding among groups and institutions'. Modern public relations means citizen voices are listened to. Advertising and PR inform citizens in the most intelligible ways about competing political parties and policies. They are a cost-effective and comprehensible means of government communication to citizens about new legislation and national developments. Digital advances mean that there is vastly more government and local institutional information now available to ordinary citizens. The internet has facilitated greater exchange and dialogue among a wide range of institutions, representatives, citizens and journalists (Beckett, 2008; Deuze, 2009). Thus the workings of government and parties are less opaque and more accessible to reporters and publics. In comparison to less-mediated times, more people are informed about the business of politics (see Shoemaker, 1989; Scammell, 1995; Norris, 2000, 2004; Newman, 1999; McNair, 2003; Schudson, 2006). As Norris (2000) and others argue, the combination of professional communication and a diverse, healthy media provides an invaluable service to an electorate needing to make informed, rational electoral choices.

However, in other ways, promotionally organized public communication has many objectives that run contrary to the idea of strong citizen-representative dialogue. Much of it involves managing media and public opinion. Indeed, looking at the adoption of promotional culture historically, governments usually increase their communication resources and personnel in times of war, industrial strife, recession and other periods of social instability (Cutlip et al., 2000; L'Etang, 2004; Miller and Dinan, 2008). In the US, state promotional efforts all rose considerably during the two world wars, during the 1930s depression and after '9/11'. The power of state media management operations was also revealed in the 2003 invasion of Iraq. Several accounts (Stauber and Rampton, 2003; Miller, 2004; Kull et al., 2004; Woodward, 2004; Snow, 2004; US Senate, 2008) describe how the US established the largest propaganda system since the Second World War. Large-scale operations, such as the Pentagon's Office of Strategic Influence and the White House's Office of Global Communications, were rolled out with multi-billion dollar budgets. These fed coordinated and continuous information to reporters at different sites. The Bush administration then disseminated a number of manufactured or misleading claims about al-Qaeda's links with Iraq and Iraq's 'weapons of mass destruction'. In this period, according to Kull et al. (2004), a majority of viewers of Fox News, CBS, ABC, CNN and NBC television channels believed in one or more of these 'misperceptions'. Pro-war coverage continued to be 'overwhelmingly more frequent' than anti-war reporting. In January 2003, 68 per cent of the US public in fact believed that Iraq had had a role in '9/11'. In 2006, a poll found that 60 per cent of Republican voters still thought Iraq had weapons of mass destruction before the 2003 invasion and 63 per cent of them thought Iraq had 'substantially' supported al-Qaeda (PIPA, 2006).

Political parties too have communication objectives that run counter to reporter and citizen needs. Journalists and critical media scholars regularly complain that media managers or 'spin doctors' have become powerful 'gatekeepers', restricting access to political institutions, representatives and public information (Jones, 1995; Kurtz, 1998; Barnett and Gaber, 2001). Information release is selective and specifically timed, either to be 'buried' or for achieving maximum coverage with a positive spin. Public party agendas generally are agreed in advance and kept within a narrow range of topics and policy responses. In addition, journalists are personally subjected to 'flak' and their organizations to legal and regulatory threats. Political coverage, whether directed by party campaigns or news media logic, becomes full of 'pseudo-events', 'soundbites', 'horse-race' stories, negative and confrontational reporting, political personalities and scandal (Boorstin, 1962; Hallin, 1994; Ansolabehere and Iyengar, 1995; Hall Jamieson, 1996; Delli Carpini and Williams, 2001; Franklin, 2004; Esser, 2008). In effect, political parties and institutions have deployed promotional activity as much to restrict as to facilitate public communication and debate.

All of this suggests that promotional politics is likely to produce distorted news content and citizens who are more poorly informed about political and national affairs. Public disengagement is one response. This certainly seems to be the case in the UK, where political reporting is focused increasingly on political personalities, conflict and scandals and less on policy issues. A study of the 2005 general election by Deacon and his colleagues (2005) found that, in the best-selling tabloid press, the three party leaders alone accounted for 60 per cent of direct quotations. They also found that 44 per cent of coverage focused on the electoral process itself ('horse-race' issues) and 8 per cent on 'political propriety'. The most important electoral issues, according to polls (Ipsos-MORI, 1997–2010), such as health and taxation, were each covered in only 3 to 4 per cent of stories.

Unsurprisingly, the UK public does not have much faith in news coverage. Ofcom (2007) found that 55 per cent of people said that 'much of the news on TV was not relevant to them'. In 2012, just 19 per cent of the public trusted journalists to 'tell the truth' (Ipsos-MORI, 2012).

In the US, there is a very similar focus on personalities, negative attacks and horse-race stories in political advertising and news coverage during elections (Dover, 2010; Owen, 2010: 173). In the 2008 election, 20 per cent of stories covered policy matters and 5 per cent the public records of candidates. The rest was comprised of polling news, candidate strategies or personal lives. According to Owen, 'a mere 12 per cent of coverage was useful to voters' decision-making.' Thus, in the current times, the US public's faith in its news media is no better than that in the UK. According to Pew (2009b), in 2008 only 25 per cent of the US public 'believed all or most of what they read' in the *Wall Street Journal*. The figure was 18 per cent in the *New York Times*, 16 per cent in *Newsweek*, and 5 per cent in the *National Enquirer*.

US party politics, political marketing and representation

Has political marketing made parties more responsive to citizens and encouraged public engagement? In all mature democracies, major parties now carry out extensive market research using commercial techniques. Policies, campaign positions, party brands and political leaders are all market-tested. Opinion polls register responses by class, profession, age, race and gender. Psychographic and lifestyle research is also used to develop a more qualitative and in-depth view of voter motivations, cognitions and behaviours. Electoral patterns are analysed state by state. Key voting issues, floating voter groups and swing states are all identified. Communication strategies, messages and choice of media outlets are focus-group tested and developed accordingly.

For political marketing advocates, the aggregate result is positive in terms of improving citizen relationships with representatives. Lees-Marshment (2004, 2008; Lilleker and Lees-Marshment, 2005) has done most to develop a positive account of what political marketing has brought to democracy. Her historical analysis (2008) presents a normative and developmental line with regard to parties and their phased adoption and implementation of political marketing. According to her model, parties traditionally were sold as 'product-oriented parties'

(POPs). They came up with an ideologically driven set of policies and then sold those rather crudely to the electorate. In the next phase, parties became more sophisticated as they developed marketing and other promotional practices. Marketing techniques were then used by 'sales-oriented parties' (SOPs) to sell in a more professional and informed way. In the third phase of professionalization, 'market-oriented parties' (MOPs) began using such marketing tools as part of the initial policy-formation process. Successful or 'good' parties, which adopt modern political marketing, therefore also benefit the public and democracy. Ideological dogma and vested interests, which previously corrupted the policy process, are replaced by meritocratic, responsive government. The electoral highs and lows of parties in democracies can be linked to their adoption, or not, of the MOP approach (Lilleker and Lees-Marshment, 2005). Thus, in Lees-Marshment's words, 'Political marketing is making politics more responsive to its market: political organizations, such as political parties, are identifying the needs and wants of those they seek to serve and attempting to meet those demands.'

However, there are several problems with this positive account of political marketing. First, marketing and other promotional experts, often with weaker party allegiances, have been elevated in importance in party hierarchies. They have a greater influence on party governance than ordinary members or local bureaucracies because of their impact on national elections and media (Swanson and Mancini, 1996; Crouch, 2004; Wring, 2005; Hay, 2007). Second, overlaying marketing onto politics is not that simple, as citizenship is not the same as consumption. Consumption is an individual activity whereas citizenship is a communal one requiring wider social engagement. Policies are not discrete, self-contained products with a simply defined consumer base. They are complex, evolve over time, impinge on other policies and citizens, and have to be delivered. Third, in practice, outside promotional experts are employed by parties, first and foremost, to win elections and good poll ratings, not necessarily to engage with citizens. Campaigning and, to an extent, policy-making become increasingly focused on capturing the electoral 'centre ground' so as to maintain wide appeal. Indeed, as several writers have noted, since the 1960s there has been considerable convergence in the ideologies and policy stances of major political parties (Entman, 1989, 2005; Giroux, 2010; Norris, 1999; Heath et al., 2001; Curtice, 2005). Regardless of actual position, presentation deliberately plays down controversial policy ideas and plays up centre-ground policies, populist social themes and personalities. This leaves voters making choices based more on the personal appeal of leaders. Thus, Lees (2005) looked at Gerhard Schröder's SPD victory over Edmund Stoiber's CDU-CSU in the 2002 German election. This was secured, according to polls, on the strength of his stronger 'character traits' rather than on greater public support for his policies.

Recent elections in the US offer evidence to support both advocates and critics of political marketing in relation to public representation and engagement. Advocates can point to recent promotional efforts encouraging renewed public participation. From 1996 to 2008, campaign spending increased significantly (see above), but so did election turnouts. 1996 saw a new low, of 51.7 per cent turnout, when Bill Clinton was re-elected. Since then turnouts have edged up again, to reach 61.6 per cent in 2008 – a level not seen since the 1960s. As McDonald (2009: 1–2) points out, turnout was also significantly higher – 4 per cent on average – in those battleground states where candidates had devoted most campaign resources. In such states, 49 per cent of those polled said they had been contacted by one or more of the campaigns, as opposed to 25 per cent elsewhere. FairVote (2004: 6) calculated that participation was up 10 per cent in the most closely contested states of the 2004 election.

It has also become clear that, in the successful campaigns of George W. Bush (2000, 2004) and Barack Obama (2008), great efforts were made to galvanize voters who were most disenchanted. In advance of the 2000 election (Knuckey and Lees-Marshment, 2005), Bush's team conducted widespread market research in developing a set of policies that would have broader electoral appeal while not alienating traditional Republicans. In 2004, according to Bush's campaign strategist Matthew Dowd (see Hall Jamieson, 2006), the Republicans conducted extensive polling and micro-targeting research. Half their efforts were focused on re-engaging and registering disenchanted Republicans. They were rewarded, as Republican voter turnout increased substantially as compared with the 2000 election. In 2008, the Obama campaign increased Democrat participation significantly by galvanizing those citizens who traditionally opted out of US politics (Pew, 2009a; Gronebeck, 2009; Hendricks and Denton, 2010; Magleby, 2011). Obama's promotional messages, personal appeal and use of digital media proved extremely successful in re-engaging young, ethnic minority and poor voters. His team had ninety people devoted to an online campaign, using websites and social media to fund-raise, organize and engage. The My.BarackObama.com website was used to register 3 million cell-phone numbers, gather

13 million email addresses, and organize 150,000 events and 35,000 groups. Obama's Facebook page had 3.18 million supporters, while 1,820 campaign videos, produced by the campaign and supporters, were posted on YouTube and were viewed 90 million times. Such actions contributed to 66 per cent of voters under the age of thirty, and 69 per cent of new voters, supporting Obama in 2008 (figures in Hendricks and Denton, 2010: xii, 7–11). According to Pew (2009a), the numbers of 18- to 29-year-old voters increased from 2004 by 4.6 per cent. Black voters increased by 6.4 per cent and Hispanics by 21.4 per cent.

However, there is also much evidence to suggest that promotional efforts have done a great deal to disengage voters. One clear concern is with the way campaigns are targeted strongly on swing states and voters, thereby ignoring the majority who reside in safe states. According to FairVote (2004, 2008), by 2004 the number of 'battleground' states had steadily declined, from twenty-four to just thirteen, which were responsible for 159 electoral college votes. Just three of the largest swing states (Florida, Ohio and Pennsylvania) dominated the campaign. Although containing only 14 per cent of the US population, they received 57 per cent of the total campaign advertising spend and 45 per cent of presidential and vice-presidential candidate visits. Eleven states in total, with 27 per cent of the population, got 92 per cent of all candidate visits and 96 per cent of the advertising. The rest were ignored almost entirely. In 2008, 98 per cent of all campaign events and advertising took place in fifteen states. In 2012 just nine swing states monopolized campaign attention. Unsurprisingly, there has been a long-term drop in voter turnout in such uncontested states. Between 1972 and 2004, the ten safest states had between 12 and 19 per cent lower turnout compared with the battleground states. The average gap was 17 per cent among 18- to 29-year-olds in those states.

Studies of campaign strategy and advertising (Hall Jamieson, 2006, 2010; Dover, 2010; Magleby, 2011) also reveal how similar campaigns have become, thus making it hard for voters to see differences. Both sides follow almost identical 'textbook' approaches, as particular tropes and narratives are repeated by incumbents and challengers. According to Dover (2010), challengers always emphasize character more than policy and sell a vision of 'change'. Incumbents sell their 'experience' and 'leadership' qualities. Following the primaries, both candidates and parties become increasingly negative. In 2008, 70.6 per cent of party ads and 75.8 per cent of coordinated ads were 'attack' adverts (Magleby, 2011: 17). Candidate adverts continue to stress the personal and make general statements of intent rather than putting down clear policy positions. That, combined with personality rather than policy news coverage (see above), means that voters are left confused about what exactly the candidates stand for. Accordingly, citizens frequently fall back on voting for candidates on the basis of perceived character traits, even if those candidates do not represent the voter's own interests and beliefs. So, in the 2000 election, polls revealed that, on four of seven key policy issues, Al Gore was considered the better candidate. In terms of ideological alignment, Bush and the Republicans were considered to be to the right of the electorate. However, Bush won in four out of seven character trait measures (Knuckey and Lees-Marshment, 2005: 48–9). Once again, in 2004, Kerry won greater approval than Bush in four out of seven key policy issues, but Bush won in four out of seven character traits (Kenski and Kenski, 2009: 281–3). In 2008, Obama had the higher approval ratings in a majority of both policy issues and character traits. Although, according to Kenski and her colleagues (2010: 5), ideological alignment was closer to McCain in most areas, 'In the end, a centre right electorate was persuaded that a candidate perceived to be a liberal shared its values more so than a person thought to be closer to its ideological bent.'

Regardless of appearances, there is much to suggest that both Democrats and Republicans remain far more connected to big donors and corporate interests than to party members and ordinary citizens. The vast sums of money that are now required to win elections mean that candidates are far too tied to special interests with big pockets. In each of the elections from 2000 to 2008, the candidate with the most funds won. At vital points, extreme differences in available funds left one side advantaged (see Dover, 2010; Farrar-Myers, 2011; Magleby, 2011). In 2008, Obama spent three times as much on television advertising as McCain. Much has been made of Obama's generation of funds through ordinary, small donors giving up to $200. However, according to Farrar-Myers (2011: 52), the 83 per cent of Obama's donors who fell into this category supplied only 26 per cent of the funds raised. In the 2008 election, just 0.001 per cent of US individuals were responsible for 24 per cent of all political donations (Ferguson, 2012: 297).

Lastly, it can be argued that heavily promoted and personality-centred elections are ultimately likely to disappoint. This is especially the case if big donor and public interests diverge considerably. Bush had some of both the highest and the lowest approval ratings of any president since polling began. He went from 90 per cent approval and 6 per cent disapproval in September 2001 to 25 per cent approval and 71 per cent disapproval in October 2008. It was among many sets of traditional Republican voters where voter turnout dropped most in 2008. For many allied to the Democratic cause, Obama has proved to be a failure whose policies have been far closer to vested, corporate interests than the young, poor and ethnic minorities he so successfully engaged before (Giroux, 2010; Hodge, 2010; Chomsky, 2012). In Giroux's words (2010: 7): 'The courage to take on predatory capitalism, state violence, the reach of the prison-industrial complex . . . is traded with the apparently more fierce urgency of popular poll ratings . . . and a shot at a second term in office.' His initial strong poll ratings of 67 per cent approval in January 2009 dropped considerably later. Indeed, in the summer of 2012 political disenchantment had returned generally. Neither Mitt Romney nor Barack Obama was garnering strong support from their traditional supporter bases. Gallup polls (on 13 and 24 July 2012) showed considerably less 'enthusiasm' for voting, or less 'intention' to vote, compared to 2004 and 2008. The biggest drops were among those same disenchanted groups that Obama successfully persuaded in 2008. In July 2012, polls show voting intention had dropped to 58 per cent, from 78 per cent in 2008, among 18- to 29-year-olds. It had also dropped from 83 per cent to 70 per cent for non-white voters.

Thus, for many, it seems that neither the Democrats nor the Republicans still represent their interests. Promotional politics may be good at winning elections but does little to instil long-term faith and trust in America's political institutions and representatives in Washington. In which case, it seems no surprise that movements such as Occupy and the Tea Party have made such an impact (see chapter 9).

UK politics, promotional professionalization and the mediatization of parties and politicians

This third section explores what happens to parties as a consequence of being more media-oriented for promotional reasons. As argued here, parties and politicians have become more 'mediatized' and thus more detached from publics. The section draws on an extended study of UK politicians and political journalists (see Davis, 2007, 2010) in which some sixty politicians and twenty-five political journalists and bloggers were interviewed.

Traditionally, studies of politician–media relations have been concerned with the issue of political media management and journalist autonomy (see above and chapter 6). However, in recent years, another question has been posed: What happens to organizations and individuals themselves as a result of having regular and intense relationships with media? Discussions addressing this issue have variously used the terms 'media logic' (Altheide and Snow, 1979; see also Hallin, 1994; Delli Carpini and Williams, 2001; Altheide, 2004), 'mediation' or 'mediatization' (Mazzoleni and Schulz, 1999; Meyer, 2002; Davis, 2007; Livingstone, 2009; Lundby, 2009). The debates overlap considerably. Each offers stronger and weaker versions of mediatization as a process.

In stronger versions, a sort of media determinism increasingly drives organizations and individuals. For Krotz (2007), 'mediatization' is a 'meta-process' as powerful a force of social change as globalization or commercialization. For Meyer (2002), as political elites adapt to news media logic, so the media 'colonize' politics. Politics becomes dominated by an 'iron triangle' of politicians, pollsters and media executives who collectively conceive problem definitions and their policy solutions. Alternatively, softer forms offer a more interactionist, reflexive account of organizational and individual relations with media. Authors (Thompson, 1995; Livingstone, 1999, 2009; Davis, 2007; Lundby, 2009) ask how individuals and institutions *use* media and communications and become reshaped in the process. How, in other words, do individuals, in their use of media, inadvertently alter their behaviours, relations and discursive practices? In each of these, media, individuals and social practices are 'co-determining'.

Whether taking a softer, reflexive or stronger, determinist line, the concern is still one of how media interaction might be reshaping politics and society. In this case, the question is: How do politicians and parties, driven by a promotional focus on gaining favourable media coverage, adapt their communication strategies? Much of the above literature has noted that parties adapt themselves to the news values and timetables of media organizations in order to gain coverage. To maintain reporter interest, politicians emphasize the personal, deliver ideas in soundbites, keep 'on message' and avoid complex policy statements.

The next step is to ask how parties might be adapting more substantially to their mediated environment. Does mediatization also mean significant changes to actual policies, party hierarchies, or the selection and elevation of politicians themselves? Such adaptations, to national media rather than local publics, may entail a further erosion of representation.

Looking at the case of the UK, there is quite a bit of evidence to suggest varied forms of reflexive adaptation to media have taken place. One clear indication of this is the way the demographic profile of senior party figures has shifted as public personal appeal and/or promotional skills become more important in politics. Previously important sets of skills, such as occupational expertise, negotiating skills and parliamentary experience, thus become downgraded. A comparison of the twenty younger and twenty-nine older members of the front benches of the two main parties in 2007–8 (those aged over and under fifty) found such tendencies (see Davis, 2010). The older generation, on average, had fifteen-year careers, usually in areas such as business, law, education and trade union work, before their election. The majority also spent many years in Parliament before working their way up to a senior party position. Over half also had local council experience. Among the younger generation, the average work experience time was seven and a half years. The majority joined the senior ranks of their party within their first term of office. Less than a quarter had local council experience. Eleven of the twenty had been policy advisors or researchers working for politicians, parties and political think tanks, often involving media relations duties. Ten had actually worked in journalism and/or public relations. All of this suggests that the newer generation of party figures may be better attuned to senior-level party politics and more able to engage with a range of outside policy experts, journalists and media. However, at the same time, their life experiences and links to non-political occupations, local politics and ordinary party members all appear to be rather weaker (see also Dalton and Wattenberg, 2000; Crouch, 2004; Hay, 2007).

The three current party leaders in UK politics typify this pattern of selection. Ed Miliband, the Labour Party leader, had a brief career in television journalism before becoming a Labour Party advisor/ researcher. Nick Clegg, leader of the Liberal Democrats, had brief careers in journalism, political lobbying and as an MEP. Both arrived in Parliament in 2005, were fast-tracked into their cabinets or shadow cabinets, and were several years younger than the average age of their fellow party MPs. David Cameron, the Conservative prime minister, spent six years as a policy advisor for several of the party's most senior figures (see Elliott and Hanning, 2007). He then had a seven-year stint as a director of communications and corporate affairs at Carlton Communications. Throughout, he gained extensive media experience and an established journalist network – all before he became an MP (see chapter 7 case study).

Looking beyond the leaders of UK parties, it is also evident that most politicians have extensive relations with media and journalists. The majority of MPs interviewed were self-confessed 'news junkies'. On average, they consumed four to five different news sources, including three newspapers, each day. This finding matched up with data from a MORI survey (Duffy and Rowden, 2005: 30). Many were tuned in to a constant news media presence in their offices, with 24-hour news channels or the Parliament channel, and news websites displayed on computers. The majority of politicians also had developed media knowledge of journalism, journalists and news production. Just over four-fifths had had formal media training (the majority) and/or previous experience in journalism or public relations/affairs. Many appeared to have a wide-ranging knowledge of 'news values', news routines, individual publications and journalists. Indeed, many senior and junior politicians explained that the gaining of media coverage, by any means, often became an objective in itself and could dictate decisions.

Such levels of news consumption and interaction suggest that media are a key information source on new policy areas and also have a certain agenda-setting or 'priming' role (Iyengar and Kinder, 1987). Just over half of MPs stated that 'news media' were a 'main source of information' to them when informing themselves about 'policy and legislative issues'. For many, news was a starting point for their day and gave clues as to what issues needed to be looked at further. A quarter of MPs directly suggested that the news, in some way, contributed to setting the political agenda in Parliament for the day. News stories could become the prominent issues and talking points for MPs, journalists and other parliamentarians.

Such media influences were also apparent in senior party circles. Former government ministers and shadow ministers explained that discussions of policy were frequently linked to the issue of how the policy would play in the media. Almost every interviewee who had served in a cabinet or a shadow cabinet since the late 1980s talked in such terms. Such accounts were echoed by several political journalists. As a consequence, an 'anticipatory media effect' can be said to have developed, as party leaders increasingly make policy decisions with future news headlines in mind. This encouraged a greater focus on issues with a 'strong headline impact', that were 'emotive' or 'sensitive', that had a 'human interest' angle, or that were a source of party conflict. Crime, law and order, and immigration were such cases. Conversely, many policy areas were under-debated and covered. This was either because parties were afraid to raise the issue for fear of negative coverage, or because journalists would not report it on account of a perceived lack of editorial or popular interest. Topics regarded as 'technical', 'complex' or 'boring' were often cited. Constitutional affairs, pensions, energy policy and foreign affairs were all mentioned as issues that were rarely covered unless a crisis occurred. Above all, debates about Europe and the National Health Service (NHS) were avoided. All sides felt that the topic of the NHS, as well as welfare-state funding and organization, was too politically sensitive and too complex to discuss. In addition, Europe was seen as a divisive issue for parties and a way for media to highlight party splits.

MPs also had a very high level of personal contact with political journalists and so were well acquainted with the authors of the news they were consuming. In all, just over two-thirds talked to journalists, on average, at least once a day, and usually several times a day. At busy periods some said they could have between ten and twenty conversations with journalists in a day. The other third, with two exceptions, talked to journalists once or a few times a week. In several US studies (Protess et al., 1991; Baumgartner and Jones, 1993; Cook, 1998), it is clear that such exchanges between politicians and journalists contribute to political agendas, debates and moods, just as they do to news agendas, public debates and moods.

This also turned out to be the case in the UK Parliament. All sides spoke of the hothouse atmosphere of the political 'lobby', where reporters constantly exchanged information and opinion as they shared facilities and attended briefings and political events. These journalists continually picked up and circulated what they knew about multiple aspects of the political process itself. Individual politicians, in turn, sought out such politically significant information from journalists. A third of the political reporters spoke about MPs and ministers seeking information on some aspect of the political process itself. Similarly, just under a third of politicians, when asked about why they talked to journalists, said they were seeking information from informed reporters about their party, the government or some aspect of Westminster politics. In effect, MPs read news and talked to journalists with a view to asking: How did key columnists and correspondents, who mix with MPs on a daily basis, assess political issues and legislation? What were other MPs saying and thinking and what were the 'moods' within the parties? How were senior party figures and leaders viewed? This seemed to be particularly the case with back-bench MPs, who found themselves further removed from decision-making at the top ends of their parties. Such conversations and exchanges also appeared to influence the rise and fall of individual (shadow) ministers and party leaders. Just under half the politicians asked stated that journalists and the media had a role to play in the rise and fall of ministers and in leadership contests. Consequently, journalists both reported on the politics of a policy or individual and, by circulating opinions and moods, had a role in those political outcomes.

In effect, a great deal of actual political behaviour and decision-making in UK politics is promotionally oriented and filtered through news texts and interactions with journalists. Promotional politics has facilitated greater mediatization of politics itself. British politics, promotion and media are as systematically and structurally intertwined as they have ever been.

Conclusion

Undoubtedly, many promotional practices have been beneficial to the healthy workings of the political process in representative democracies. Market research methods have made politicians more sensitive to what matters to citizens. Communication about politics is more targeted and user-friendly. There are multiple means and forums for generating feedback, dialogue and debate.

However, as also argued here, promotional politics does much to put off citizens and disengage them. Media management, in conjunction with the media's own workings, weakens news coverage about political affairs and leaves the public confused and ill-informed. Political marketing narrows policy and campaign agendas to focus on the small sets of voters who might turn an election. Promotional imperatives mean that media requirements are overly influential when it comes to making political decisions about policy and leadership.

9

Conflict and Pluralism in Civil Society

Introduction

This chapter draws on research in political sociology and media sociology to explore the use of promotion by groups and organizations operating across civil society. In recent decades a range of public institutions, organized interest groups, charities and social movements have adopted promotional personnel and practices. These have become vital for communicating with publics, members and funders. They are also centrally involved in forms of promotional conflict as organizations try and compete to influence political and media agendas. Thus, society-based promotional struggle has become a feature of modern democracies.

The question is: How pluralistic is such promotional conflict? For many, promotional democracy is dominated by powerful corporate bodies and state institutions that exploit existing economic, symbolic and organizational resource advantages. 'Resource-poor' and 'outsider' groups gain relatively few campaign victories or positive political outcomes. Promotional struggle thus further reduces pluralism in democracies. For others, promotional techniques offer new opportunities for weaker and more excluded groups to compete in ways that were previously impossible. Various interest-group objectives have been successful in terms of impacting on mainstream political agendas in the long run. The latter part of this chapter illustrates the discussion with three case studies where campaigners took on governments and corporations. The first is the UCW union's successful opposition to Post Office privatization in the 1990s. The second reviews the divisions within, and problematic outcomes of, the Make Poverty History campaign of 2005. The third looks at the varied impacts of the Occupy movement, ongoing since September 2011.

The rise and spread of professional campaigning in promotional civil society

A wide range of organizations in civil society now use promotional strategies and practitioners to achieve specific political and socio-economic goals. Traditionally, the corporate sector has been the biggest employer of promotional professionals for political as well as commercial objectives. However, over time, other types of organization have developed their campaign operations along similar lines. Local and regional government, religious institutions, NGOs and social movements, trade unions and consumer groups, have all come to use such means to achieve their objectives. These include developing their 'brand' images with publics, increasing private and public income sources, and improving communication with employees and members. It has also become part of competition and conflict, as campaigns are launched to win industrial and market disputes or influence news media, policy-makers and regulators.

In all the promotional professions it is the corporate sector which employs the majority of practitioners and resources. Of these, public relations units, often encompassing public affairs and advocacy, are most involved in campaigns. The corporate PR industry grew considerably in the postwar period and expanded impressively in the UK from the 1970s onwards (Davis, 2002). By the mid-1980s (Carl Byoir, 1986), 85 per cent of the UK's 100 largest companies and 69 per cent of its largest 500 companies were employing PR consultancies. The consultancy sector in the UK, which almost exclusively serves the corporate sector, rose by a factor of thirty-one (or eleven-fold in real terms) between 1979 and 1998 (Miller and Dinan, 2000: 10). Similar corporate expansions have been recorded in the US (see Dreier, 1988; Cutlip et al., 2000; Sussman, 2011; Ferguson, 2012).

In recent decades, a range of non-corporate institutions and organizations in civil society followed the trend, albeit on a much reduced scale. Looking at the case in the UK, by the mid-1990s, according to Franklin (1994: 7), 90 per cent of metropolitan local authorities had established PR departments. In 1979, Buckingham Palace employed three 'information officers'; by 2012 this figure had reached twelve. The Metropolitan Police went from six to sixty-eight in the same period. The Inland Revenue increased from five to forty-six and the CBI (Confederation of British Industry) from eight to twenty-three (COI directories 1979–2012). A similar influx of promotional professionals was recorded in charities, trade unions and interest groups. Deacon's (1996) survey of the voluntary sector found that 31 per cent of such organizations had press or publicity officers, 43 per cent used external PR agencies, and 56 per cent monitored the media. These figures were increased to 57 per cent, 81 per cent and 78 per cent for medium and larger organizations. The CIPR (Chartered Institute of Public Relations) has had a 'fifth estate', not-for-profit sector since 1990 and has regularly recognized third-sector campaigns in its annual awards. There is now a growing literature documenting interest-group and union campaigning on a range of issues (Manning, 1998; Allan et al., 2000; Davis, 2002; Cottle, 2003; de Jong et al., 2005; Dinan and Miller, 2007; Kumar, 2008; Sireau, 2009; Hansen, 2010).

The general dispersal of public relations across society also shows up in industry surveys. In 1998, the CIPR membership survey (IPR, 1998) found that 45 per cent of members worked for consultancies (mainly for corporations), 23 per cent in-house for private companies, 16.6 per cent for government and public institutions, and 6.4 per cent for NGOs and charities. In 2011, the survey (CIPR, 2011) recorded that 29 per cent of its members worked in-house in the public sector, 23 per cent for consultancies, 21 per cent in-house for private companies, and 13 per cent for NGOs and charities (14 per cent were freelance). In the US in 2010 (US Bureau of Labor Statistics, 2010), the majority continued to work in the private sector but, as with the UK, PR employment had become more widely distributed. An estimated 17.3 per cent worked in consultancies or freelance, 6.4 per cent in local or state government (excluding health or education), 12 to 14 per cent in private or state education, 2.4 per cent in interest groups and unions, and 3.4 per cent in broadcasting, sports and performing arts.*

The plurality issue in political sociology debates

What is the significance of the spread of promotional practices across civil society? In political sociology, a long-running debate has been focused on the ability of democratic states to act as arbiters between

* Figures compiled from US Bureau of Labor Statistics (2010) from National Employment Matrix. Percentages from aggregating different categories from list of 163.

competing societal interests. The concern is with political power and whether or not it is sufficiently pluralist, balanced and reflective of wider interests. Thus, the question is whether promotional democracies increase or decrease pluralism.

Classic liberal pluralist thought, as presented by Truman (1951) and Dahl (1961), argues the exercise of power is 'fragmented' and 'non-cumulative'. It is shared and competed over by numerous, usually powerful, groups in democracies. Even though power is not evenly distributed, the point is that it remains contested and pluralistic in nature. This ideal picture has been challenged from a variety of critical perspectives: the inability of large, collective groups to act as effectively as small organized and powerful interests (Olson, 1965; Offe and Wiesenthal, 1985); the way in which decision-making regularly excludes the concerns of certain, less powerful groups in society (Bachrach and Baratz, 1962); the role of the state in actively supporting the interests of the capitalist class (Miliband, 1969; Poulantzas, 1975); and the need for the state to yield to the demands of business and established groups in order to sustain economic prosperity, and therefore its own long-term survival (Lindblom, 1977; Offe, 1984).

Similar arguments have been played out in studies of pressure groups and 'policy communities/networks'. For Grant (1978), groups may be located along a scale between 'insiders' – close to government – and 'outsiders' – on the periphery of the political (and legal) process. Insiders, usually powerful groups and large corporations, have regular, almost institutionalized contact with government and direct input into policy networks (Marsh and Rhodes, 1992; Marsh, 1998). At the same time, insider power remains restricted in practice as business groups pursue conflicting aims, often cancelling each other out (Jordan and Richardson, 1987; Grant, 1993, 1995). A wide range of anti-business groups have flourished in the gaps that emerge, often managing to engage both public and political support.

Indeed, the shifting political and economic landscape appears to be increasingly favourable to the growth of new interest groups and social movements (Castells, 1997; Della Porta and Diani, 1999; Norris, 2002; Albrow et al., 2008). Just as political party memberships have declined in mature democracies (see chapter 8), so interest-group memberships and activities have increased impressively. Such shifts suggest a positive change in the 'political opportunity structures' (Kriesi, 1991; Gamson and Meyer, 1996) available to new campaign organizations. In Norris's estimation (2002), healthy interest-group politics is being reborn for the twenty-first century. Thus, political promotional activity, be it aimed at governments, local councils, or international institutions and corporations, is having a significant impact on wider society and institutional politics itself.

However, others remain sceptical (Hutton, 1996; Mitchell, 1997; Crouch, 2004; Hay, 2007; Moran, 2007). They continue to argue that the corporate sector and other powerful interests retain significant influence. This is because business leaders maintain their privileged access to government decision-makers; economic power is more highly concentrated in a diminishing number of large corporations; the financial sector is growing in strength; and there is greater corporate involvement in the management of state politics and bureaucracies. All such trends have been aided by the employment of expensive lobbying firms (Jordan, 1990; Crouch and Dore, 1990; Mitchell, 1997; Dinan and Miller, 2007; Ferguson, 2012). In fact, they have become all the more exacerbated as multiple global forces challenge and erode state autonomy itself. In many accounts (Reich, 1991; Habermas, 1999; Strange, 1996; Crouch, 2004; Cerny et al., 2005) the transnational corporations and markets of 'turbo capitalism' have come to control or influence capital flows that are far in excess of those managed by nations (see Held and McGrew, 2000; chapter 10). Even if not directly challenged, state politics is now increasingly embedded in international, multi-layered political, industrial and financial systems (Slaughter, 2000; Held, 2002). Such developments disadvantage locally or nationally based outsider groups even more.

Looking at actual legislative outcomes in the US, the UK and elsewhere over the last three decades, corporations do appear to have had far greater influence over many areas of state policy. Since the late 1970s, government interventions in the economy, in aggregate, have worked to support the interests of international finance and multinational corporations at the expense of national wage labour, ordinary consumer-citizens and the state itself. Certain trends are clear and include increasing corporate conglomeration; rising economic inequality and poverty on the local and global scales; overproduction, environmental degradation and economic crises; the steady lowering of corporation and higher individual levels of tax; extensive privatization programmes and deregulation of industries; the rising power of the international financial sector, an increase in corporate and high-level tax avoidance and tax havens; the rise of sovereign debt, transferred from private banking debt; restrictive union legislation, longer working hours and casualized employment; and attacks on the welfare state and public spending (see Hutton, 1996, 2010; Stiglitz, 2002, 2010; Crouch, 2004, 2011; Harvey,

2005, 2011; Krugman, 2008; Elliott and Atkinson, 2009; Chang, 2010).

The plurality issue in media sociology debates

Similar debates, about plurality, societal interests, access and power, have been applied by media sociologists to the mass media. Some argue that powerful, mainly corporate organizations use promotional culture to consolidate their control and influence over the media and public discourse. Alternatively, others suggest that outsider, 'resource-poor' groups, such as unions and interest groups, are managing to exploit promotional conditions to improve their access and influence.

Several explanations account for why corporate and powerful entities are likely to use promotional culture to dominate media and public communication. The first comes down to closer institutional and organizational alignments. Most media are owned by private corporations with corporate agendas. Media political economists (Herman and Chomsky, 1988; Golding and Murdock, 2000; Curran, 2002; Bagdikian, 2004) have documented the ability of corporate interests to influence corporate media through advertising and linked networks of shareholders and directorships. Corporate-owned or -influenced media is more likely to favour pro-business arguments and pro-market policies while marginalizing oppositional organizations (see also GUMG, 1976; Gitlin, 1980; Curran et al., 1986; Parenti, 1993). The daily organization of news itself also advantages large institutions. News-gathering is driven by news beats and routines and is remarkably bureaucratic. Large institutions and corporations have a 'bureaucratic affinity' (Fishman, 1980) with media organizations – i.e., they attract journalists because they are usually physically accessible, well resourced, and provide a regular supply of 'information subsidies' (Tiffen, 1989; Ericson et al., 1989). The same cannot be said of small or dispersed interest groups and social movements, which often campaign on complex and long-term problems that do not fit the news cycle.

Second is the resource advantage. Businesses are the greatest users of public relations, advocacy and advertising (see above). Several studies (Goldenberg, 1975; Gandy, 1980; Herman and Chomsky, 1988; Miller, 1994; Deacon, 1996) have emphasized the correlation between economic resources and public relations efficacy. Greater resources mean more communications equipment and professional personnel. This brings more media contacts, greater production of news 'information subsidies', multiple modes of communication and continuous media operations. In effect, well-resourced organizations can inundate the media and set agendas while the attempts of 'resource-poor' organizations quickly become marginalized. So, Miller (1994: 132–3), for example, recorded that, in Northern Ireland in 1989, Sinn Fein, with five voluntary press staff and a budget of £7,000, attempted to compete against official government sources with 145 communications staff and a budget of £20 million. Herman and Chomsky (1988: 20–1) make a similar point about the US military and its oppositions. In the early 1980s, the US Air Force produced 150 times as many press releases as its two strongest challengers combined (the National Council of the Churches of Christ and American Friends Service Committee) and held 94 times as many press conferences. Clearly, big business promotional budgets are far beyond the meagre finances of those NGOs and unions which attempt to hold corporations to account.

Third, large corporations and public institutions have cultural and symbolic advantages in the way they are framed and presented in mass-media texts. The work of Hall and his colleagues (1978) on UK media coverage of mugging explained that journalists, in their search for 'objective' and 'authoritative' accounts, automatically sought out established sources. These sources, already legitimated by their status and expertise, became the *de facto* 'primary definers' of news agendas and story frameworks. Alternative sources, and journalists themselves, were relegated to the status of 'secondary definers' with primarily responsive roles. Goldenberg (1975) and Gitlin (1980), writing about US interest groups, similarly identified a strong link between an organization's 'legitimacy' and 'authority' and its ability to gain regular and favourable coverage. Once again, outsider sources struggled to gain regular news access by reasonable means. As Cracknell (1993) observed, this leaves such groups struggling both to 'command attention' and to 'claim legitimacy' (see also Anderson, 1997; Wilson, 2000; de Jong, 2005).

Each of these factors favours corporations and institutional leaders as they attempt to win ongoing political, promotional battles with interest groups and trade unions. Their dominant position as sources is supported by almost all social and content studies of news. Such sources are consistently cited or featured in news coverage over and above others (Hall et al., 1978; Gans, 1979; Gandy, 1980; Bennett, 1990; Hallin, 1994; Manning, 2000; Davis, 2002). However, such powerful source dominance does not always ensure an equivalent dominance of news in its entirety. There are now many documented cases of NGOs, unions and social movements successfully using promotional strategies to take on larger businesses and institutions. Such organized actions have resulted in changes to legislation and regulation, institutional u-turns, and long-term shifts in political agendas. This suggests that alternative groups have found ways of neutralizing opponents and exploiting advantages of their own.

In terms of institutional and organizational advantages, certain factors do mitigate the influences of corporate owners and advertisers. Some of these are attributable to reporter news values and public interest expectations. Journalists want to appear to offer a balance of viewpoints and need to produce stories sympathetic to ordinary readers as well as advertisers (Gans, 1979; Harrison, 1985; Tiffen, 1989; Deuze, 2005; Schudson, 2006). Thus, market-oriented pragmatism and professionalism offer a balancing influence. Studies of journalists, in both the UK and the US, have shown greater sympathies with centre-left politics and interest groups than with centre-right, pro-corporate positions (Jones, 1986; Lichter and Rothman, 1988; Seaton, 1991). Lichter and Rothman's (1988) surveys found that over 80 per cent of US journalists had voted Democrat over the previous two decades. Similarly, interest groups themselves have become better attuned to servicing news routines, reporting beats and news values. Studies of environmental movement campaigns (Anderson, 1997; Hansen, 1993, 2010), as well as of other protest areas (Wilson, 1984; Deacon and Golding, 1994; Manning, 2000; Cottle, 2003), have documented more professionalized media strategies. Interest groups and charities have built up and sustained journalist contacts and become regular suppliers of information subsidies (news stories and research) to reporters.

Although corporations have large resource advantages, this does not guarantee advantages when it comes to framing public debate. Studies of business elites (Grant, 1993, 1995; Mitchell, 1997; Boswell and Peters, 1997) stress how often there are great divisions within such communities and their messages. The same has been observed in studies of sources from parties and government institutions (Deacon and Golding, 1994; Hallin, 1994; Miller, 1994; Entman, 2004). When such elites come into conflict, their messages can cancel one another out, as well as opening up spaces for alternative sources and arguments to be heard. Similarly, corporate and political sources risk being ignored if their communication does not chime with appropriate news values. In addition, not all promotional activity requires extensive resources. Advertising and lobbying may be expensive but news coverage is free. The basic communication costs (phones, email, post) are relatively cheap. Large numbers of volunteers and members may be pulled in to work on campaigns for free (see Davis, 2002).

Lastly, corporate cultural and symbolic advantages are not so clear cut. Interest groups may piggy-back off celebrities and established political figures who then publicly present their views (Sireau, 2009). Thus, the 'primary definer' status of elites may be used by non-elite sources. Public legitimacy and symbolic capital are not rigid, unchanging things (Schlesinger, 1990). Established public sources can lose public status during promotional conflicts with each other and outsiders. They can come to be regarded as 'unreliable' by journalists and may be seen to lose their standing as legitimate sources altogether (Deacon and Golding, 1994; Hallin, 1994; Miller, 1994; Davis, 2000a; de Jong, 2005). At such times, alternative sources may gain greater access to, and legitimacy from, journalists. Both they and journalists themselves can then become 'primary definers' in the short term. Over time, reliable interest-group sources can build up a sense of legitimacy and authority, thus drawing journalists to use them more in certain reporting areas. Amnesty International, Liberty, the World Wildlife Fund and the British Medical Association are such examples.

In effect, corporate and powerful institutional dominance of media, through the use of promotional activity, is not assured. Indeed, it can be cyclical, temporary and unstable. Media coverage can fluctuate considerably and according to news media needs. Alternative organizations, such as interest groups and unions, can be very effective in their use of promotional campaign techniques. Mainstream political and commercial agendas on a variety of policy areas, from smoking and environmental regulation to race and gender equality legislation, have shifted considerably over decades.

However, we are still left to wonder about the cumulative long-term changes to the contemporary media and political environments of promotional democracies. Can alternative interests continue to compete against ever larger conglomerates in an era of weakened states, sovereign debt and economic depression? Similarly, what organizational objectives, ideals and messages become compromised when alternative groups push for greater access to institutional politics and mainstream media coverage? Alternatively, is it possible for outsider interest groups to be effective while maintaining a distance from institutional politics and bypassing mainstream media? Such questions are explored in the three case studies below.

Trade unions and the promotional battle against Post Office privatization in the UK

The labour movement has done much to organize opposition to long-term pro-market policies enacted by successive governments of the last three decades. In addition to arguing over pay and conditions, trade unions have battled governments over corporate deregulation, economic policy, and the privatization of government businesses and services. Several observers have noted how old union campaign strategies have become more professional (Davis, 2002; O'Neill, 2007; Kumar, 2008). Shifts in organizational practices have included the employment of former journalists and PR professionals, media training programmes, and the use of consultants. According to Davis (2002), the large majority of UK medium and large unions had their own communication departments. More than half employed other types of agency or consultancy for communications work (advertising, lobbying, media monitoring, media training, etc.). Despite the kinds of resource disadvantages noted above, unions have come to build up their media contacts and to identify and exploit certain advantages of their own, such as using their extensive memberships for campaigning and employing their 'expert' knowledge and public figures to source stories.

One outstanding example of a union campaign has been the CWU's (Communication Workers Union, then UCW) ongoing operations to prevent the privatization of the UK Post Office (see Davis, 2002). This was attempted by both the Conservative government in the 1990s and the Labour government in the 2000s. The following case is of their first campaign, which took place over four months in 1994. It was the only major privatization to be successfully opposed during eighteen years of Conservative government.

Much about the campaign suggests that the pro-privatization forces, of Post Office management and John Major's government, had many advantages and should have won. They had a majority in Parliament and privileged access to MPs and civil servants. The Post Office had a network of 460 communications staff. The government's Department of Trade and Industry (DTI), led by Michael Heseltine, had sixty-seven such staff. Communication budgets were extensive. Media access and coverage was systematic. In contrast, the then UCW had a handful of communications staff and a limited budget. The newspaper content analysis of the time showed that government and corporate sources dominated, making up 55.3 per cent of all sources cited. The UCW and other unions made up just

12.6 per cent. The views of Heseltine and the DTI were discussed in, or contributed to, 89 per cent of articles, while the unions were mentioned in only 37 per cent.

In spite of these differences, the union did manage to win through. Part of the victory can be attributed to the UCW's innovative use of resources and campaign strategy. The union made up for its economic and symbolic resource disadvantages in a number of ways. It hired several promotional consultants, in public affairs, public relations and from economic think tanks. The UCW also made extensive use of its 100 local UK branches and 160,000 members, giving media training campaign packs to all branch representatives. Every union postman and woman was given information cards and encouraged to discuss the issues with their customers during their rounds. Public opinion polls, opposing privatization, were conducted and released to the media. The union worked closely with a number of interest groups, often funding them and supplying them with information subsidies, campaign materials and contacts. They also worked closely with the Labour Party, which pushed the union case in Parliament and to the media. These allied organizations, which were often presented as independent groups, themselves made up 34.4 per cent of newspaper citations overall. Since many of these came in the final weeks of the campaign, anti-privatization sources came to dominate the news coverage during the vital endgame. Public opinion hardened against privatization.

The UCW media and advocacy strategy was also successful because it legitimized the union itself, while also dividing and delegitimizing its corporate and political opponents. Industrial action was avoided. The campaign emphasis at all times was on the protection of public services, Britain's long Post Office 'heritage' and its vital community role. Instead of arguing for jobs or obstructing change, the union offered its own alternative of greater commercial freedom within the public sector. To do so, it commissioned reports from the Economists Advisory Group (1993) and London Economics (1994), two pro-free-market think tanks. These argued that the privatization proposals were unworkable. The UCW also hired Lowe Bell Political, headed by Tim Bell, a former advisor to Margaret Thatcher and the Conservative Party. The consultancy brought good contacts with Conservative MPs and access to the right-wing press. Such reports and consultants were used to split the Conservative government and business support for privatization. Local UCW campaigns also targeted Conservative rebel MPs and those with small electoral majorities. In the weeks that remained before the final government decision, party support had weakened considerably for all privatization options on offer. The plans were considered to be politically impossible and had to be withdrawn.

Interest groups and the challenge to global poverty: the Make Poverty History campaign

As interest groups have become more professional and ambitious in their campaigning, pushing for greater political access and media coverage, so they have been confronted with new dilemmas. Obtaining closer access to government ('insider status') has risked political co-option and diluted objectives. Similarly, being more mass media-oriented has risked media co-option by news values and practices. In effect, gaining success through mainstream politics and media may well mean campaign groups losing their critical distance and public messaging (see also Gitlin, 1980; Clarke, 2001; Ross, 2004).

Such problems became apparent in the Make Poverty History (MPH) campaign of 2005 (see Sireau and Davis, 2007; Sireau, 2009), which brought together a large number of NGOs to campaign during the UK's presidency of the European Union and its hosting of the G8 summit in Scotland. A total of 540 member organizations joined together, including leading NGOs such as Oxfam, Christian Aid, Action Aid, Comic Relief, Cafod and Save the Children. The campaign worked closely with the New Labour government as well as with public figures and celebrities, such as Bob Geldof, Bono and the film director Richard Curtis. It also attempted to generate mass-media coverage and raise public awareness, thus creating greater pressure on the UK and other G8 governments. The high point was the July summit, around which a major MPH rally and the international Live 8 concert were organized. However, such strategies and alliances meant organizations being forced into a series of political and communicative compromises that left many campaigners dissatisfied.

The NGO coalition contained a variety of interests with conflicting campaign goals and strategies. Some took a more 'outsider', radical line, seeking to present G8 leaders and corporations as the cause of economic injustice. They appealed to critical activists and wanted to protest directly against government policies, particularly on international trade. However, the majority, including the larger, established NGOs, took a more 'insider', moderate and consensual approach. This focused on the need to offer aid, cancel debt and alleviate suffering, without directly confronting governments. They also attempted to gain mass-media coverage, using professional marketing consultants, by presenting simple messages and using celebrities. Consequently, messages became blurred, and the campaign became co-opted by politicians, celebrities and the media. Certain key campaign objectives were not achieved.

Political co-option became a concern from the start, as the Labour government attempted to associate itself closely with the campaign. Labour saw Make Poverty History as a clear opportunity for demonstrating public support for its policies. Ministers frequently referred to the MPH campaign in speeches, took on its key discourse on aid and debt, and even adopted the symbol of the white band. A significant proportion of the public even believed that MPH was a government idea (Fenyoe and Darnton, 2005). On the campaign side, the moderate majority took charge and adopted a sympathetic government line. For them, the campaign needed to present government actors as potential heroes of the poor, encouraging them to act. Advertising staff from Abbot Mead Vicker (AMV) were given instructions to produce non-challenging messages that encouraged government decision-makers. Draft ads circulated including phrases such as 'G8: Make Poverty History' and 'G8: Do Something Great'. However, several smaller, more radical groups were not happy, as it meant that the campaign did not directly challenge government trade policy, seen as a key cause of poverty. Tensions became evident in the press coverage. Richard Curtis (vice-chair of Comic Relief), the AMV agency, and close links to New Labour all came to be the focus of the radicals' anger (Quarmby, 2005; Hodkinson, 2005a, 2005b, 2005c). *The Independent* (Hodkinson, 2005b) revealed that campaign disagreements had escalated 'between the powerful right-wing grouping of government-friendly aid agencies and charities effectively running MPH . . . and the more progressive yet smaller NGOs such as War on Want and the World Development Movement'.

The larger insider member organizations ultimately had more input into the framing of the issues in the run-up to the crucial G8 summit. For them there were significant successes. That co-option had taken place was to be judged not as a failing but, in certain ways, as the true signifier of success itself (Martin et al., 2006). For critics, however, this resulted in a failure to tackle government on the more crucial issue of trade, which became the campaign's focus in the second half of the year.

Just as Make Poverty History had to deal with the problem of political co-option, so it was also faced with the parallel problem of media co-option. From the start, a mass-media campaign took place alongside the political campaign. This involved widespread use of corporate, mass-marketing techniques used by AMV in its work for Comic Relief. The strategy combined celebrity endorsement, mass advertising, corporate sponsorship and strong branding. However, in so doing, the complex causes of poverty came to be oversimplified or were lost altogether in the attempt to gain mass-media interest. Celebrities used to generate media coverage went 'off message' and inadvertently misrepresented the campaign.

The early strategic choice was for a mass-media campaign which used simple messages and celebrities to appeal to news editors. MPH's click advert involved a number of public personalities, including Bob Geldof, Bono, Brad Pitt, Kate Moss, Kylie Minogue and George Clooney. They were seen clicking their fingers to symbolize a child dying from extreme poverty every three seconds. It worked, as the campaign gained extensive media coverage. Unfortunately, because the broad coalition had no clear central spokespersons, celebrities tended to be presented as *de facto* leaders. Consequently, messaging and the campaign's larger profile became distorted. Many of these difficulties came to be typified in the campaign's relationship with Bob Geldof. Geldof, while supporting MPH, was also leading an Africa campaign and working closely with the government, and so had conflicting interests. His independent decision to stage the Live 8 concert during the G8 summit directly clashed with the rally in Edinburgh on 2 July that the coalition had been organizing. Live 8 and Make Poverty History messages became confused.

A particularly difficult moment came during the press conference just after the G8 summit. Following the announcement of the G8 package on international development Geldof gave an enthusiastic assessment. He spoke of a 'great day', gave the G8 summit '10 out of 10 on aid, 8 out of 10 on debt'. He concluded that 'never before have so many people forced a change of policy onto a global agenda' (BBC, 2005a, 2005b). It soon became clear that this was not the message that the MPH campaign wanted to convey. Oxfam's policy advisor, Max Lawson, said that there was 'an incentive on the part of Number 10 Downing Street and even Bob Geldof to portray these announcements as a huge deal' (Beattie, 2005). The more radical elements of Make Poverty History were furious and publicly criticized Geldof through the press. As Hodkinson (2005b) wrote: 'There has been little coverage of how bitterly most MPH members feel about the concerts, which were organized separately by Geldof and Curtis . . . Their focus was not on global poverty, but Africa.

And their demands were not those of MPH, but of the Commission for Africa, a Government-sponsored think-tank committed to free-market capitalism.'

Clearly, campaigners knew that they needed to simplify the issues, and get celebrities such as Geldof on board, to gain access to the international media and the support of the wider public. Yet, they also felt frustration at the simplistic explanations of poverty and the lack of control they were able to exercise when the issues were relayed through such high-profile figures.

Taking on the power of global finance and the 1 per cent: the Occupy movement

This third case study looks at the Occupy movement. In various ways it can be described as being at the far end of the promotional spectrum of progressive campaigning groups. Unlike labour unions and established interest groups, it is a social movement with few financial resources and no obvious leaders and is devoid of a centralized operational hierarchy. It has also deliberately maintained its distance from conventional mainstream media and political parties. It is an example of what Tormey (2012) calls 'post-representative, disorganized politics'. The real questions are: What, if anything, has the movement achieved? Can such movements bring about change and, if so, on what levels?

The Occupy movement officially began on 27 September 2011. A few dozen people decided to make a statement by Occupying Wall Street (OWS) and ended up setting up camp in New York's Zuccotti Park. This demonstration, partly inspired by the recent 'Arab Spring' and Spanish 'Indignados' camps, was one of a rolling set of protest actions in 2011. However, the movement quickly snowballed as the camp grew, and allied Occupy initiatives sprang up across the US and many other countries. On 15 October several hundred protests took place in over eighty countries, often with thousands or tens of thousands coming together. In Spain and Italy it was hundreds of thousands. In the US, the mainstream media, after first ignoring the action, gave it extensive coverage. For roughly two months it remained one of the top five weekly news stories. In the week of 10 to 16 October it took up 10 per cent of all US news coverage and, from 14 to 20 November, 13 per cent (Pew News Coverage Index, 2011). At its peak, 52 per cent of New Yorkers and 29 per cent of the US public overall considered themselves to be 'supporters' of OWS (Polling Report; Enten, 2012). Then, in mid-November, Mayor Bloomberg ordered the dismantling of the Zuccotti Park camp and forcible eviction of protestors. Similar actions followed, as camps and protests were shut down, often using brutal methods. By August 2012 there had been over 7,400 arrests in the US (OccupyArrests). By February 2012, the last of the large, high-profile camps, in Washington, DC, and at St Paul's Cathedral, London, had been cleared. By the summer of 2012, the movement appeared to have passed into history, a receding memory for most voters and journalists.

Occupy is characterized by several things. It is a large, globally dispersed social movement that rejects centralization, organizational hierarchies, leaders and conventional, representative politics. At its sites it practises forms of direct, participatory democracy organized through 'general assemblies' and working groups (a 'progressive stack'). The movement makes extensive use of digital media and social networking to organize and publicize its activities and to connect to allied and associated groups. In Gitlin's (2011) account, its 'horizontal democracy is spunky, polymorphic, energetic, theatrical, scattered and droll . . . it tends to care about process more than results.' It has no clear manifesto, set of demands or identifiable objectives. But its various groups and supporters are united by a set of concerns around wealth, inequality and power, summed up by the slogan 'We are the 99 per cent'. Its protests highlight the stagnation of ordinary incomes next to the huge income rises of the top 1 per cent (or 0.001 per cent) and the economic and political power of the 1 per cent and the financial sector. It also voices a general disenchantment with a political system that supports such trends (see figures in Chang, 2010; CBO, 2011; Ferguson, 2012; chapter 10). In Chomsky's view (2012: 54), it is 'the first major public response, in fact, to about thirty years of a really quite bitter class war'.

Occupy has been compared to many other movements and interest groups, past and present. Chief among them is the right-wing, Republican-linked Tea Party, which emerged in 2009. It is also directly contrasted with the protests and movements for change in Egypt, Tunisia, Spain, Italy and Greece (see Krugman, 2011; Rosenthal, 2011; Bruff, 2012; Chomsky, 2012). Next to these, Occupy appears to have promised much and delivered little. The Tea Party has maintained a steady influence on US politics, getting representatives elected in 2010, forcing Republican politicians to adopt many of their policies, and obstructing Congress. They have continued to gain mass-media coverage and have kept their public 'support' levels in the low to mid-30s over an extended period. The movements in Tunisia and Egypt have toppled their political regimes, albeit with many old, reactionary institutional structures left standing. The demonstrations in Spain, Greece and Italy have been far larger and have continued over longer periods. Next to all of these, Occupy's achievements seem rather modest. For many in mainstream politics and media, its time has come and gone. Like the anti-globalization protests in the late 1990s or the anti-poverty initiatives of the 2000s, it is easily forgotten. Authorities survived the storm, and another rudderless progressive initiative failed to achieve a substantive political breakthrough.

In many accounts, even from sympathetic supporters, the movement's organizational structure, practices and ideals are key contributors to its failure (see Gitlin, 2011; Wainwright, 2012; Tormey, 2012). Journalists and politicians have regularly derided Occupy for its lack of clear demands and objectives. Gitlin (2011), early on, predicted its likely demise, 'since an evolving alliance demands concrete goals, strategies and compromises'. As Tormey (2012: 132, 135) says: 'History is littered with disaffiliated, non-programmatic groups who wanted to contest inequality in quite general terms . . . immobilism and inefficacy seem at one level built into OWS.' In contrast to the Tea Party, Occupy has remained suspicious and distant from the Democrats, as well as their linked funders, organization and media. In effect, the Occupy experiment has shown that cutting all links to conventional media and representative politics, no matter the justification, is self-defeating in mature, wealthy democracies. The US is far removed from the conditions of 1930s Europe, the twenty-first-century Middle East or, at the moment, Spain and Greece. Thus, a policy of extreme institutional and media de-alignment fails.

However, there is also much to suggest that, as with many social movements of the past, substantive progress may be achieved in the longer term. Gitlin (2011) and Wainwright (2012) more aptly compare Occupy with the student and women's movements of the 1960s and 1970s. Like Occupy, they had general objectives and avoided imposed leaders and hierarchies. Other comparisons may also be made with long-running movements and interest-group networks formed around racial equality, anti-nuclear concerns and environmental protection. In these cases, movements, initially ignored or derided, came over time to influence mainstream media, culture and politics. For many, Occupy indeed represents a growing zeitgeist, a 'subterranean' mass feeling, bubbling to the surface. It has inspired related union activities and protest initiatives worldwide. Politicians and journalists continue to use its language, terms and arguments, even if not referring directly to Occupy. Jobs, the economy and inequality were key themes in the 2012 US presidential race. For Rosen (2011), 'The Occupy movement has changed the national conversation in America', making 'class' an issue once again and legitimating critiques of unbridled capitalism in mainstream debate. For Chomsky (2012: 69), 'One of the really remarkable and almost spectacular successes of the Occupy movement is that it has simply changed the entire framework of discussion on many issues.'

In such circumstances, it is far too early to say what the true impact of Occupy will be on US culture and politics. It may well go down in history as a loud but insignificant event. Alternatively, it may also be one important step among many in the making of a substantial political and social shift. Promotional politics in civil society may be effective (or ineffective) on many planes.

Conclusion

Clearly, the use of professional promotional techniques and person-nel to achieve political and economic goals is now fairly widespread in civil society. The shifting political and communication environment appears to offer more opportunities to interest groups to take on powerful corporations and institutions and influence elite decisions. There is a growing list of successful campaigns by 'resource-poor' and 'outsider' groups. In some ways, promotional civil society can be said to have made democracies more pluralist.

However, at the same time, the odds remain stacked in favour of the major employers of the promotional professions. Resource differences mean that the gains of smaller opposition groups continue to be relatively infrequent or on smaller issues. Large corporations carry on getting bigger and more influential. Institutional politics remains relatively 'captured' by corporate, free-market thinking. Inequality keeps on rising. The rights of workers and consumers, as well as many elements of welfare state provision, continue to be eroded. International action on global warming and environmental issues has ground to a halt.

Since 1994, governments have managed to sell off several parts of the UK Post Office. In 2011, the new UK coalition government passed the Postal Services Act, making a full future privatization of the Royal Mail more likely. They have also made great strides towards privatizing the NHS and higher education. As also demonstrated with the MPH case, the adoption of corporate-style lobbying and media-friendly campaign strategies may be detrimental to a group's long-term goals. Greater political access and mass-media coverage may result in forms of political and news media co-option and the achievement of more limited objectives. However, as the case of Occupy shows, maintaining outsider autonomy and distance from the political centre and mass media may also mean inevitable marginalization. Increased promotional and political plurality does not automatically mean that actual power is any less centralized.

10
Economies, Speculative Markets and Value

Introduction

This chapter looks at how promotional culture influences economies, speculative markets and values. Such markets include those in high finance, such as stocks, bonds, currencies and derivatives, as well as real estate, art and ageing musical instruments. In each of these cases, unlike ordinary commodities markets, the values of the objects traded often appear to have little connection to their material conditions of production. The markets involved come to operate under their own internal logics and may be prone to extreme fluctuations.

At the heart of the discussion lies a challenge to conventional economics and economic conceptions of markets, market participants and value. For neo-classical economists, their discipline is close to a science. According to their analytical framework, in properly functioning markets, values are set by competing sets of buyers and sellers (supply and demand) who operate rationally in their own self-interest. In so doing, they contribute to long-term market equilibrium. Under such conditions, social and cultural factors, including promotional culture, have negligible impacts.

However, as argued here, all markets and participants are affected by social, cultural and psychological factors. Indeed, such markets are more, not less, prone to such influences. Values are guided as much by the symbolic and the promotional as they are by any logical or conventional accounting measures. In effect, such markets are able to form their own 'disembedded' cultures and trading logics within which promotional activity makes forceful interventions. Promotion not only influences calculations of value, it also affects the tools of calculation as well as the cultural and psychological conditions within which actors make their valuations. In fact, in many ways, economics and accountancy have become promotional disciplines. That they still successfully present themselves as science-like and rational is, in itself, indication of their inherent promotional qualities.

The first part of the chapter discusses orthodox economics and the challenges to it from economic sociology, cultural economy and heterodox economics. The main case study material looks closely at promotion in financial markets. It is in three parts. The first examines the rise of financialization and how the financial lobby has become so influential in the US and the UK. The second records how promotion affects stock markets and can lead to bubbles and crashes. In particular it focuses on the dot.com bubble of 2000. The third details what happened in property and investment banking in the lead up to the financial market crisis of 2007–8. In each case, the consequences of promotional culture, direct and indirect, have been profound on the markets concerned, as well as on wider economies and societies.

Markets, actors and value: economic rationality, sociological irrationality and promotional markets

Neo-classical, orthodox economics

For over a century neo-classical economics has provided the dominant analytical framework for conceiving of and assessing markets, market actors and values. It became distinguished as a separate discipline, distinct from political economy, in the nineteenth century, and has become steadily more consolidated as modern economics has built on and refined its foundational starting points. Its perspectives have also come to have a dominant influence over practitioners and policy-makers. As a discipline, economics brackets out the social and the psychological, as well as other external factors. Thus promotional culture is not a consideration. This section questions this position, introducing alternative ways of conceptualizing and analysing markets, actors and values. Such ways allow for and engage with promotional factors.

Before the establishment of mainstream economics, there was the notion that all goods had a 'natural' or 'intrinsic' value that could be deduced independently of social or market factors. In the nineteenth century, political economists such as Smith, Ricardo and Marx calculated that the value of goods was determined by the costs of their production. Most of this was the result of human labour. Buyers purchased commodities because of their 'use value' but paid prices determined by a good's 'exchange value' – as calculated by individuals to be of relative equivalence to other goods. Under ideal conditions the costs of production ('labour value'), incurred by sellers, would be matched by the perceived 'use value' of buyers. For Smith and Ricardo, markets became the intermediary apparatuses by which individual self-interests were reconciled, and larger economies came to function best.

However, it became clear that such definitions of value appeared far too arbitrary and volatile. As markets became larger, more dispersed and more complex, they appeared all the more redundant. The breakthrough, for economists at least, was the 'marginal revolution' (Menger, Jevons, Walrus) at the end of the nineteenth century. This identified the market itself as the means of value determination via the mechanism of price. Marginalists argued that rational consumers were deemed capable of calculating the 'marginal utility' of one commodity over another and deciding the price they should pay accordingly. Value is the outcome of a competition between buyers and sellers. Prices, and therefore values, are most stable when supply matches demand in perfect market conditions. When supply outstrips demand, marginal utility and prices go down, and vice versa. In this new foundation of economic thought, all other conceptions of value and individual behaviour, as well as social or external influences, are bracketed out. Over the twentieth century, while debates in the discipline continued and a range of arguments and models evolved, this continued to provide the framework for interpreting markets, market actors and value. Thus, neo-classical economics, at root, has treated the economic as separate from the social and as an independent subject of research. Market transactions involve entirely rational individuals who attempt to maximize their resources while in competition with other rational market actors. Markets and the multiple transactions that take place within them are entirely autonomous from all other social and cultural activity.

Such thinking finds its purest form and application in financial markets. Here, the Efficient Market Hypothesis (EMH; see Fama, 1970) is given a central place in finance textbooks (e.g., Reilly and Brown, 2000; Bodie et al., 2003). According to the EMH, prices and market equilibrium are reached by the absorption of all market-relevant information by large numbers of self-serving buyers and sellers in competition. Each rational participant knows what they want and logically calculates the prices at which they will trade. If some individuals act irrationally – i.e., not in their own best interests or not using rational calculation – there are enough rational buyers and sellers to cancel them out. 'Arbitrageurs' (professional, short-term profit-seekers) will always move in to take advantage of individual and market irrationalities to make a profit. In so doing, all relevant information will come to be reflected in market prices, and market equilibrium will be quickly restored. Irrational participants, because of their losses, are automatically traded out of the market altogether. Thus, financial markets are assumed to be populated by rational individuals and always find their logical equilibrium.

Such thinking, however, does not explain the wild price swings that can occur with individual products or whole markets. Markets in shares, commodities, real estate and art are examples where values can fluctuate wildly, bubbles can form and markets can crash. There are many well-known past examples, such as in South Sea stocks, Dutch tulip bulbs, British railways, and the 1929 Wall Street Crash. In recent years, such behaviour seems to have become more regular. Between 1970 and 1999, twenty-one different national financial markets experienced increases in value of over 100 per cent in a year; seventeen of those same markets experienced drops of over 50 per cent in a subsequent year (Shiller, 2001: 119–20). The value of commodities such as copper, gold, wheat and coffee have also been subject to quite dramatic shifts. Oil, for example, hovered between $10 and $30 a barrel from the mid-1980s to the mid-2000s. It then shot up to peak at just under $150 a barrel in mid-2008, before falling back to just over $30 again a few months later (and it continues to fluctuate). According to Ferguson (2012: 238, 213), daily oil futures (agreements to buy existing goods at set prices in the future) are currently worth ten times the current value of real oil supply. He also noted that, between 2001 and 2005, the net value of US homes doubled, from $6 trillion to $13 trillion, before slumping back down to £6 trillion again in 2010. Art provides another example. For the 1990s, the average sale price at auction of an artwork moved between $22,791 and $45,135 (bar a spike in 1996). Then between 2002 and 2007 the average suddenly climbed, from $49,763 to $329,824, increasing by a multiple of more than six and a half (Artnet). Such 'abnormal' movements appear both increasingly common and in spite of regulations and information technologies encouraging more 'perfect' market conditions. In many cases, market participants and economists will usually offer quite logical explanations for these dramatic shifts in value before restating a belief that market equilibrium will return again.

Heterodox economics, social and cultural perspectives

However, there are many alternative bodies of work which suggest that more convincing explanations of erratic market behaviours and values can be found outside of mainstream economics. Heterodox economists, including economic historians, post-Keynesians, behavioural economists, development economists and political economists, have all been sceptical about orthodox economic assumptions and financial market theory (Keynes, 1936; Minsky, 1982; Shiller, 1989, 2001; Kahnemann and Tversky, 2000; Kindleberger, 2000; Harvey, 2005; Akerlof and Shiller, 2009; Chang, 2010). In their varied works, market instabilities, bubbles and crashes, and irrational calculative behaviour (animal spirits) are considered to be regular rather than abnormal features. These studies look outside markets to long-term historical market data, to wider socio-economic trends and relationships, and to social and psychological factors.

For economic sociologists and anthropologists, economic action is always social. Early postwar work by Talcott Parsons, Smelser and, above all, Polanyi (1944) insisted that all economic action was a form of social action that was socially situated. Markets are socially constructed. They require social and political prerequisites to function. So too do money, accounting tools, contract and property law, market institutions and, indeed, the discipline of neo-classical economics. As such, the pure, rational participants of market theory do not exist. Markets and the price mechanism are not neutral systems by which market equilibrium is reached or stable values are achieved. Instead, values are determined by individuals and market systems which are themselves subject to a range of social, cultural and psychological influences. In recent decades, other authors have gone further. Increasingly they have emphasized the power of the cultural and the symbolic over the material in contemporary society (Baudrillard, 1988a [1972]; Featherstone, 1991; Lash and Urry, 1994; Lash and Lury, 2007; and see chapter 4). Production, goods, markets and values are driven by the production and circulation of symbolic signs. There are no innate 'use values', institutions or individual subjects that exist outside of a world of signs. Thus, the value of the 'commodity-sign' created is completely arbitrary and temporary. 'Symbolic values' determine exchange values across a variety of markets.

Weaving a way between the extremes of orthodox economics and the 'cultural' or 'postmodern' turn in sociology come several alternatives. New Economic Sociologists (see Granovetter and Swedberg, 1992; Guillen et al., 2002; Smelser and Swedberg, 2005) emphasize the dynamic, social construction of markets and industries, historically and within social networks. Granovetter (1992 [1985]) argued that the rules, regulations and norms of markets were established through the ongoing social interaction of rational agents. Thus, actors retain their agency but, at the same time, make economic decisions and take economic actions that are embedded in the social relations of the market. Several studies have revealed the substantive influences of local cultures, belief systems and social networks on market participants, processes of numerical calculation and trading decisions. Trader assessments are concerned as much with judgements about managers, sources of information, rival traders, business rhetoric, risk and spotting regulatory loopholes as they are about the raw accounting issues or simple profit maximization (Lazar, 1990; Abolafia, 1996; De Bondt, 2005; Davis, 2007; Ho, 2009).

Elsewhere, emerging out of science and technology studies and actor network theory, has come the concept of 'metrological performativity' (Callon, 1998b, 1998c). The 'performative' both describes something and enacts it, thus bringing it into being. 'Metrological performativity' applies this logic to markets and economic actors. Here markets are conceived as 'actor networks' which are 'disentangled' from wider social influences. Economic agents enter into such networks on a temporary basis. All parts of a market actor network – individuals, institutions, tools, prices and measures – are so constituted in ongoing social practices within the market itself. Economics and associated metrological professions play a central part in that they both observe and configure markets and the wider economy. By such means, 'economics, in the broad sense of the term, performs, shapes and formats the economy, rather than observing how it functions' (Callon, 1998b: 2). Agents then calculate and act according to the logics of the market which, in turn, are guided by economics, accounting and other market professions (P. Miller, 1998; Cochoy, 1998). Rational, calculating agents, the *homo economicus* of economic theory, exist, but also calculate according to the social circumstances of the market in which they find themselves.

All these bodies of work suggest several things. Markets are far from being socially autonomous. Market participants are influenced by a range of social, psychological and cultural factors in their decision-making. Numerical forms of calculation have a social component, and calculative rationality may be based on non-numerical factors. As such, there are many ways that promotional culture and promotional intermediaries may intervene and influence prices, market conditions and the shapes of entire markets.

Promotion and markets

In fact, what is observable across financial, art, property and other such markets is the presence of promotional intermediaries and activities. In each case the core activity is to sell objects using a range of financial and non-financial information. Narratives, futurology, cults of the individual (artist, CEO, trader, etc.), brands and symbols are all blended with hard financial data to boost demand and therefore value. At another level, promotion is also about selling the market itself, be it in Impressionism or Young British Art, antiques or ageing violins, exclusive London property, the BRIC economies (Brazil, Russia, India and China) or the German bond market. Such markets have to entice investors in to sustain market buoyancy and prices. At a third level, promotion involves the lobbying of regulators, professional associations and governments. Favourable decisions about public funding, law and regulation are also important for markets trying to sustain themselves and grow.

In the case of the art market, promotion works across multiple networks and formats (see Thornton, 2008; Lewis, 2009, 2011). Individual contemporary artists promote themselves, as do their dealers, collectors, museums and auction houses. But promotion is also applied to whole art styles and movements, nations and periods. As Thornton (2008: xiv) states: 'Great works . . . are made – not just by artists and their assistants but also by the dealers, curators, critics, and "collectors" who "support" the work.' Those professional insiders she observes are as likely to view modern art acquisitions as part of an 'investment portfolio' as they are to value them on 'meaningful' or 'aesthetic' grounds. In her account, collectors and dealers inflate values, spread rumours and entice media coverage with a view to influencing prices. The archetypal example of the last two decades has been Charles Saatchi and his promotion of Young British Artists. Saatchi, of the international advertising agency Saatchi and Saatchi, propelled contemporary British and other art markets for over two decades, both promoting and dealing in those works. According to Lewis (2011: 22), 'Having played a central role in inventing a new kind of art, Charles [Saatchi] then led the way in inventing a new kind of art economy . . . a fusion of the art collector and dealer/ speculator who drove the art boom of the last decade.'

Promotional activity is also a core activity for financial markets. Fundamentally, they are about buying and selling paper (or electronic) representations of real-world items with unpredictable future values: companies (shares), commodities (e.g., oil, gold, rice), real estate and currencies. Over time they have additionally become about trading more virtual items such as debt (government, corporate and personal) and financially constructed products such as complex derivatives (see below). And they have become about pushing particular market sectors (e.g., shares versus bonds, banking versus telecommunication, BRICs versus European economies) and financial markets themselves (London versus Frankfurt or New York). Lastly, financial industries are concerned to sell themselves and their general functions to national and international regulators and governing institutions. Thus, selling is at the core of what takes place in financial markets, and promotional activity is fundamental to selling.

Indeed, in the postwar period, financially based forms of advertising, public relations and advocacy have all steadily increased. In the UK, according to Curran (1978) and Newman (1984), financial advertising in newspapers grew enormously, outpacing many other advertising forms (see also Mintel, 1995). As Davis (2002) recorded, it was financial and investor public relations that led the expansion of corporate PR in the last decades of the twentieth century. Parsons (1989) and Davis (2002) suggested that financial news has become one of the most PR-reliant forms of coverage. A poll produced by the Public Relations Consultants Association (*PR Week*, 1994) found that the *Financial Times* used considerably more public relations material than any other national paper, with 26 per cent of its total output and 62 per cent in its 'Companies and Markets' section being PR-generated. Over the years, the UK financial lobby has also developed powerful links to UK governments and the Conservative Party. Davis (2002) recorded the links that developed in the 1980s and 1990s between the top PR and public affairs consultancies, the Conservative government, and FTSE 100 companies. More recently, CRESC (2009) and Engelen and his colleagues (2011) have observed the power of London's financial lobby successfully to resist attempts to restore stronger regulations on banking and finance after the 2008 crisis. Following the 2010 UK election, 134 Conservative MPs and Lords were (or still are) employed in the financial sector, and financiers have provided over 50 per cent of the party's funds (Robert Peston, BBC report, 2 September 2011). The Bureau of Investigative Journalism (2012) identified 129 organizations engaged in lobbying for finance and estimated that £92.8 million had been spent lobbying the UK government just in 2011.

Similar trends are observable in the US. FIRE sector advertising (finance, insurance, real estate) increased, from 2 per cent of total advertising spend in 1945 to 12 per cent in 2005. In 2005, financial corporations were spending almost $20 billion annually on advertising (McChesney et al., 2011: 35). Corporate and financial public relations and 'advocacy advertising' grew tremendously from the 1970s onwards (Dreier, 1988; Ewen, 1996; Cutlip et al., 2000; Miller and Dinan, 2008; Sussman, 2011; Ferguson, 2012). Billions of dollars were invested in promotional activities, including executive media training; larger public affairs units; the establishment of pro-finance think tanks; corporate-sponsored business and financial journalism courses; and the funding of academic economists to publish favourable papers and testify to committees on behalf of the financial industry. Annual lobbying expenditure from the securities and investment sectors between 1998 and 2012 amounted to $932 million. From the insurance sector it was $1,700 million (Opensecrets, 2012). Both Taibbi (2011) and Ferguson (2012) have documented the revolving doors that have come to operate between US financial regulators and large financial companies, as well as the repeated failures of authorities to pursue and prosecute senior financial figures since the 1990s.

The promotion of financial products, financial markets and financialization

The remainder of this chapter looks at what has happened in banking and financial markets in recent decades in the US and the UK. It argues that promotion has been ever present and has aided the startling growth of international financial centres and banks. It has also become inextricably intertwined with these financial markets, being used to promote and misrepresent a variety of financial goods, from companies and commodities to debt and derivatives. Such activity has, in turn, contributed to a series of bubbles and crashes, causing a wave of personal and institutional bankruptcies and pushing financial centres and whole nations to the brink of collapse. In the varied accounts of the causes of the recent financial and economic crisis, promotional activity does not figure high on the lists of most people – although, of course, in various ways, it has been an essential ingredient.

Selling financial markets, free markets and financialization to governments

Over three decades, a process of financialization has taken place and is particularly advanced in the US and the UK (see descriptions in, for example, Philips, 2006; Palley, 2007). Financial markets have swallowed up and now control significantly larger amounts of capital than either governments or non-financial corporations. Consequently, financiers have become increasingly influential in the economy as well as other policy-making areas. At the same time, much of what they do takes place in under-regulated environments, hidden from public or regulator view. Promotion, be it through lobbying, public relations or advertising, has played its part in this transition. Indeed, financiers have proven extremely adept at promoting themselves as well as neo-liberal economic thinking to governments and other elites. Their current size, autonomy, influence and unaccountability are all testimony to their promotional powers.

A critical element has been convincing regulators and politicians that, in today's globalized world, the UK and the US excel in the business of finance (see Wigley, 2008; Bischoff and Darling, 2009; and critiques in Cable, 2009; CRESC, 2009; Ferguson, 2012). Since the early 1980s, the City of London and Wall Street have been presented as key engines of growth and prosperity for their respective national economies. They have argued that their success will be disseminated through to the wider population in terms of business expansion, growth and employment, and wider home and share ownership. In effect, healthy financial markets have been presented as being synonymous with healthy economies. Such a line has clearly had a significant impact on central banks, external investors and government policy-makers. Through legislation and budgetary measures, these 'stakeholder elites' then encouraged the growth of finance and facilitated a large transfer of public and personal capital into the hands of financial markets. There were multiple privatizations of state businesses and assets, as well as demutualizations of life assurance companies and building societies. Most ended up being traded on stock markets. Pensions, retirement plans and pooled savings funds were all similarly directed towards professional fund managers operating in large financial markets.

In many ways, the promises of financial prosperity have been fulfilled. In recent decades, both the New York and London stock exchanges have brought rising employment, large tax revenues, and positive national trade balances in financial services. In the UK, in 2000, the City employed an estimated 300,000 people, had seen an average growth of 7 per cent per year for twenty-five years, and had an overseas trade surplus of £31 billion (Golding, 2003: 10). Between 2002 and 2008, financial company taxes raised £193 billion for the UK government (CRESC, 2009). In the US in 2007, although it made up only 8 per cent of the economy, the financial sector was responsible for 40 per cent of domestic corporate profits (Bootle, 2009: 113).

However, behind the positive financial figures there have also been several concerning developments. One of these has been the creation of powerful financial systems that have come to tower over industry and democratically elected governments. So, in the case of the UK up until the 1970s, bank assets had been equal to roughly 50 per cent of GDP for a century. Following changes, they have now risen to 500 per cent of GDP (Haldane, 2011). When the Thatcher government came to power in 1979, the value of the FTSE 100 was roughly 40 per cent of government-managed income. By 1997, after eighteen years of Conservative government, the FTSE 100 was valued at three and a half times government income (HMSO, 1980/81, 1997/98; London Stock Exchange, 1998). In 2007, the total managed annual expenditure of the UK government was £587 billion and total national GDP was estimated to be £1.24 trillion. However, in that same year, members of the UK-based Investment Management Association managed £3.4 trillion worth of funds (IMA, 2007) and the international banking system operated funds of $512 trillion, or ten times the GDP value of the entire world economy (Cable, 2009: 30, 146).

Of equal significance is that financial markets have managed to persuade governments and regulators that they would be more profitable and efficient if left alone. The EMH-style argument (see above) was that financial markets, if properly functioning and free from outside influences, would always be right, stable and prosperous. They were self-correcting as well as being the most efficient way to invest capital in society. In such respects, 'financial innovation' was a necessary and productive, wealth-creating activity, similar to innovation in industry, medicine, science and other sectors. Of related significance were the notions that globalization and free trade could only be positive things, and that the world contained a finite pool of floating, talented 'entrepreneurs' who need to be attracted to nations. To attract them, countries need to reduce their rates of personal and corporation tax, deregulate markets, and free them up from the interference of states and trade unions. Such thinking provided the rational and directive parameters for successive waves of deregulation of financial markets (Lazar, 1990; Hutton, 1996; Davis, 2007; Elliott and Atkinson, 2009; Krugman, 2008; Akerlof and Shiller, 2009; Bootle, 2009; Ferguson, 2012).

In the UK, legislation in 1979 and 1980 brought the release of exchange and credit controls and thus initiated a new credit boom. Financial deregulation continued, most notably with the 1986 Financial Services Act, leading to the frenzied activity of the 'Big Bang'. During the years of New Labour (1997–2010) the government continued to encourage a 'light-touch', self-regulatory environment. In the US, the Reagan years began an aggressive era of financial deregulation which continued through the administrations of Clinton and Bush Jr. Many of the very safeguards put into the system in the 1930s after the 1929 Wall Street Crash, such as the 1933 Glass–Steagall Act, were systematically dismantled. The mostly local and mutually owned savings and loan system was deregulated and opened up to financial markets. Deregulation cut the barriers that existed between different banking and trading functions. There emerged large consolidated firms that undertook commercial and investment banking, stock broking, trading and insurance. However, there were large conflicts of interest in these companies, which could work for all sides, in terms of who they worked for and the functions they performed. All of this has had dangerous consequences.

By 2007–8, when things started to deteriorate, it had become clear that relations between finance, industry and government had changed considerably. Since then, the flaws in financial market ideology and promotional rhetoric have been exposed. Critics have pointed out that, far from boosting their economies, the financial sectors of the US and the UK may very well have been damaging them (Hutton, 1996; Froud et al., 2006; Krugman, 2008; CRESC, 2009; Chang, 2010; Ferguson, 2012). For example, almost all studies of takeovers have shown that they destroy wealth rather than create it (Golding, 2003; Bootle, 2009). An increasing proportion of company profits have gone to shareholders rather than to investment, research and development (Hutton, 1996). 'Productive investment' in business itself in the UK declined between 1996 and 2008, from 30 per cent to 12 per cent (CRESC, 2009: 6–7). According to Adair Turner (2011), chair of the Financial Services Authority, most of the new, financially engineered products of recent years, from collateralized debt obligations to asset-backed securities, are 'socially useless' and designed merely to extract wealth from businesses and individuals. Similarly, in the US, Ferguson (2012: 210, 8) shows that, since 1960, the financial sector's share of GDP growth and corporate profits has eased upwards, while overall economic GDP growth has eased steadily downwards. The income of the top 1 per cent, including many CEOs and financiers, has increased tremendously, far beyond any rises in company profits or productivity. The top 1 per cent now own a third of US net worth, including 40 per cent of its financial wealth. Middle- and lower-class incomes have stagnated or declined. Despite these issues, the promotional power of finance remains strong, as financialized states such as the US and the UK have done little to change matters.

The over-promotion of companies and stock markets to outside investors: the 2000 dot.com boom

Financial elite promotion has not been just about promoting the merits of financial markets to governments and regulators. On a day-to-day basis it has also been about selling a variety of products such as company shares, bonds and currencies. In each case promotional activity can be intense and prices fluctuate wildly. Company stock markets, historically regarded as the best markets in which to invest, are particularly prone to such tendencies. Industry reports and investor guides (e.g., Siegal, 1998; Glassman and Hassett, 1999) have regularly argued that wise investors should always put most of their capital into equities rather than other markets (e.g., bonds, property, currency). Certainly, such thinking proved very persuasive to a range of pension fund trustees, small investors and others.

The promotion of shares markets continues to be strong despite the ups and downs of recent decades. On the one hand, companies are sold with regular flows of positive financial data, such as corporate earnings, assets, profits and dividends. On the other, much is unknown and speculative when it comes to those companies and industry sectors. Things such as expected 'growth rates', the future 'market share' in a sector, wider patterns of consumption, and so on, are difficult to predict. This has left ample scope for financial spin operations to present future expectations of profit, charismatic CEOs and management teams, and engaging investment narratives (Soros, 1994; Davis, 2002, 2006; Shiller, 2001; Golding, 2003; Froud et al., 2006).

The overselling of stocks, manipulation of financial data, and general promotional creativity were clearly apparent throughout the 1990s and in the lead up to the 2000 dot.com crash. In this case, the part played by vague narratives and fairy-tale accounting is now evident (see accounts in Shiller, 2001; Cassidy, 2002; Golding, 2003; Davis, 2007; Krugman, 2008). The TMT boom (telecommunications, media, technology) made a good story to sell to investors and was talked up by entrepreneurs, financiers and financial media. This focused on 'the new era economy', 'the creative' or 'knowledge-based economy', and the 'end of the traditional business cycle'. However, these new industries did not have a trading history, often had no assets, and produced no profits or dividends and, therefore, could not be valued by usual accounting measures. So, instead, stock-brokers, analysts, investors and companies came up with their own means of evaluation. These ignored conventional economic measures and historical patterns. Brokers became increasingly reluctant to make 'sell' recommendations for fear of offending the companies they analysed or of going against the market mainstream. According to FSA research (FSA, 2002: 12), 'buy' recommendations in 2000 outnumbered 'sell' by a ratio of 9 to 1. Even through the period 2000–2, when share prices fell heavily, the ratio remained at five 'buys' to one 'sell'.

Consequently, stock markets exploded. The Dow Jones went from 3,600 points in 1994 to 11,000 in 1999 (Shiller, 2001: 9). The London stock market went from just over 3,000 points to almost 7,000. These stock market values, as a whole, became entirely detached from long-term, traditional, real-world measures. One such measure is the P/E ratio. The P/E, or price–earnings, ratio of a company is the total price of the shares divided by the actual annual earnings of the company: the higher the ratio, the smaller the returns and the riskier the investment. By the peak of the dot.com boom, the P/E ratio of the US stock market had gone from 15 in the late 1980s to 45 in 2000 (it was only 32.6 in 1929; Shiller, 2001). The London stock exchange's P/E ratio was almost as detached from its long-term average (Wetherilt and Weeken, 2002). Individual internet companies with no assets or profits became worth billions. Priceline.com, an online company for selling excess airline capacity, was worth $150 billion, or more than the entire airline industry (Cassidy, 2002). Ultimately, in the collapse that began in 2000, both the US and the UK stock markets lost over half their value. Most internet companies collapsed, and many that survived were worth a small fraction of their peak stock market values.

The over-promotion of credit, debt and financial products to financiers: the 2008 financial crisis

Perhaps the most dangerous promotional activity that took place in recent decades was the creation and selling of easy credit and complex financial products across financial institutions themselves. These increased financial flows and investments. They took up debts, risky developments and market anomalies and, through securitization and financial engineering, turned them into valuable, tradable items. These were then promoted as devices for spreading debt, reducing risk and maintaining market stability. However, in practice, they spread financial insider risk to others, created huge instabilities and imbalances, and produced virtual valuations and profits that were entirely divorced from real values. Financial insiders then paid themselves with real money created out of virtual values and profits. The ability of financiers to convince themselves and others that risk and debt were actually sources of value and profit was a persuasive sleight of hand of Orwellian proportions.

In the under-regulated environments that developed in the UK, the US and elsewhere (see above) there emerged a huge, barely monitored and regulated 'shadow banking sector'. In the US, by the time of the collapse, the regulated banking system accounted for some $12 trillion of funds, but the unregulated shadow banking system was worth $16 trillion (UNCTAD, 2009: 13). Global financial markets became sources of an endless supply of cheap, unregulated credit to any banks, fund managers, investors and governments who asked. These institutions took on capital amounts that were far in excess of their asset bases. Easy money was then lent out to others further down the chain or used by governments eager for short-term budget fixes and tax cuts. Government debt, as a proportion of GDP, grew, and many banks borrowed and lent out capital worth up to thirty or forty times their actual asset base (Bootle, 2009; Ferguson, 2012). By the time Northern Rock collapsed in 2007, the first of many bank casualties, it had assets of £1.5 billion and loans worth over £100 billion, 80 per cent of which was financed by the global money markets (Elliott and Atkinson, 2009: 52).

Financial deregulation also enabled the growth of a multiplicity of complex financial products, barely understood by those who traded them. These new creations, presented as a means of spreading risk and of bringing stability throughout the financial sector, became entirely disconnected from the real-world items and values they were supposed to represent. Over-the-counter commodity derivatives, between 2002 and 2008, increased twentyfold to total $13 trillion (UNCTAD, 2009: 25). The total derivatives market rose in value, over the space of a decade to 2008, from $15 trillion to $600 trillion, or nearly twelve times total world output (Cable, 2009: 34). Since derivatives are constructed and valued according to estimates of future values of real assets, the market had somehow risen to impossible values.

Credit default swaps enabled rising debts to be repackaged and presented as vehicles for hedging risks but, at the same time, also increased potential debts several times over. It is through such forms of financial engineering that subprime mortgages could be packaged up into mortgage-backed securities and then further complicated and spliced, using collateralized debt obligations, to hide the risks (see account in Krugman, 2008). This resulted in lots of these packages being given AAA risk ratings by credit ratings agencies, thus encouraging normally cautious institutions, such as pension funds, and ordinary banks to buy them. Not only were mortgages sold to the poorest and least educated in society, they were then repackaged up and sold on in complex entities as safe investments to investors and lenders around the world.

The new waves of financial products, which produced impossible, virtual values, were all traded making large profits. Banks then paid their employees equally large bonuses out of the virtual capital and profits acquired. In effect, financial elites, subprime borrowers, governments and fund managers all bought into the accompanying, if varied, forms of persuasion and propaganda. But, ultimately, what was created was a series of 'giant chain letters' or 'naturally occurring Ponzi schemes' (Krugman, 2008; Elliott and Atkinson, 2009). Money accrued in abundance for those financial institutions and insiders at the head of such schemes and, eventually, everyone else was left nursing the losses. When the complex scams unravelled, as interest rates went up and debt and credit became more expensive, so too the complex networks of IOUs began to unravel and fall apart. Banks did not want to loan money to anyone because no one knew where all the IOUs were hidden. Individuals, financial institutions and governments all had their debts called in, and each was faced with the same threats: bankruptcy and repossession.

We are still trying to gauge the consequences of the collapse that followed. Economies have been wrecked and pension funds devastated, unemployment levels have soared, and many have been left in a deep poverty trap. Governments in many countries have had to nationalize or part-nationalize their retail banks as well as other institutions deemed 'too big to fail'. Freddie Mac and Fannie Mae, the largest mortgage lenders in the US, required $200 billion of public money to bail them out. Four US banks (Bear Stearns, Morgan Stanley, Citigroup and Merrill Lynch) were each loaned between $1.5 and $2 trillion to survive. The total cost to the UK of assorted bank bailouts, loans and state guarantees to maintain the banking system had reached £1.2 trillion by 2012 (Chakrabortty, 2012). Governments everywhere have had to borrow large amounts to do all this, as well as to prop up their struggling economies. US national debt increased 50 per cent. The UK's external debt rose from 22.5 per cent of GDP in 2007 to 66.5 per cent in 2009. In 2008, Greece's national debt had reached 110 per cent of GDP; by 2012 it was 170 per cent. In the same period, Spain's debt went from 40 per cent to 60 per cent of GDP, and Portugal's from 25 per cent to 110 per cent (Ferguson, 2012: 214). At the same time, personal levels of debt have shot up (see chapter 3) and many homeowners have fallen into negative equity. In the US, by 2008, 12 million households were in negative equity and ordinary homeowners faced cumulative losses of $7 trillion (Krugman, 2008: 169, 189). Many financial elite actors have lost their jobs and/or seen their incomes reduced. However, the salaries and bonuses they gathered over the years, as well as pay-offs and pension schemes they have since received, have left them very wealthy.

Conclusion

Promotional practices have had a significant part in the presentation of orthodox economic thinking in speculative markets and in high finance. Economists and financiers have been very successful at presenting their disciplines and institutions as rational, logical, stable entities, operating according to scientific-like laws. The prevailing public image of financial markets has been one of sober institutions, with long-established histories, being run by highly intelligent, respectable individuals. They are promoted as stable centres for economies, offering services vital to businesses, governments and citizens. If things go wrong and markets suffer unstable periods, it is down to ignorant government interference, external obstacles or rogue traders.

Such presentations have been hugely successful. They have convinced a succession of government decision-makers that they were essential to the health of economies, that states should get out of the way, and that they should be left alone and allowed to expand. They have managed to persuade pension fund managers and CEOs to invest in and work with their financial markets. They have directed ordinary people towards placing their savings, pension pots and debts into their hands. Lastly, they convinced one another that money and value could be conjured out of thin air and that what goes up never has to come down. All this took a well-oiled promotional machine, working through its lobby, private networks, and financial advertising and public relations.

However, real-world economies, financial markets and profes-sional traders do not behave according to either economic theory or their public image. Economies do not run themselves and, if left too much alone, become unstable, less efficient and exploitative. Financial markets are characterized more by instability, opportun-ism and irrational behaviour. They are zero-sum games, where great profits and losses are made, but where those who work on the inside have the edge and are always paid. They offer temporary credit and elite employment, not real assets, productive investment or general employment in the wider economy. Those who do best push the boundaries hardest. Rogue traders, such as Michael Milken, Bernie Madoff, Nick Leeson, Jeffrey Skilling and Fabrice Tourre, are just the ones that pushed too hard and/or got caught. The focus on them and their Ponzi schemes distracts from the fact that financial markets, in effect, are large Ponzi scheme-creating machines. These operate on a small scale on a daily basis as well as on a large scale during bubbles. The suckers, as with all Ponzi schemes, are those outsiders who were persuaded to join late in the cycle: governments, pension funds, non-financial corporate institutions and ordinary citizens.

11
Conclusions

Promotion has always been a part of human communication and social interaction. Individuals and organizations have actively engaged in promotional practices, no matter how basic or instinctive, for many centuries. However, what has changed is that promotional culture has become a more central, influential part of communication and social relations, just as financialization, globalization and new communication technologies have. The shift towards greater promotion has taken place largely over the course of a century. Its growth and wider dissemination gathered pace in the postwar years and developed faster still from the 1980s.

Undoubtedly, the evolution of the promotional industries played a key part in promotional culture's inexorable rise. Such industries have provided institutionalized bases for education and practices to develop. They not only sold their services to a variety of occupational fields, they sold the idea of promotion itself. In so doing, a promotional arms race has been triggered in many work sectors and parts of society. Whether or not it is effective, a wide array of organizations and individuals feel they cannot avoid promotion for fear of losing the race. Consequently, promotional professionals and practices have become incorporated into many ordinary occupations, in many cases becoming institutionalized and systematic. Organizations, and those who work for them, have internalized and come to reproduce, often unconsciously, a series of promotional responses and routines. This can run right the way through an organization, from the CEO, to the designers and engineers, to the ordinary service staff on the shop floors and in the call centres. Similarly, as the technologies and practices of promotional communication have developed, so individuals have also adopted them in their personal lives. Choices of clothes and everyday commodities, personal website and social media presences, and participation in all manner of groups, clubs and networks all have strong self-promotional elements.

As demonstrated through these chapters, the greater emphasis on promotion, in turn, has reshaped those same individuals, organizations, and fields of leisure and work. This has not been a simple, unidirectional and deterministic form of impact. Promotional influences have combined with other developments, such as new technologies, demographic changes or new forms of capitalism. Degrees of personal adoption or rejection have varied considerably. But, in many cases, behaviours, beliefs, budgets, choices and practices have been significantly altered in response to heighted promotional imperatives. For example, decisions may be made to repackage existing commodities and services rather than to invest in risky new research into unknown products. Promoting political leaders on the basis of their personality rather than their policies or skills can become a defining political strategy. Films and prime-time television series may be more likely to be 'green-lighted' if they can be turned into 'commercial intertexts' with a generic appeal to youth or international markets. Great writers, artists, inventors and performers (and academics) are more likely to invest in the promotion of their own public personas as a means of disseminating their work. The attention we all devote to the promotional and symbolic qualities of material goods, cultural products and people often surpasses our concern with their practical uses or core personal values and abilities. Accordingly, we may feel obliged to devote more of our personal energies to our own self-presentation.

How should we evaluate such developments? Can we make normative judgements about our promotional times? In my own view, many promotional practices and practitioners have a fairly neutral or even positive role. Proper marketing and consumer-citizen consultation does make producers and politicians more responsive. Good public relations and transparency improves relations and understanding, both within organizations and between organizations and publics. Many campaigners and lobbyists work for progressive causes they believe in. Unscrupulous, mind-controlling figures are not representative of the promotional industries as a whole, just as unscrupulous investment bankers are not representative of general savings and loan-type banking. Nor are most consumers easily duped by promotional campaigns. Audiences avoid many typical adverts and are cynical about overt forms of promotion and promotionally influenced media. Promotional campaigns fail far more often than they succeed.

However, I also believe promotional culture is implicated in many negative short-term outcomes and longer-term social trends. In the short term, it matters that large states can persuade their publics of the case for illegitimate wars abroad using propaganda. It is problematic that those presidential candidates with the biggest advertising budgets and best spun personalities have a strong electoral advantage. It is destabilizing when billion-dollar contracts are won under false pretences or junk is turned into respectable investments with clever financial promotion. In the longer term, it is very alarming that large oil companies are able to undermine legitimate scientific research about global warming to the extent that political and public doubts remain. It is concerning that individuals over-consume to levels that are unsustainable both personally and globally, while debt and obesity levels rise, finite resources are depleted and large-scale poverty continues. It is unjust that women, ethnic minorities and the poor are made subtly to feel inadequate or second-class citizens by promotional content. It also matters that fundamental qualities of art, culture, political representation, public debate and market economies can be significantly altered by promotional activities.

Under such circumstances, arguments about knowing, active audiences, or how the symbolic now dominates the material, or the interactive, liberating capabilities of Web 2.0 promotion are intellectual distractions. They all make valid points. But, even the smartest audiences can be persuaded or misdirected with promotional techniques. Material realities such as poverty, inequality and environmental degradation are very real for a majority, regardless of how sign-saturated our society has become. Social media capabilities are more than matched by exclusive, elite electronic communication networks and off-line power structures.

Individualism as a dominant discourse

Several themes flow through multiple chapters in this book. One of these is the discourse of individualism, something that promotional culture encourages in various ways. For years, critics have noted that advertising focuses on individual rather than collective needs and wants. Promotional messages are frequently targeted at single actors, encouraging self-reflection and dissatisfaction, as well as the promise of personal enhancement. Personal goal-setting and notions of individual 'choice', 'liberty' and 'advancement' are all wrapped up in promotional appeals. In turn, individuals are encouraged to promote themselves. Personal self-promotion is perceived as a practice that is necessary for achieving social and career success.

Notions of the individual are further reinforced by various promotional activities that, cumulatively, reinforce a discourse of the self. Celebrity promotion is one such activity which emphasizes the 'cult' of the individual 'leader', sporting 'hero' or entertainment 'star'. Sporting world champions are feted by national governments and media. So, too, corporate and political promotion is often presented through individual leaders. The cult of the corporate leader, from Henry Ford and John D. Rockefeller to Steve Jobs and Jack Welch, has been used to promote companies to publics and financial investors alike. Political parties and governments come to be overly represented by single leaders. In both cases, a head figure becomes the brand representative of an organization. Personal and large-scale investment decisions and voting patterns are then based on assessments of such leaders. Products, ideas and causes are all sold using celebrity endorsement and associations with individual public figures. A common strategy, now adopted by charities and interest groups, is to recruit celebrity spokespersons. The world of haute couture typically exploits this dynamic, with designers presented as celebrities, celebrities turned designers, and celebrity audiences.

The media sells itself through a focus on individual celebrities, victims, criminals and personalized human interest stories. The successes or failures, tragedies and dramas of individuals are generally preferred to macro-, technical and statistical accounts of major issues and trends. So dependent on celebrities have news and entertainment media become, they have turned systematically to creating their own public personalities. Reality and talent shows produce and then dispose of a steady stream of temporary 'celetoids'. News producers locate fleeting news personalities, based on association, notoriety and publicly captured misbehaviour. Gossip magazines produce weekly trawls through the personal ups and downs of celebrities and celetoids alike.

The discourse of individualism is also promoted through corporate, political and economic rhetorics. Corporations absorb cynicism and discontent through an appeal to individual choice and rebellion. Politicians promote themselves as being in tune with ordinary people and individual aspiration. Neo-liberal economics is based on the rational, self-interested profit-maximizing tendencies of individuals. It reconciles individual fulfilment with wider market and society fulfilment. Selfish self-advancement, as well as the freedom of powerful individuals, benefits all. The consequences of an enhanced focus on individualism are a frequent sense of personal failure, disappointed consumption, a false sense of individual choice and control, and the tendency to focus on individual rather than collective problems and issues.

Trust, certainty and values

Over time, promotional culture has also influenced a series of cultural and cognitive anchors and values. It feeds into a larger, longer-term erosion of 'trust', 'ontological security' and wider value systems. Part of this can be put down simply to promotion's false promises. Promotional hard sells invariably fail to deliver on their semi-subliminal claims. Gold jewellery does not bring everlasting love. New mobiles do not bring alienated teens lots of new friends. Fast cars and leather jackets do not make middle-aged men more sexually appealing. 'Hope', 'change', 'compassionate Conservativism' and the 'third way', said with a charismatic smile, can prove to be quite meaningless in practice. The more that skilful promotional strategies convince, the greater the sense of disillusion and distrust when post-sale delivery fails. In the longer term this is likely to erode trust in those parties, institutions and corporations that over-promote themselves and their wares.

Part of the erosion of ontological security can also be put down to the pace of change. 'Time–space compression' is a distinct feature of turbo-charged promotional capitalism. The turnover of goods gets ever faster. Top clothing stores change their lines every three to four weeks. Prime-time television series have a handful of episodes to attract sizeable Nielson ratings. Hollywood films have a weekend to make their impact. Company shares are held for days or weeks rather than months or years. News editors are preoccupied with daily sales, CEOs with quarterly periods, and politicians with two- to five-year election cycles. For individuals, in-built redundancy is a feature of contemporary personal consumption. New fashions in clothing and entertainment provision move on just as consumers and fans are becoming accustomed to the old ones. New televisions, recording devices, computers and mobile phones arrive rapidly, fight for market share, and then decline. In effect, consumption can be a precarious, insecure and unstable occupation. One's favourite items or collections can be made culturally or physically redundant in a short space of time.

Many postmodernist observations about sign-saturation, displaced meaning, fragmentation and shifting identities also make sense in terms of how people encounter promotional culture. Adverts and promotional imagery repeatedly pick up, cut and paste, and rearrange accepted images, norms and values. What it is to be male or female, or to relate to one's class, age, race, religion or home town, are subject to faster, more fragmented and contradictory shifts. Promotional culture adds to the sense that meaning, identities, places and values are only temporary, superficial things. This is not to say that all norms, values and relations are simply social constructions with no substantive basis or 'truth', or that all modernist aspirations are to be rejected simply as 'meta-narratives'. Many social values, modernist ideals, and elements of identity are far more enduring than that. But, it is to say that subjection to promotional overflows both erodes personal levels of faith in norms and values and creates greater ontological insecurity.

Media logic, mediation and mediatization

Another key theme running through several chapters is 'mediatization' (or 'media logic' or 'mediation'). As promotionally minded individuals and organizations increase their engagement with media, so they shift their cognitive processes, behaviours, relations and practices accordingly. Promotional intermediaries, whether geared to traditional or digital media, greatly facilitate such shifts. In order to be reported by news journalists, organizations and individuals think in terms of news values, beats and cycles. To raise one's online profile one has to conform to the operational parameters of Facebook, Twitter, Google and YouTube.

Clearly, some occupations and organizations rely more than others on using promotion to gain media visibility or 'media capital'. In attempting to engage with media in such ways, so they are subjected to mediatization. Organizations and individuals devote larger resources to 'reputation management' and building their brand equity through multiple media. Everyday goods come to be redesigned and repackaged with an eye on increased symbolic and media appeal. Watches and computers are made into branded fashion accessories, to be presented with a stylish flourish at mass-media events, in fashion magazines, and through viral, social media 'buzzes'. Political parties spend millions on grand televised conventions and other 'pseudo-events' designed only to gain news coverage. Policies and leaders are chosen with an eye on their newsworthiness and mediagenic characteristics. Company CEOs and heads of public institutions and charities undergo media training. Campaigning groups go to extremes to catch the eye of otherwise uninterested news journalists.

The promotional push towards media exposure and the accumulation of media capital can be rather problematic for those involved. Media interest in celebrities, companies and events is often cyclical and can be very volatile. Industries, promotional professions and media all combine to increase the speed of story turnover, be it for new commodities, leaders, celebrities or cultural phenomena. Like other fashions, reporting is likely to be intense for short periods and then move on entirely. Such has been the fate of media-created celebrities and large-scale campaigns such as Make Poverty History or the Occupy movement. Similarly, those organizations and individuals which employ promotional media strategies to gain rapid exposure and high poll ratings risk equally quick declines. So, recent presidents and prime ministers (George W. Bush, Obama, Blair, Sarkozy) have endured extreme highs and lows in their public support. Musicians, sports stars and actors, considered more adept at self-promotion than at their profession, can be rapidly downgraded as a cynical public and media move on. Simple public transgressions can end careers, if not through direct professional demotion, indirectly through simple media disinterest. She who lives by the media dies by it too.

Marketization, neo-liberalism and Anglo-American promotional capitalism

Another key theme running through the book is the role of promotion in the increasing marketization of society. The rise of market power and the growth of promotion go hand in hand. Since the economic crises of the 1970s, neo-liberal free-market thinking has driven policy-making in the US, the UK and many leading economies. In turbo-charged Anglo-American-style capitalism, marketization and competition and, therefore, promotion have become more extreme. The US leads the way, both in developing an aggressive free-market form of weakly regulated capitalism and in the per capita resources it puts into promotion itself. Advertising, public relations, marketing, lobbying and branding all developed first and fastest in America. So, too, it led the industrialized world in other related trends, such as financialization, growing inequality, long-term income stagnation for median wage earners, deregulated public news media and media conglomeration, and poorly regulated advertising and campaign financing. The UK is in second place when it comes to the development of the promotional professions. In terms of general market deregulation, financialization, growing inequality and media conglomeration, it has been following closely in the footsteps of the US. There is thus a strong case to be made for linking developed promotional culture with uncompromising neo-liberal market systems. In fact, promotional culture might be considered to be the Trojan horse of marketization.

In Anglo-American promotional capitalism, economics and accountancy have been transformed into promotional professions for pushing the advancement of free-market extremism. Chicago School economics graduates have come to dominate state bureaucracies and international institutions such as the IMF and World Bank. Traditional economists and financiers blind political elites and publics with complex numbers, pseudo-science, incomprehensible jargon and 'expert' status. In truth, their models can be highly subjective, based on narrow parameters and imaginary, two-dimensional actors. The continuing elevation of neo-classical economic thought over all alternatives, in spite of repeated failures, demonstrates a degree of ideological fundamentalism. But rarely are such doubts or subjectivities conveyed in public. Accountancy too has succeeded in presenting itself as objective, commanding, neutral and authoritative. Yet accountancy has become inextricably intertwined with promotion. It enables companies and treasury officials to create a temporary picture of steady quarterly growth and economic health where none may actually exist. It facilitates the transformation of debts into assets and highly risky investments into AAA-rated ones. It turns celebrities, brands, assetless start-ups, and gambles on the future into quantifiable financial investments and current profits. Indeed, the great promotional trick of economists, accountants and financiers has been to convince the world that they are rational, objective, non-political and authoritative. In reality, they can be as ideological, subjective and skilled in promotion as any 'spin doctor' or advertising executive.

In Anglo-American promotional capitalism, the push to market deregulation and competition has moved beyond markets and economic management. Large parts of national state infrastructures have been shrunk, privatized, contracted out, restructured by private management consultants, or had competition forced upon them. Accordingly, increased marketization has involved greater use of market practices and promotional personnel outside of markets. Thus public health and education providers are forced to promote themselves in a competition for consumers and public resources.

Charities, cultural institutions and religious organizations contend for recognition and state support using promotional consultants. In the UK and the US, so much that might once have been considered a public resource is now for sale and has become promotable: prisons and policing, primary schools and kindergartens, air traffic controllers and water supplies, public hospitals and health systems, states and national cultures. Even stock exchanges, large parts of government bureaucracies and political party policy-making itself are run by self-promoting commercial organizations.

Risk, creativity and innovation

Risk, creativity and innovation has been another theme running through *Promotional Cultures*. On the one hand, promotion has proved essential for smoothing unpredictable markets and maintaining levels of stability. Good marketing and targeted advertising link producers and consumers more efficiently. Self-indulgent creatives may be better reined in, and forced to respond to real demand, by promotional intermediaries. The maximization of profits from 'hits' and mainstream fare underpins investment in riskier, innovative productions, be they prescription drugs, music, films or hi-tech gadgets.

However, in many ways, promotion can be said to stifle innovation and creativity. This can be seen very clearly in the various ways that media conglomerates use promotional media. The bigger the perceived investment risk, the larger the role for promotional intermediaries. Marketers pre- and post-test everything. Producers are funnelled towards the mainstream, encouraged to use well-known stars, to repeat successful formulas, and to draw on existing markets and fan bases. Promoters suck up production budgets with multiple teasers, trailers, online viral marketing campaigns, openings and press junkets. In addition, 'synergy'-obsessed conglomerates use 'cross-media promotion' to create a series of 'commercial intertexts'. This in itself pushes media production towards creating outputs that may be reproduced in multiple media. Big budget films, television series and computer games are now conceptualized as multi-media creations, to be repackaged, franchised and sold in multiple formats. A film may also be a television series, a computer or board game, a theme-park ride, an interactive website and a fanzine – all in addition to being a sequel, a prequel, a DVD, or a digital download for computers and mobile phones.

Innovation and risk are similarly restrained in industrial production.

New product development is risky and expensive. New patents are hard to enforce and market leads are difficult to maintain in the globalized, digital economy. Consequently, copying, redesigning and repackaging with skilful promotional professionals is often the cheaper option. CEOs, who have to please big investors with short-term profit expectations, find it easier and less risky to repackage and promote rather than to invest and innovate. It is also easier to use promotional accounting and creative financial narratives to keep investors interested and share prices moving up. In addition, promotion can be used to blame over-regulating governments and unionized workforces, thereby justifying cutting wages or outsourcing operations abroad rather than innovating. In effect, promotion can be used to avoid creativity, innovation and long-term investment.

Ironically, although promotional culture is often employed as a risk-reduction strategy, it often adds greater risk and uncertainty. Promotion itself can add considerably to the costs of producing something, thus making it more risky, not less. If Hollywood films now spend 38 per cent of their budgets on promotion, many more millions have to be found and invested in a new project. Large promotional budgets are now gambled on big-bang opening weekends or on generating high music chart entries or immediate Nielson ratings. This equates to making big bets under fairly unpredictable circumstances (bad weather, rival productions, rival news stories). However, the most significant examples of promotion increasing risk in recent times can be found in financial markets. Promotion, or perhaps high-end propaganda, turned sub-prime mortgages into safe investments. It also persuaded financiers that hedge funds, derivatives, futures and so many other financial products were ways of spreading risk and maintaining market stability. In many cases, the exact opposite has proved to be the case.

Democracy, politics, information and power

The subject of democracy, politics, information and power also comes up frequently. As with markets, it is hard now to envisage politics without marketing, advertising, lobbying and public relations. Promotional methods and personnel are employed by all governments and political parties as well as most public institutions and large campaign organizations. In some respects, it can be argued that promotional practices have improved citizen exchanges with states, parties, institutions and interest groups.

However, there are also very real problems associated with promotional politics. Several were discussed in chapters 2, 8 and 9. Governments now employ extensive communication resources to provide important public information and facilitate consultations. However, these are also used to manage media and public opinion, especially in times of crisis. When combined with 'news values', media management turns election news into personalized, negative and 'horse-race' coverage, leaving little discussion of policy or candidate records. Political marketing and advertising mean that politicians focus far more on a small proportion of swing voters and states and ignore the majority. The electoral importance of media means that politicians with media contacts or promotional experience are more likely to be promoted. Media and news value considerations then have an influence on legislative agendas.

Promotional politics has additional consequences attached. One of these is its reliance on money. Quite simply, greater promotional resources usually bring greater influence over important public information content, from news and advertising to lobbying and 'independent' research reports. The deployment of billions of dollars in US election campaigns is of prime concern. Clearly, those who have more funds exploit their advantage with extensive television advertising blitzes, big media events and market-tested presentations. Big funding also tends to have big, primarily business, donor strings attached. Large corporations, in addition to making sizeable political donations, have far greater promotional power than ordinary interest-group campaigners. This enables them to pay for permanent advocacy services at the world's political centres and to fund any number of think tanks and public researchers. They can also bankroll astro-turf front groups, extensive advocacy advertising campaigns and general PR initiatives. All of this has a considerable influence on information sources used for public and political decision-making. Journalists are rarely forthcoming about just how much they rely for what they publish on press releases, promotional contacts and other information subsidies. Politicians and bureaucrats too are disinclined to admit their use of commercially funded research for policy-making.

Of equal importance is the way promotional politics is used to restrict public information and transparency. Much promotional activity is organized around blocking journalist access, smothering problematic stories and maintaining secrecy. Public relations staff in parties and governments are likely to spend much of their time keeping stories out of the press and in defensive PR. Corporations go to great lengths to maintain minimal exposure in public media spheres. Little is known about the internal workings of large financiers, fund managers and bankers unless something goes badly wrong. Even less is known about some of the world's largest privately owned corporations or their CEOs. Almost nothing is published about the funding and true political affiliations of many think tanks and lobby groups. In effect, large amounts of publicly relevant information, as well as the sourcing of published policies and news, remain hidden by promotional activity.

Finally, promotional politics inadvertently creates a misleading associational link between public appearance and power. Many celebrities, who have accumulated substantial amounts of symbolic or economic capital, personally have little power. Increasingly, this is also the case for democratically elected and accountable politicians. At the same time they have adapted to mediated forms of politics, so raising their personal levels of symbolic capital, their political power seems to have been in decline. In contrast, unknown senior civil servants, powerful corporate and financial figures, and the heads of international institutions remain relatively anonymous while wielding considerable economic and political power. Thus promotional culture directs media and public attention to public figures, often with less power, all the while allowing many powerful actors to remain obscured from view.

Final thoughts? What now?

I can't disclose any now ... but all will be revealed in *Promotional Cultures: The Sequel*, starring Kim Kardashian, Boris Johnson and Justin Bieber (I'm played by George Clooney) and available at all good bookshops, shopping websites and cinema screens next year.

References

AA (Advertising Association) (2011) website at www.adassoc.org.uk/Home.

Abolafia, M. (1996) *Making Markets: Opportunism and Restraint on Wall Street*. Cambridge, MA: Harvard University Press.

Adorno, T. (1991) *The Culture Industry: Selected Essays on Mass Culture*, ed. J. Bernstein. London: Routledge.

Adorno, T., and Horkheimer, M. (1979 [1947]) *Dialectic of Enlightenment*. London: Verso.

Agins, T. (1999) *The End of Fashion: How Marketing Changed the Clothing Industry*. New York: Quill/HarperCollins.

Aglietta, M. (1987) *A Theory of Capitalist Regulation: The US Experience*. London: Verso.

Akerlof, G., and Shiller, R. (2009) *Animal Spirits: How Human Psychology Drives the Economy, and Why it Matters for Global Capitalism*. Princeton, NJ: Princeton University Press.

Alberoni, F. (2007 [1960]) 'The Powerless "Elite": Theory and Sociological Research on the Phenomenon of the Stars', in S. Redmond and S. Holmes, eds, *Stardom and Celebrity: A Reader*. London: Sage.

Albrow, M., Anheier, H., Glasius, M., Price, M., and Kaldor, M., eds (2008) *Global Civil Society 2007/08: Communicative Power and Democracy*. London: Sage.

Alexander, J. C. (1981) 'The Mass News Media in Systemic, Historical and Comparative Perspective', in E. Katz and T. Szesco, eds, *Mass Media and Social Change*. Beverly Hills, CA: Sage, pp. 17–51.

Allan, S., Adam, B., and Carter, C., eds (2000) *Environmental Risks and the Media*. London: Routledge.

Altheide, D. (2004) 'Media Logic and Political Communication', *Political Communication*, 21(3): 293–6.

Altheide, D., and Snow, R. (1979) *Media Logic*. Beverly Hills, CA: Sage.

Althusser, L. (1971) *Lenin and Philosophy and Other Essays*, trans. Ben Brewster. London: Verso.

Amin, A., and Thrift, N., eds (2003) *The Blackwell Cultural Economy Reader.* Oxford: Blackwell.

Anderson, A. (1997) *Media, Culture and the Environment.* London: UCL Press.

Andrejevic, M. (2002) 'The Work of Being Watched: Interactive Media and the Exploitation of Self-Disclosure', *Critical Studies in Media Communication*, 19(2): 230–48.

Andrews, D., and Jackson, D., eds (2001) *Sports Stars: The Cultural Politics of Sporting Celebrity.* London: Routledge.

Ang, I. (1985) *Watching Dallas.* London: Methuen.

Ang, I. (1991) *Desperately Seeking the Audience.* London: Routledge.

Ansolabehere, S., and Iyengar, S. (1995) *Going Negative: How Political Advertisements Shrink and Polarize the Electorate.* New York: Free Press.

Arnold, R. (2001) *Fashion, Desire and Anxiety: Image and Morality in the 20th Century.* London: I. B. Tauris.

Artnet (2012) website at www.artnet.com.

Arvidsson, A. (2006) *Brands: Meaning and Value in Media Culture.* London: Routledge.

Bachrach, P., and Baratz, M. (1962) 'Two Faces of Power', *American Political Science Review*, 56(4): 947–52.

Bagdikian, B. (2004) *The Media Monopoly.* 6th edn, Boston: Beacon Press.

Baltruschat, D. (2011) 'Branded Entertainment and the New Media Economy', in G. Sussman, ed., *The Propaganda Society: Promotional Culture and Politics in Global Context.* New York: Peter Lang.

Barker, M. (2008) 'Analysing Discourse', in M. Pickering, ed., *Research Methods for Cultural Studies.* Edinburgh: Edinburgh University Press.

Barnett, S., and Gaber, I. (2001) *Westminster Tales: The Twenty-First-Century Crisis in Political Journalism.* London: Continuum.

Barrett, M. (1980) *Women's Oppression Today: Problems in Marxist Analysis.* London: Verso.

Bartels, R. (1988) *The History of Marketing Thought.* 3rd edn, Homewood, IL: Irwin.

Barthes, R. (1968) *Elements of Semiology.* New York: Hill & Wang.

Barthes, R. (1970) *S/Z.* London: Jonathan Cape.

Barthes, R. (1973 [1957]) *Mythologies.* London: Paladin Books.

Barthes, R. (1977) *Image, Music, Text.* London: Fontana.

Baudrillard, J. (1983) *Simulations.* New York: Semiotext(e).

Baudrillard, J. (1988a [1972]) 'For a Critique of the Political Economy of the Sign', in M. Poster, ed., *Jean Baudrillard: Selected Writings.* Cambridge: Polity.

Baudrillard, J. (1988b) *Selected Writings*, ed. M. Poster. Cambridge: Polity.

Bauman, Z. (2005) *Work Consumerism and the New Poor.* 2nd edn, Maidenhead: Open University Press.

Bauman, Z. (2007) *Consuming Life.* Cambridge: Polity.

Baumgartner, F. R., and Jones, B. D. (1993) *Agendas and Instability in American Politics*. Chicago: University of Chicago Press.

BBC (2005a) 'Government Defends G8 Aid Boost', 9 July, http://news.bbc.co.uk/1/hi/business/4666743.stm.

BBC (2005b) 'African Head Defends G8 Agreement', 9 July, http://news.bbc.co.uk/1/hi/business/4666769.stm.

Beattie, A. (2005) 'NGOs Grow Weary of World Leaders' "Empty" Initiatives', *Financial Times*, 5 July.

Beckett, C. (2008) *Supermedia: Saving Journalism so it Can Save Itself*. Oxford: Wiley-Blackwell.

Beesley, M. (1996) *Markets and the Media*. London: Institute of Economic Affairs.

Bell, D. (1973) *The Coming of the Post-Industrial Age: A Venture in Social Forecasting*. London: Penguin.

Beltran, M. (2007) 'The Hollywood Latina Body as Site of Social Struggle: Media Constructions of Stardom and Jennifer Lopez's "Crossover Butt"', in S. Redmond and S. Holmes, eds, *Stardom and Celebrity: A Reader*. London: Sage.

Benjamin, W. (1970) *Illuminations*. London: Jonathan Cape.

Bennett, T., and Woollacott, J. (1987) *Bond and Beyond: The Political Career of a Popular Hero*. Basingstoke: Macmillan.

Bennett, W. L. (1990) 'Towards a Theory of Press–State Relations in the United States', *Journal of Communication*, 40(2): 103–25.

Berger, J. (1972) *Ways of Seeing*. London: BBC/Penguin.

Bird, S. E. (2000) 'Audience Demands in a Murderous Market: Tabloidization of U.S. Television News', in C. Sparks and J. Tulloch, eds, *Tabloid Tales: Global Debates over Media Standards*. Lanham, MD: Rowman & Littlefield.

Bischoff, W., and Darling, A. (2009) *UK International Financial Services – the Future: A Report from UK-Based Financial Service Leaders to the Government*. London: HM Treasury.

Blackett, T. (2009) 'What is a Brand?', in R. Clifton, ed., *Brands and Branding*. 2nd edn, London: Economist.

Blumer, H. (1969) 'Fashion: From Class Differentiation to Collective Selection', *Sociological Quarterly*, 10(3): 275–91.

Blumler, J., and Gurevitch, M. (1995) *The Crisis of Public Communication*. London: Routledge.

Bocock, R. (1993) *Consumption*. London: Routledge.

Bodie, Z., Kane, A., and Marcus, A. (2003) *Essentials of Investment*. 5th edn, London: McGraw-Hill.

Boltanski, L., and Chiapello, E. (2007) *The New Spirit of Capitalism*. London: Verso.

Boorstin, D. (1962) *The Image*. London: Weidenfeld & Nicolson.

Bootle, R. (2009) *The Trouble with Markets: Saving Capitalism from Itself*. London: Nicholas Brealey.

Boswell, J., and Peters, J. (1997) *Capitalism in Contention: Business Leaders and Political Economy in Modern Britain*. Cambridge: Cambridge University Press.

Bourdieu, P. (1984) *Distinction: A Social Critique of the Judgement of Taste*. London: Routledge.

Bourdieu, P. (1986) 'The Forms of Capital', in J. Richardson, ed., *Handbook of Theory and Research for the Sociology of Education*. New York: Greenwood Press.

Bourdieu, P. (1993) *The Field of Cultural Production: Essays on Art and Literature*, ed. R. Johnson. Cambridge: Polity.

Bourdieu, P., Darbel, A., and Schnapper, D. (1990) *The Love of Art: European Museums and their Public*. Stanford, CA: Stanford University Press.

Bowlby, R. (2000) *Carried Away: The Invention of Modern Shopping*. London: Faber.

Boxofficemojo, website at http://boxofficemojo.com/.

Braham, P. (1997) 'Fashion: Unpacking a Cultural Production', in P. du Gay, ed., *Production of Culture/Cultures of Production*. London: Sage.

Brands, H. (1999) *Masters of Enterprise: Giants of American Business from John Jacobs Aster and JP Morgan to Bill Gates and Oprah Winfrey*. New York: Free Press.

Braudel, F. (1981) *Civilization and Capitalism, 15th–18th Century: Structures of Everyday Life*, Vol. 1, trans. Sian Reynolds and M. Kochan. London: HarperCollins.

Breward, C. (1995) *The Culture of Fashion: A New History of Fashionable Dress*. Manchester: Manchester University Press.

Brierly, S. (1995) *The Advertising Handbook*. London: Routledge.

Bruff, I. (2012) 'Authoritarian Neoliberalism, the Occupy Movements, and IPE', *Journal of Critical Global Studies*, no. 5: 114–16.

Bureau of Investigative Journalism (2012) website at www.thebureauinvestigates.com.

Burston, J. (2000) 'Spectacle, Synergy and Megamusicals: The Global-Industrialisation of the Live-Entertainment Economy', in J. Curran, ed., *Media Organisations in Society*. London: Arnold.

Cable, V. (2009) *The Storm: The World Economic Crisis and What it Means*. London: Atlantic Books.

Callon, M., ed. (1998a) *The Laws of the Markets*. Oxford: Blackwell.

Callon, M. (1998b) 'The Embeddedness of Economic Markets in Economics', in M. Callon, ed., *The Laws of the Markets*. Oxford: Blackwell.

Callon, M. (1998c) 'An Essay on Framing and Overflowing: Economic Externalities Revisited by Sociology', in M. Callon, ed., *The Laws of the Markets*. Oxford: Blackwell.

Campbell, C. (1989 [1940]) *The Romantic Ethic and the Spirit of Modern Consumerism*. Oxford: Blackwell.

Carl Byoir (1986) Carl Byoir Survey Research, in *Public Relations Yearbook*. London: PRCA.

Cashmore, E. (2006) *Celebrity/Culture*. London: Routledge.

Cassidy, J. (2002) *Dot.Con: The Greatest Story Ever Told*. London: Allen Lane.

Castells, M. (1996) *The Rise of the Network Society*. Oxford: Blackwell.

Castells, M. (1997) *The Power of Identity*. Oxford: Blackwell.

Castells, M. (2001) *The Internet Galaxy: Reflections on the Internet, Business and Society*. Oxford: Oxford University Press.

CBO (2011) *Trends in the Distribution of Household Income between 1979 and 2007*, 25 October. Washington, DC: Congressional Budget Office.

Cerny, P. G., Menz, G., and Soederberg, S. (2005) 'Different Roads to Globalization: Neoliberalism, the Competition State, and Politics in a More Open World', in S. Soederberg, G. Menz and P. G. Cerny, eds, *Internalizing Globalization: The Rise of Neoliberalism and the Decline of National Varieties of Capitalism*. Basingstoke: Palgrave Macmillan.

Chakrabortty, A. (2012) 'You've Been Bankered', *The Guardian*, 3 July.

Chandler, D. (2002) *Semiotics: The Basics*. London: Routledge.

Chang, H. (2010) *23 Things They Don't Tell You about Capitalism*. London: Allen Lane.

Chaudhuri, M. (2001) 'Gender and Advertisements: The Rhetoric of Globalisation', *Women's Studies International Forum*, 24(3/4): 373–85.

Childs, S., Lovenduski, J., and Campbell, R. (2005) British Representation Study, unpublished report.

Chomsky, N. (2012) *Occupy*. Harmondsworth: Penguin.

Christopherson, S. (2008) 'Labor: The Effects of Media Concentration on the Film and Television Workforce', in P. McDonald and J. Wasko, eds, *The Contemporary Hollywood Film Industry*. Oxford: Blackwell.

Christopherson, S., and Storper, M. (1986) 'The City as Studio, the World as Back Lot: The Impact of Vertical Disintegration on the Location of the Motion Picture Industry', *Environment and Planning D: Society and Space*, 4: 305–20.

Chung, K., Derdenger, J., and Srinivasan, K. (2011) *Economic Value of Celebrity Endorsements: Tiger Woods' Impact on Sales of Nike Golf Balls*. Tepper School of Business Paper, Pittsburgh: Carnegie Mellon University.

CIM (Chartered Institute of Marketing, UK) website at www.cim.co.uk.

CIPR (2011) *State of the PR Profession: Benchmarking Survey*. London: CIPR/ComRes.

Clarke, J. (2001) 'Ethical Globalization: The Dilemmas and Challenges of Internationalizing Civil Society', in M. Edwards and J. Gaventa, eds, *Global Citizen Action*. Boulder, CO: Lynne Rienner.

Clifton, R. (2009) 'Introduction', in R. Clifton, ed., *Brands and Branding*. 2nd edn, London: Economist.

CMD, Centre for Media and Democracy, website at www.prwatch.org/.

Cochoy, F. (1998) 'Another Discipline for the Market Economy: Marketing as Performance Knowledge and Know-How for Capitalism', in M. Callon, ed., *The Laws of the Markets*. Oxford: Blackwell.

COI (1979–2012) *The IPO Directory: Information and Press Officers in Government Departments and Public Corporations*. London: Central Office of Information.

Cole, C., and Andrews, D. (2001) 'America's New Son: Tiger Woods and America's Multiculturalism', in D. Andrews and D. Jackson, eds, *Sports Stars: The Cultural Politics of Sporting Celebrity*. London: Routledge.

Connell, I. (1992) 'Personalities in the Popular Media', in P. Dahlgren and C. Sparks, eds, *Journalism and Popular Culture*. London: Sage.

Cook, G. (2001) *The Discourse of Advertising*. 2nd edn, London: Routledge.

Cook, G. (2004) *Genetically Modified Language: The Discourse of Arguments for GM Crops and Food*. London: Routledge.

Cook, T. (1998) *Governing with the News: The News Media as a Political Institution*. Chicago: University of Chicago Press.

Coombe, R. (1998) *The Cultural Life of Intellectual Properties: Authorship, Appropriation and the Law*. Durham, NC: Duke University Press.

Corner, J. (1991) 'Meaning, Genre and Context: The Problematics of "Public Knowledge" in the New Audience Studies', in J. Curran and M. Gurevitch, eds, *Mass Media and Society*. London: Arnold.

Corner, J., and Pels, D. (2003) 'Introduction: The Restyling of Politics', in J. Corner and D. Pels, eds, *Media and the Restyling of Politics: Consumerism, Celebrity and Cynicism*. London: Sage, pp. 1–18.

Cottle, S., ed. (2003) *News, Public Relations and Power*. London: Sage.

Cracknell, J. (1993) 'Issue Arenas, Pressure Groups and Environmental Agendas', in A. Hansen, ed., *The Mass Media and Environmental Issues*. Leicester: Leicester University Press.

Crane, D. (2000) *Fashion and its Social Agendas: Class, Gender and Identity in Clothing*. Chicago: Chicago University Press.

Crang, P. (1997) 'Introduction: Cultural Turns and the (Re)constitution of Economic Geography', in R. Lee and J. Wills, eds, *Geographies of Economies*. London: Arnold.

CRESC (2009) *An Alternative Report on UK Banking Reform: A Public Interest Report from CRESC*. Manchester: Centre for Research on Socio-Cultural Change.

Cronin, A. (2000) *Advertising and Consumer Citizenship: Gender, Images and Rights*. London: Routledge.

Crouch, C. (2004) *Post-Democracy*. Cambridge: Polity.

Crouch, C. (2011) *The Strange Non-Death of Neo-Liberalism*. Cambridge: Polity.

Crouch, C., and Dore, R., eds (1990) *Corporatism and Accountability: Organized Interests in British Public Life*. Oxford: Clarendon Press.

Culler, J. (1981) *The Pursuit of Signs: Semiotics, Literature, Deconstruction*. London: Routledge & Kegan Paul.

Currah, A. (2009) *What's Happening to our News*. Oxford: Reuters Institute for the Study of Journalism.

Curran, J. (1978) 'Advertising and the Press', in J. Curran, ed., *The British Press: A Manifesto*. London: Macmillan.

Curran, J. (1986) 'The Impact of Advertising on the British Mass Media', in R. Collins, J. Curran, N. Garnham, P. Scannell, P. Schlesinger and C. Sparks, eds, *Media, Culture and Society*. London: Sage.

Curran, J. (1990) 'The New Revisionism in Mass Communications Research: A Reappraisal', *European Journal of Communication*, 5: 130–64.

Curran, J. (2002) *Media and Power*. London: Routledge.

Curran, J. (2010) 'Technology Foretold', in N. Fenton, ed., *New Media: Old News*. London: Sage.

Curran, J., and Seaton, J. (2003) *Power without Responsibility*. 6th edn, London: Routledge.

Curran, J., Ecclestone, J., Oakley, G., and Richardson, A. (1986) *Bending Reality*. London: Pluto Press.

Curran, J., Fenton, N., and Freedman, D. (2012) *Misunderstanding the Internet*. London: Routledge.

Curtice, J. (2005) 'Turnout: Electors Stay Home Again', in P. Norris, and C. Wlezien, eds, *Britain Votes 2005*. Oxford: Oxford University Press.

Cutlip, S. M., Centre, A. H., and Broom, G. M. (1985, 2000) *Effective Public Relations*. 6th and 8th edns, Englewood Cliffs, NJ: Prentice Hall.

D'Acci, J. (1994) *Defining Women*. Chapel Hill: University of North Carolina Press.

Dahl, R. (1961) *Who Governs? Democracy and Power in an American City*. New Haven, CT: Yale University Press.

Dahl, R. (1971) *Polyarchy, Participation and Opposition*. New Haven, CT: Yale University Press.

Daily Telegraph (2012) 'Leveson: Prime Minister David Cameron Gives Evidence – as it Happened', *Daily Telegraph*, 14 June.

Dalton, R. (2004) *Democratic Challenges, Democratic Choices: The Erosion of Political Support in Advanced Industrial Democracies*. Oxford: Oxford University Press.

Dalton, R. J., and Wattenberg, M. P., eds (2000) *Parties without Partisans: Political Change in Advanced Industrial Democracies*. Oxford: Oxford University Press.

Danesi, M. (2006) *Brands*. New York: Routledge.

Davies, N. (2008) *Flat Earth News*. London: Chatto & Windus.

Davis, A. (2000a) 'Public Relations Campaigning and News Production: The Case of New Unionism in Britain', in J. Curran, ed., *Media Organisations in Society*. London: Arnold.

Davis, A. (2000b) 'Public Relations, Business News and the Reproduction of Corporate Elite Power', *Journalism: Theory, Practice and Criticism*, 1(3): 282–304.

Davis, A. (2002) *Public Relations Democracy: Public Relations, Politics and the Mass Media in Britain*. Manchester: Manchester University Press.

Davis, A. (2006) 'Media Effects and the Question of the Rational Audience: Lessons from the Financial Markets', *Media, Culture and Society*, 28(4): 603–25.

Davis, A. (2007) *The Mediation of Power: A Critical Introduction*. London: Routledge.

Davis, A. (2010) *Political Communication and Social Theory*. London: Routledge.

Davis, A., and Seymour, E. (2010) 'Generating Forms of Media Capital Inside and Outside the Political Field: The Strange Case of David Cameron', *Media, Culture and Society*, 32(5): 1–20.

Davis, F. (1992) *Fashion, Culture, and Identity*. Chicago: University of Chicago Press.

De Bondt, W. (2005) 'The Values and Beliefs of European Investors', in K. Knorr Cetina and A. Preda, eds, *The Sociology of Financial Markets*. Oxford: Oxford University Press.

De Certeau, M. (1984) *The Practice of Everyday Life*. Berkeley: University of California Press.

DeCordova, R. (1990) *Picture Personalities: The Emergence of the Star System in America*. Urbana: University of Illinois Press.

De Jong, W. (2005) 'The Power and Limits of Media-Based Opposition Politics – a Case Study: The Brent Spar Conflict', in W. de Jong, M. Shaw and N. Stammers, eds, *Global Activism, Global Media*. London: Pluto Press.

De Jong, W., Shaw, M., and Stammers, N., eds (2005) *Global Activism, Global Media*. London: Pluto Press.

De Vries, J. (1975) *The Dutch Rural Economy in the Golden Age, 1500–1700*. New Haven, CT: Yale University Press.

Deacon, D. (1996) 'The Voluntary Sector in a Changing Communication Environment', *European Journal of Communication*, 11(2): 173–99.

Deacon, D., and Golding, P. (1994) *Taxation and Representation*. London: John Libby Press.

Deacon, D., Wring, D., Billig, M., Downey, J., Golding, P., and Davidson, S. (2005) *Reporting the 2005 UK General Election*. Loughborough: Loughborough University Communication Research Centre.

Della Porta, D., and Diani, M. (1999) *Social Movements: An Introduction*. Oxford: Blackwell.

Delli Carpini, M. S., and Williams, B. A. (2001) 'Let Us Infotain You: Politics in the New Media Environment', in W. L. Bennett and R. M. Entman, eds, *Mediated Politics: Communication in the Future of Democracy*. Cambridge: Cambridge University Press.

Demoor, M., ed. (2004) *Marketing the Author: Authorial Personae, Narrative Selves and Self-Fashioning, 1880–1930*. Basingstoke: Palgrave Macmillan.

Deuze, M. (2005) 'What is Journalism? Professional Identity and Ideology of Journalists Reconsidered', *Journalism*, 6(4): 442–64.

Deuze, M. (2009) 'Journalism, Citizenship and Digital Culture', in Z.

Papacharisi, ed., *Journalism and Citizenship: New Agendas in Communication*. New York: Routledge.

Dinan, W., and Miller, D. (2007) *Thinker, Faker, Spinner, Spy: Corporate PR and the Assault on Democracy*. London: Pluto Press.

Douglas, M., and Isherwood, B. (1979) *The World of Goods: Towards an Anthropology of Consumption*. London: Routledge.

Dover, E. D. (2010) *On Message: Television Advertising by the Presidential Candidates in Election 2008*. Lanham, MD: Lexington Books.

Drake, P. (2008) 'Distribution and Marketing in Contemporary Hollywood', in P. McDonald and J. Wasko, eds, *The Contemporary Hollywood Film Industry*. Oxford: Blackwell.

Dreier, P. (1988) 'The Corporate Complaint against the Media', in R. Hiebert and C. Reuss, eds, *Impacts of Mass Media*. 2nd edn, New York: Longman.

Du Gay, P., ed. (1997) *Production of Culture/Cultures of Production*. London: Sage/Open University Press.

Du Gay, P., and Pryke, M., eds (2002) *Cultural Economy*. London: Sage.

Duffy, B., and Rowden, L. (2005) *You Are What you Read?* London: MORI.

Durham, F. (2007) 'Framing the State in Globalization: The *Financial Times*' Coverage of the 1997 Thai Currency Crisis', *Critical Studies in Media Communication*, 24(1): 57–76.

Dwyer, T. (2011) 'Net Worth: Popular Social Networks as Colossal Marketing Machines', in G. Sussman, ed., *The Propaganda Society: Promotional Culture and Politics in Global Context*. New York: Peter Lang.

Dyer, G. (1982) *Advertising as Communication*. London: Routledge.

Dyer, R. (1979) *Stars*. London: BFI.

Dyer, R. (1986) *Heavenly Bodies*. Basingstoke: Macmillan/BFI.

Economists Advisory Group (1993) *Commercialisation of the Post Office: How to Secure Financial Independence without Risking Service Quality*. London: EAG.

Ehrenreich, B. (2001) *Nickel and Dimed: Undercover in Low-Wage USA*. London: Granta Books.

Elliott, F., and Hanning, J. (2007) *Cameron: The Rise of the New Conservative*. London: Fourth Estate.

Elliott, L., and Atkinson, D. (2009) *The Gods that Failed: How the Financial Elite Have Gambled Away our Futures*. London: Vintage.

Engelen, E., Erturk, I., Froud, J., Johal, S., Leaver, A., Moran, M., Nilsson, A., and Williams, K. (2011) *After the Great Complacence: Financial Crisis and the Politics of Reform*. Oxford: Oxford University Press.

Enten, H. J. (2012) 'Occupy Wall Street's People Power Loses Popularity', *The Guardian*, 14 May.

Entman, R. (1989) *Democracy without Citizens: Media and the Decay of American Politics*. Oxford: Oxford University Press.

Entman, R. (2004) *Projections of Power: Framing News, Public Opinion, and US Foreign Policy*. Chicago: University of Chicago Press.

Entman, R. (2005) 'Media and Democracy without Party Competition', in J. Curran and M. Gurevitch, eds, *Mass Media and Society*. 4th edn, London: Arnold.

Epstein, E. (2005) *The Big Picture: Money and Power in Hollywood*. New York: Random House.

Ericson, R. V., Baranek, P. M., and Chan, J. B. L. (1989) *Negotiating Control: A Study of News Sources*. Milton Keynes: Open University Press.

Esser, F. (2008) 'Dimensions of Political News Cultures: Sound Bite and Image Bite News in France, Germany, Great Britain, and the United States', *Harvard International Journal of Press/Politics*, 13(4): 401–28.

Evans, J., and Hesmondhalgh, D. (2005) *Understanding Media: Inside Celebrity*. Milton Keynes: Open University Press.

Ewen, S. (1996) *PR! A Social History of Spin*. New York: Basic Books.

Ewen, S. (2001) *Captains of Consciousness: Advertising and the Social Roots of the Consumer Culture*. 2nd edn, New York: Basic Books.

Fairclough, N. (1991) *Language and Power*. London: Longman.

Fairclough, N. (1995) *Media Discourse*. London: Arnold.

Fairclough, N. (2000) *New Labour, New Language?* London: Routledge.

FairVote (2004) *Who Picks the President?* Takoma Park, MD: Center for Voting and Democracy; at: www.fairvote.org/who-picks-the-president/.

FairVote (2008) *Presidential Election Inequality: The Electoral College in the 21st Century*. Takoma Park, MD: Center for Voting and Democracy; at: http://archive.fairvote.org/media/perp/presidentialinequality.pdf.

Fama, E. (1970) 'Efficient Capital Markets: A Review of Theory and Empirical Work', *Journal of Finance*, 25(2): 383–417.

Farrar-Myers, V. (2011) 'Donors, Dollars and Momentum', in M. Bose, ed., *From Votes to Victory: Winning and Governing the White House in the Twenty-First Century*. College Station: Texas A&M University Press.

Featherstone, M. (1991) *Consumer Culture and Postmodernism*. London: Sage.

Fenyoe, A., and Darnton, A. (2005) *Public Perceptions of Poverty: Qualitative Research Findings, Wave 2*. London: Synovate.

Ferguson, C. (2012) *Inside Job: The Financiers Who Pulled Off the Heist of the Century*. Oxford: Oneworld.

Fish, S. (1980) *Is There a Text in this Class? The Authority of Interpretive Communities*. Cambridge, MA: Harvard University Press.

Fishman, M. (1980) *Manufacturing the News*. Austin: University of Texas Press.

Fiske, J. (1987) *Reading the Popular*. London: Unwin Hyman.

Fiske, J. (1989) *Understanding Popular Culture*. London: Unwin Hyman.

Fiske, J. (1996) *Media Matters: Everyday Culture and Political Change*. Minneapolis: University of Minnesota Press.

Fiske, J., and Hartley, J. (1978) *Reading Television*. London: Methuen.

Fletcher, W. (2008) *Powers of Persuasion: The Inside Story of British Advertising, 1951–2000*. Oxford: Oxford University Press.

Forbes (1999–2012) *The World's Most Powerful Celebrities*, at www.forbes.com/wealth/celebrities.

Foucault, M. (1971) *Madness and Civilization: History of Insanity in the Age of Reason*. London: Tavistock.

Foucault, M. (1975) *Discipline and Punish: The Birth of the Prison*, trans. A. Sheridan. Harmondsworth: Penguin.

Foucault, M. (1979) *The History of Sexuality*, Vol. 1, trans. Robert Hurley. London: Allen Lane.

Foucault, M. (1980) *Power/Knowledge: Selected Interviews and Other Writings, 1972–1977*, ed. C. Gordon. Hemel Hempstead: Harvester Wheatsheaf.

Fowles, J. (1996) *Advertising and Popular Culture*. London: Sage.

Frank, T. (1997) *The Conquest of Cool: Business Culture, Counter Culture and the Rise of Hip Consumerism*. Chicago: University of Chicago Press.

Franklin, B. (1997) *Newszak and News Media*. London: Arnold.

Franklin, B. (1994 and 2004) *Packaging Politics: Political Communications in Britain's Media Democracy*. 1st and 2nd edns, London: Arnold.

Franklin, B. (2005) 'McJournalism: The Local Press and the McDonaldization Thesis', in S. Allan, ed., *Journalism: Critical Issues*. Maidenhead: Open University Press.

Freedman, D. (2009) 'The Political Economy of the "New" News Environment', in N. Fenton, ed., *New Media, Old News: Journalism and Democracy in a Digital Age*. London: Sage, pp. 35–50.

Frith, K., Show, P., and Chung, H. (2005) 'The Construction of Beauty: A Cross-Cultural Analysis of Women's Magazine Advertising', *Journal of Communication*, 55(1): 56–70.

Frith, S. (1988) *Music for Pleasure: Essays in the Sociology of Pop*. Cambridge: Polity.

Froud, J., Johal, S., Leaver, A., and Williams, K. (2006) *Financialization and Strategy: Narrative and Numbers*. London: Routledge.

FSA (2002) *DP15 Investment Research: Conflicts and Other Issues*. London: Financial Services Authority.

Fuchs, C. (2011) 'Contemporary World Wide Web: Social Medium or New Space of Accumulation?', in D. Winseck and D. Jin, eds, *The Political Economies of Media: The Transformation of the Global Media Industries*. London: Bloomsbury.

Galbraith, J. K. (1991 [1958]) *The Affluent Society*. Harmondsworth: Penguin.

Gallup Polls (2012) 'Young US Voters' Turnout Intentions Lagging', 13 July, and 'Obama Character Edge Offsets Romney's Economic Advantage', 24 July, at: www.gallup.com/poll/politics.aspx.

Galtung, J., and Ruge, M. (1965) 'The Structure of Foreign News', *Journal of International Peace Research*, 1: 64–90.

Gamson, J. (1992) 'The Assembly Line of Greatness: Celebrity in Twentieth-Century America', *Critical Studies in Mass Communication*, 9(1): 1–24.

Gamson, W., and Meyer, D. (1996) 'Framing Political Opportunity', in

D. McAdam, J. McCarthy and M. Zald, eds, *Comparative Perspectives on Social Movements: Political Opportunities, Mobilizing Structures, and Cultural Framings*. Cambridge: Cambridge University Press.

Gandy, O. (1980) 'Information in Health: Subsidised News', *Media, Culture and Society*, 2(2): 103–15.

Gandy, O. (1982) *Beyond Agenda Setting: Information Subsidies and Public Policy*. Norwood, NJ: Ablex.

Gans, H. J. (1979) *Deciding What's News: A Study of CBS Evening News, NBC Nightly News, Newsweek and Time*. New York: Pantheon.

Garfinkel, H. (1967) *Studies in Ethnomethodology*. Englewood Cliffs, NJ: Prentice Hall.

Garnham, N. (1990) *Capitalism and Communication: Global Culture and the Economics of Information*. London: Sage.

Garofalo, R., ed. (1992) *Rockin' the Boat: Mass Music and Mass Movements*. Boston: South End Press.

Gates, B. (1996) *The Road Ahead*. New York: Penguin.

Gendron, B. (1986) 'Theodore Adorno Meets the Cadillacs', in T. Modleski, ed., *Studies in Entertainment*. Bloomington: Indiana University Press.

Gibbons, G. (2009) 'The Social Value of Brands', in R. Clifton, ed., *Brands and Branding*. 2nd edn, London: Economist.

Giddens, A. (1991) *Modernity and Self-Identity: Self and Society in the Late Modern Age*. Cambridge: Polity.

Gillan, J. (2011) *Television and New Media: Must-Click TV*. London: Routledge.

Giroux, H. A. (2010) *Politics after Hope: Obama and the Crisis of Youth, Race, and Democracy*. Boulder, CO: Paradigm.

Gitlin, T. (1980) *The Whole World is Watching*. Berkeley: University of California Press.

Gitlin, T. (1994) *Inside Prime Time*. 2nd edn, London: Routledge.

Gitlin, T. (2011) 'The Left Declares its Independence', *New York Times*, 8 October.

GUMG (Glasgow University Media Group) (1976) *Bad News*. London: Routledge.

GUMG (Glasgow University Media Group) (1980) *More Bad News*. London: Routledge.

GUMG (Glasgow University Media Group) (1982) *Really Bad News*. London: Routledge.

Glasser, T., ed. (1999) *The Idea of Public Journalism*. London: Guilford Press.

Glassman, J., and Hassett, K. (1999) *Dow, 36,000: The New Strategy for Profiting from the Coming Rise in the Stock Market*. New York: Random House.

Goddard, A. (1998) *The Language of Advertising: Written Texts*. London: Routledge.

Goffman, E. (1979) *Gender Advertisements*. Cambridge, MA: Harvard University Press.

Goffman, H. (1967) *Interaction Ritual: Essays on Face-to-Face Behavior*. New York: Anchor Books.

Goldenberg, E. (1975) *Making the Papers: The Access of Resource-Poor Groups to the Metropolitan Press*. Lexington, MA: D. C. Heath.

Golding, P., and Murdock, G. (2000) 'Culture, Communications and Political Economy', in J. Curran and M. Gurevitch, eds, *Mass Media and Society*. 3rd edn, London: Arnold.

Golding, T. (2003) *The City: Inside the Great Expectation Machine*. 2nd edn, London: FT/Prentice Hall.

Goldman, R. (1992) *Reading Ads Socially*. London: Routledge.

Goldman, R., and Papson, S. (1996) *Sign Wars: The Cluttered Landscape of Advertising*. New York: Guilford Press.

Goldman, R., and Papson, S. (1998) *Nike Culture: The Sign of the Swoosh*. London: Sage.

Goodman, R. (2002) 'Flabless is Fabulous: How Latina and Anglo Women Read and Incorporate the Excessively Thin Body Ideal into Everyday Experience', *Journalism and Mass Communication Quarterly*, 79(3): 712–27.

Gore, A. (2006) *An Inconvenient Truth: The Planetary Emergency of Global Warming and What We Can Do About It*. London: Bloomsbury.

Gramsci, A. (1988) *A Gramsci Reader: Selected Writings 1916–1935*, ed. D. Forgacs. London: Lawrence & Wishart.

Granovetter, M. (1992 [1985]) 'Economic Action and Social Structure: The Problem of Embeddedness', in M. Granovetter and R. Swedberg, eds, *The Sociology of Economic Life*. Boulder, CO: Westview Press.

Granovetter, M., and McGuire, P. (1998) 'The Making of an Industry: Electricity in the United States', in M. Callon, ed., *The Laws of the Markets*. Oxford: Blackwell.

Granovetter, M., and Swedberg, R., eds (1992) *The Sociology of Economic Life*. Boulder, CO: Westview Press.

Grant, W. (1978) *Insider Groups, Outsider Groups and Interest Group Strategies in Britain*, Department of Politics Working Paper no. 19. Warwick: University of Warwick.

Grant, W. (1993) *Business and Politics in Britain*. 2nd edn, London: Macmillan.

Grant, W. (1995) *Pressure Groups, Politics and Democracy in Britain*. New York: Harvester Wheatsheaf.

Gray, J. (2008) *Television Entertainment*. New York: Routledge.

Gray, J. (2010) *Show Sold Separately: Promos, Spoilers and Other Media Paratexts*. New York: New York University Press.

Greenberg, J. (2008) *From Betamax to Blockbuster: Video Stores and the Invention of Movies on Video*. Cambridge, MA: MIT Press.

Gronebeck, B. (2009) 'The Web, Campaign 07–08, and Engaged Citizens:

Political, Social, and Moral Consequences', in R. Denton, ed., *The 2008 Presidential Campaign: A Communication Perspective*. Lanham, MD: Rowman & Littlefield.

Grunig, J., ed. (1992) *Excellence in Public Relations and Communication Management*. Hillsdale, NJ: Lawrence Erlbaum.

Grunig, J. (2009) 'Paradigms of Global Public Relations in an Age of Digitalisation', *PRism*, 6(2): 1–19.

Grunig, J., and Hunt, T. (1984) *Managing Public Relations*. New York: Holt, Rinehart & Winston.

Guillen, M., Collins, R., England, P., and Meyer, M., eds (2002) *The New Economic Sociology: Developments in an Emerging Field*. New York: Russell Sage Foundation.

Gunther, R., Mantero, J., and Linz, J. (2002) *Political Parties: Old Concepts and New Challenges*. Oxford: Oxford University Press.

Habermas, J. (1989 [1962]) *The Structural Transformation of the Public Sphere: An Inquiry into a Category of Bourgeois Society*, trans. T. Burger. Cambridge: Polity.

Habermas, J. (1999) 'The European Nation State and the Pressures of Globalization', *New Left Review*, no. 235: 425–36.

Hague, R., and Harrop, M. (2007) *Comparative Government and Politics*. 7th edn, Basingstoke: Palgrave Macmillan.

Haldane, A. (2011) 'Control Rights (and Wrongs)', Wincott Annual Memorial Lecture, Westminster, 24 October.

Hall, S. (1973) *Encoding and Decoding in the Television Discourse*, Stencilled Paper no. 7. Birmingham: University of Birmingham Centre for Cultural Studies.

Hall, S., and Jacques, M. (1989) *New Times: The Changing Face of British Politics in the 1990s*. London: Lawrence & Wishart.

Hall, S., and Jefferson, T., eds (1976) *Resistance through Rituals: Youth Subcultures in Post-War Britain*. Birmingham: University of Birmingham Centre for Cultural Studies.

Hall, S., Critcher, C., Jefferson, T., Clarke, J., and Roberts, B. (1978) *Policing the Crisis: Mugging, the State, and Law and Order*. London: Macmillan.

Hall Jamieson, K. (1996) *Packaging the Presidency: A History and Criticism of Presidential Campaign Advertising*. 3rd edn, Oxford: Oxford University Press.

Hall Jamieson, K., ed. (2006) *Electing the President 2004: The Insider View*. Philadelphia: University of Pennsylvania Press.

Hall Jamieson, K., ed. (2010) *Electing the President 2008: The Insider View*. Philadelphia: University of Pennsylvania Press.

Hallin, D. (1994) *We Keep America on Top of the World: Television Journalism and the Public Sphere*. London: Routledge.

Hansard (2009) *Audit of Political Engagement 6: The 2009 Report*. London: Hansard Society.

Hansen, A., ed. (1993) *The Mass Media and Environmental Issues*. Leicester: Leicester University Press.

Hansen, A. (2010) *Environment, Media and Communication*. London: Routledge.

Hardy, J. (2010) *Cross-Media Promotion*. New York: Peter Lang.

Hardy, J. (2013) 'Cross-Media Promotion and Media Synergy: Practices, Problems and Policy Responses', in M. McAllister and E. West, eds, *The Routledge Companion to Advertising and Promotional Culture*. London: Routledge.

Harrison, M. (1985) *TV News: Whose Bias?* Newbury: Policy Journals.

Hartley, J. (1996) *Popular Reality: Journalism, Modernity, Popular Culture*. London: Arnold.

Harvey, D. (1989) *The Condition of Postmodernity: An Enquiry in the Origins of Cultural Change*. Oxford: Blackwell.

Harvey, D. (2005) *A Brief History of Neoliberalism*. Oxford: Oxford University Press.

Harvey, D. (2011) *The Enigma of Capital: And the Crisis of Capitalism*. London: Profile Books.

Hay, C. (2007) *Why We Hate Politics*. Cambridge: Polity.

Hayward, M., Rindova, P., and Pollock, T. (2004) 'Believing One's Own Press: The Causes and Consequences of CEO Celebrity', *Strategic Management Journal*, 25(7): 637–53.

Heath, A., Jowell, R., and Curtice, J. (2001) *The Rise of New Labour: Party Policies and Voter Choices*. Oxford: Oxford University Press.

Heath, J., and Potter, A. (2006) *Rebel Culture: How the Counter Culture Became Consumer Culture*. Chichester: Capstone.

Hebdige, D. (1979) *Subculture: The Meaning of Style*. London: Sage.

Hebdige, D. (1988) *Hiding in the Light*. London: Comedia.

Heffernan, R. (2003) 'Political Parties and the Party System', in P. Dunleavy, A. Gamble, R. Heffernan and G. Peele, eds, *Developments in British Politics 7*. Basingstoke: Palgrave Macmillan.

Held, D. (1989) *Political Theory and the Modern State*. Cambridge: Polity.

Held, D. (1996) *Models of Democracy*. 2nd edn, Cambridge: Polity.

Held, D. (2002) 'Laws of States, Laws of Peoples', *Legal Theory*, 8: 1–44.

Held, D., and McGrew, A. (2000) 'The Great Globalization Debate: An Introduction', in D. Held and A. McGrew, eds, *The Global Transformations Reader: An Introduction to the Globalization Debate*. Cambridge: Polity.

Hendricks, J., and Denton, R., eds (2010) *Communicator in Chief: How Barack Obama Used New Media Technology to Win the White House*. Lanham, MD: Rowman & Littlefield.

Herman, E., and Chomsky, N. (1988) *Manufacturing Consent: The Political Economy of the Mass Media*. New York: Pantheon Books.

Herman, E., and Peterson, D. (2011) 'Legitimizing Versus Delegitimizing Elections: Honduras and Iran', in G. Sussman, ed., *The Propaganda*

Society: Promotional Culture and Politics in Global Context. New York: Peter Lang.

Hesmondhalgh, D. (1998) 'The British Dance Music Industry: A Case Study of Independent Cultural Production', *British Journal of Sociology*, 49(2): 234–51.

Hesmondhalgh, D. (2000) 'Alternative Media, Alternative Texts? Rethinking Democratisation in the Cultural Industries', in J. Curran, ed., *Media Organisations in Society*. London: Arnold.

Hesmondhalgh, D. (2005) 'Producing Celebrity', in J. Evans and D. Hesmondhalgh, eds, *Understanding Media: Inside Celebrity*. Milton Keynes: Open University Press.

Hesmondhalgh, D. (2007) *The Cultural Industries.* 2nd edn, London: Sage.

HMSO (1980/81 and 1997/98) *Financial Statement and Budget Report.* London: HMSO.

Ho, K. (2009) *Liquidated: An Ethnography of Wall Street.* Durham, NC: Duke University Press.

Hobson, D. (1982) *Crossroads: The Drama of Soap Opera.* London: Methuen.

Hochschild, A. (1983) *The Managed Heart: Commercialization of Human Feeling.* Berkeley: University of California Press.

Hochschild, A. (2003) *The Commercialization of Intimate Life: Notes from Home and Work.* Berkeley: University of California Press.

Hochschild, A., with Machung, A. (1997) *The Second Shift.* New York: Avon Books.

Hodge, R. (2010) *The Mendacity of Hope: Barack Obama and the Betrayal of American Liberalism.* New York: HarperCollins.

Hodkinson, S. (2005a) 'Make the G8 History', July, at http://redpepper. blogs.com/g8/.

Hodkinson, S. (2005b) 'Do Stars Really Aid the Cause?' *The Independent*, 26 October.

Hodkinson, S. (2005c) 'Geldof 8 – Africa Nil: How Rock Stars Betrayed the Poor', *New Internationalist*, 9 November; at www.newint.org/features/ geldof-8/index.html.

Hoedeman, O. (2007) 'Corporate Power in Europe: The Brussels "Lobbycracy"', in W. Dinan and D. Miller, eds, *Thinker, Faker, Spinner, Spy: Spin and Corporate Power*. London: Pluto Press.

Holmes, S. (2005) '"Off-Guard, Unkempt, Unready?" Deconstructing Contemporary Celebrity in Heat Magazine', *Continuum*, 19(1): 21–38.

Horton, D., and Wohl, R. (1993) 'Mass Communication and Para-Social Interaction', in J. Corner and J. Hawthorn, eds, *Communication Studies: An Introductory Reader*. 4th edn, London: Arnold.

Hutton, W. (1996) *The State We're In.* London: Vintage.

Hutton, W. (2010) *Them and Us: Changing Britain – Why We Need a Fairer Society.* London: Abacus.

IMA (2007) *Investment Management Association Survey of Members.* London: IMA.

IPR (1998) *Membership Survey*. London: Institute of Public Relations.

Ipsos-MORI (1997–2010) *Long Term Trends: The Most Important Issues Facing Britain*. London: Ipsos-MORI.

Ipsos-MORI (2009 and 2012) *Trust in People*. London: Ipsos-MORI.

Isaacson, W. (2011) *Steve Jobs*. London: Little, Brown.

Iser, W. (1978) *The Act of Reading: A Theory of Aesthetic Response*. Baltimore: Johns Hopkins University Press.

Iyengar, S., and Kinder, D. (1987) *News that Matters*. Chicago: University of Chicago Press.

Jackson, T. (2011) *Prosperity without Growth: Economics for a Finite Planet*. London: Routledge.

Jackson, T., and Shaw, D. (2009) *Mastering Fashion Marketing*. London: Palgrave Macmillan.

Jameson, F. (1991) *Postmodernism or the Cultural Logic of Late Capitalism*. London: Verso.

Jhally, S. (1987 and 1990) *The Codes of Advertising: Fetishism and the Political Economy of Meaning in Consumer Society*. 1st and 2nd edns, London: Routledge.

Jhally, S., and Lewis, J. (1992) *Enlightened Racism: The Cosby Show, Audiences and the Myth of the American Dream*. Boulder, CO: Westview Press.

Jhally, S., and Livant, B. (1986) 'Watching is Working: The Valorization of Audience Consciousness', *Journal of Communication*, 36: 124–43.

Jones, N. (1986) *Strikes and the Media: Communication and Conflict*. Oxford: Blackwell.

Jones, N. (1995) *Soundbites and Spin Doctors: How Politicians Manipulate the Media and Vice Versa*. London: Cassell.

Jones, N. (2002) *The Control Freaks: How New Labour Gets its Own Way*. London: Politicos.

Jordan, G., ed. (1990) *The Commercial Lobbyists: Politics and Profit in Britain*. Aberdeen: Aberdeen University Press.

Jordan, G., and Richardson, J. (1987) *Government and Pressure Groups in Britain*. Oxford: Clarendon Press.

Kahnemann, D., and Tversky, A. (2000) *Choice, Values and Frames*. Cambridge: Cambridge University Press.

Kantola, A. (2006) 'On the Dark Side of Democracy: The Global Imaginary of Financial Journalism', in B. Cammaerts and N. Carpentier, eds, *Reclaiming the Media: Communication, Rights and Democratic Media Roles*. Bristol: Intellect.

Kantola, A. (2009) 'The Disciplined Imaginary: The Nation Rejuvenated for the Global Condition', in A. Roosvall and I. Salovaara-Moring, eds, *Communicating the Nation*. Stockholm: Nordicom.

Karmak, E. (2010) 'Challenges in the Mediatizing of a Corporate Brand: Identity-Effects as LEGO Establishes a Media Products Company', in L. Chouliaraki and M. Morsing, eds, *Media, Organizations and Identity*. Basingstoke: Palgrave Macmillan.

Kavanagh, D. (1995) *Election Campaigning: The New Marketing of Politics*. Oxford: Blackwell.

Keane, J. (1991) *The Media and Democracy*. Cambridge: Polity.

Kellner, D. (1995) *Media Culture: Cultural Studies, Identity and Politics between the Modern and the Postmodern*. London: Routledge.

Kelly, A., Lawlor, K., and O'Donohoe, S. (2005) 'Encoding Advertisements: The Creative Perspective', *Journal of Marketing Management*, 21(5): 505–28.

Kelso, T. (2008) 'And Now No Word from our Sponsor: How HBO Put the Risk Back into Television', in M. Leverette, B. Ott and C. Buckley, eds, *It's Not TV: Watching HBO in the Post-Television Era*. New York: Routledge.

Kenski, H., and Kenski, K. (2009) 'Explaining the Vote in the Election of 2008: The Democratic Revival', in R. Denton, ed., *The 2008 Presidential Campaign: A Communication Perspective*. Lanham, MD: Rowman & Littlefield.

Kenski, K., Hardy, B., and Hall Jamieson, K. (2010) *The Obama Victory: How Media, Money, and Message Shaped the 2008 Election*. Oxford: Oxford University Press.

Key Note (2006) *Public Relations Industry Market Assessment 2006*. Hampton, Middx: Key Note.

Keynes, J. (1936) *The General Theory of Employment, Interest and Money*. London: Macmillan.

Khan, N. (2000) 'Catwalk Politics', in S. Bruzzi and P. Gibson, eds, *Fashion Cultures: Theories, Explorations and Analysis*. London: Routledge.

Khurana, R. (2002) *Searching for a Corporate Savior: The Irrational Quest for Charismatic CEOs*. Princeton, NJ: Princeton University Press.

Kindleberger, C. (2000) *Manias, Panics and Crashes*. 4th edn, New York: Wiley.

King, G. (2005) *American Independent Cinema*. New York: I. B. Tauris.

Klein, N. (2000) *No Logo*. London: Flamingo.

Knightley, P. (2000) *The First Casualty*. London: Andre Deutsch.

Knittel, C. R., and Stango, V. (2010) *Shareholder Value Destruction following the Tiger Woods Scandal*, Department of Economics Paper. University of California, Davis.

Knuckey, J., and Lees-Marshment, J. (2005) 'American Political Marketing: George W. Bush and the Republican Party', in D. Lilleker and J. Lees-Marshment, eds, *Political Marketing: A Comparative Perspective*. Manchester: Manchester University Press.

Koss, S. (1984) *The Rise and Fall of the Political Press in Britain*. London: Hamish Hamilton.

Kourdi, J. (2011) *The Marketing Century: How Marketing Drives Business and Shapes Society*. Chichester: Wiley.

Kovach, B., Rosenstiel, T., and Mitchell, A. (2004) *A Crisis of Confidence: A Commentary on the Findings*. Washington, DC: Pew Research Center.

Kriesi, H. (1991) *The Political Opportunity Structure of New Social Movements*. Berlin: Wissenschaftszentrum für Sozialforschung.

Krotz, F. (2007) 'The Meta-Process of Mediatization as a Conceptual Frame', *Global Media and Communication*, 3(3): 256–60.

Krugman, P. (2008) *The Return of Depression Economics and the Crisis of 2008*. Harmondsworth: Penguin.

Krugman, P. (2011) 'Confronting the Malefactors', *New York Times*, 6 October.

Krzyzanowski, M., and Oberhuber, F. (2007) *(Un)Doing Europe: Discourse and Practices in Negotiating the EU Constitution*. New York: Peter Lang.

Kubey, R. (2004) *Creating Television: Conversations with the People behind 50 Years of American TV*. Mahwah, NJ: Lawrence Erlbaum.

Kull, S., Ramsey, C., and Lewis, E. (2004) 'Misperceptions, the Media and the Iraq War', *Political Science Quarterly*, 118(4): 569–98.

Kumar, D. (2008) *Outside the Box: Corporate Media, Globalization, and the UPS Strike*. Urbana: University of Illinois Press.

Kurtz, H. (1998) *Spin Cycle: Inside the Clinton Propaganda Machine*. New York: Pan Books.

Lambiase, J. (2003) 'Codes of Online Sexuality: Celebrity, Gender and Marketing on the Web', *Sexuality and Culture*, 7(3): 57–78.

Lasch, C. (1979) *The Culture of Narcissism: American Life in an Age of Diminishing Expectations*. New York: Norton.

Lash, S., and Lury, C. (2007) *Global Culture Industry: The Mediation of Things*. Cambridge: Polity.

Lash, S., and Urry, J. (1987) *The End of Organized Capitalism*. Cambridge: Polity.

Lash, S., and Urry, J. (1994) *Economies of Signs and Spaces*. London: Sage.

Lazar, D. (1990) *Markets and Ideology in the City of London*. Basingstoke: Macmillan.

Lears, T. (1994) *Fables of Abundance: A Cultural History of Advertising in America*. New York: Basic Books.

Lee, M. (2000) *The Consumer Society Reader*. Oxford: Blackwell.

Lee-Wright, P., Philips, A., and Witschge, T. (2012) *Changing Journalism*. London: Routledge.

Lees, C. (2005) 'Political Marketing in Germany: The Campaigns of the Social Democratic Party', in D. Lilleker and J. Lees-Marshment, eds, *Political Marketing: A Comparative Perspective*. Manchester: Manchester University Press.

Lees-Marshment, J. (2004) *The Political Marketing Revolution: Transforming the Government of the UK*. Manchester: Manchester University Press.

Lees-Marshment, J. (2008) *Political Marketing and British Political Parties: The Party's Just Begun*. 2nd edn, Manchester: Manchester University Press.

Leiss, W., Kline, S., Jhally, S., and Botterill, J. (2005) *Social Communication in Advertising: Consumption in the Mediated Marketplace.* 3rd edn, London: Routledge.

L'Etang, J. (2004) *Public Relations in Britain: A History of Professional Practice in the Twentieth Century.* Mahwah, NJ: Lawrence Erlbaum.

Lévi-Strauss, C. (1972) *Structural Anthropology,* trans. C. Jacobson and B. Grundfest Schoepf. Harmondsworth: Penguin.

Levy, E. (1999) *Cinema of Outsiders: The Rise of American Independent Film.* New York: New York University Press.

Lewis, B. (2009) *The Great Contemporary Art Bubble.* London: BBC [DVD].

Lewis, B. (2011) 'The Man Who Changed the Way We See', *The Observer,* 10 July.

Lewis, J. (2004) 'Television, Public Opinion and the War in Iraq: The Case of Britain', *International Journal of Public Opinion Research,* 16(3): 295–310.

Lewis, J., Williams, A., and Franklin, B. (2008) 'A Compromised Fourth Estate? UK News Journalism, Public Relations and News Sources', *Journalism Studies,* 9(1): 1–20.

Lichtenberg, J. (2000) 'In Defence of Objectivity', in J. Curran and M. Gurevitch, eds, *Mass Media and Society.* 3rd edn, London: Arnold.

Lichter, S., and Rothman, S. (1988) 'Media and Business Elites', in R. Hiebert and C. Reuss, eds, *Impacts of Mass Media.* New York: Longman.

Liebes, T., and Katz, E. (1990) *The Export of Meaning: Cross-Cultural Readings of Dallas.* Cambridge: Polity.

Liebowitz, S., and Margolis, S. (1999) *Winners, Losers & Microsoft: Competition and Antitrust in High Technology.* Oakland, CA: Independent Institute.

Lievrouw, L. (2004) 'What's Changed about New Media?', *New Media and Society,* 6(1): 9–15.

Lievrouw, L., and Livingstone, S. (2006) 'Introduction', in L. Lievrouw and S. Livingstone, eds, *The Handbook of New Media.* 2nd edn, London: Sage.

Lijphart, A. (1999) *Patterns of Democracy: Government Forms and Performances in Thirty-Six Countries.* New Haven, CT: Yale University Press.

Lilleker, D., and Lees-Marshment, J. (2005) *Political Marketing: A Comparative Perspective.* Manchester: Manchester University Press.

Lim, G. (2005) *Idol to Icon: The Creation of Celebrity Brands.* London: Cyan Communications.

Lindblom, C. (1977) *Politics and Markets: The World's Political Economic Systems.* New York: Basic Books.

Lindemann, J. (2009) 'The Financial Value of Brands', in R. Clifton, ed., *Brands and Branding.* 2nd edn, London: Economist.

Littler, J. (2007) 'Celebrity CEOs and the Cultural Economy of Tabloid Intimacy', in S. Redmond and S. Holmes, eds, *Stardom and Celebrity: A Reader.* London: Sage.

Livingstone, S. (1998) *Making Sense of Television: The Psychology of Audience Interpretation.* London: Routledge.

Livingstone, S. (1999) 'Mediated Knowledge: Recognition of the Familiar, Discovery of the New', in J. Gripsrud, ed., *Television and Common Knowledge*. London: Routledge.

Livingstone, S. (2005) 'Critical Debates in Internet Studies: Reflections on an Emerging Field', in J. Curran and M. Gurevitch, eds, *Mass Media and Society*. 4th edn, London: Hodder Arnold.

Livingstone, S. (2009) 'On the Mediation of Everything: ICA Presidential Address 2008', *Journal of Communication*, 59(1): 1–18.

Livingstone, S., and Lunt, P. (1992) *Mass Consumption and Personal Identity: Everyday Economic Experience*. Buckingham: Open University Press.

Lloyd, J. (2004) *What the Media Do to our Politics*. London: Constable.

Lockhart, T. (2007) 'Jennifer Lopez: The New Wave of Border Crossing', in M. Mendible, ed., *From Bananas to Buttocks: The Latina Body in Popular Film and Culture*. Austin: University of Texas Press.

London Economics (1994) *The Future of Postal Services: A Critique of the Government's Green Paper*. London: London Economics.

London Stock Exchange (1998) *London Stock Exchange Fact File*. London: Stock Exchange.

Lotz, A. D. (2007) *The Television Will be Revolutionized*. New York: New York University Press.

Lukacs, G. (1972) *Studies in European Realism*. London: Merlin Press.

Lull, J. (2001) 'Superculture for the Communication Age', in J. Lull, ed., *Culture in the Communication Age*. London: Routledge.

Lumby, C. (1999) *Gotcha! Life in a Tabloid World*. London: Allen & Unwin.

Lundby, K., ed. (2009) *Mediatization: Concept, Changes, Consequences*. New York: Peter Lang.

Lury, C. (1996) *Consumer Culture*. Cambridge: Polity.

Lury, C. (2004) *Brands: The Logos of the Global Economy*. London: Routledge.

Lury, C., and Warde, A. (1997) 'Investments in the Imaginary Consumer: Conjectures Regarding Power, Knowledge and Advertising', in M. Nava, A. Blake, I. MacRury and B. Richards, eds, *Buy This Book: Studies in Advertising and Consumption*. London: Routledge.

Lyon, D. (2007) *Surveillance Studies: An Overview*. Cambridge: Polity.

Lyotard, J. (1979) *The Postmodern Condition: A Report on Knowledge*. Manchester: Manchester University Press.

Maarek, P. (1995) *Political Marketing and Communication*. Eastleigh: John Libby Press.

Maarek, P. (2011) *Campaign Communication and Political Marketing*. Oxford: Wiley-Blackwell.

McCabe, J., and Akass, K. (2008) 'It's Not TV: It's HBO's Original Programming', in M. Leverette, B. Ott and C. Buckley, eds, *It's Not TV: Watching HBO in the Post-Television Era*. New York: Routledge.

McChesney, R. (2008) *The Political Economy of Media: Enduring Issues, Emerging Dilemmas*. New York: Monthly Review Press.

McChesney, R., and Nichols, J. (2010) *The Death and Life of American Journalism*. New York: Nation Books.

McChesney, R., and Pickard, R., eds (2011) *Will the Last Reporter Please Turn Out the Lights: The Collapse of Journalism and What Can be Done to Fix It*. New York: New Press.

McChesney, R., Stole, I., Foster, J., and Holleman, H. (2011) 'Advertising and the Genius of Commercial Propaganda', in G. Sussman, ed., *The Propaganda Society: Promotional Culture and Politics in Global Context*. New York: Peter Lang.

McDonald, C. (1996) *Sampling the Universe: The Growth, Development and Influence of Market Research in Britain since 1945*. Henley on Thames: NTC.

MacDonald, M. (2000) 'Rethinking Personalization in Current Affairs Journalism', in C. Sparks and J. Tulloch, eds, *Tabloid Tales: Global Debates Over Media Standards*. Oxford: Rowman & Littlefield.

McDonald, M. P. (2009) 'The Return of the Voter: Voter Turnout in the 2008 Presidential Election', *The Forum*, 6(4): 1–10.

McDonald, P. (2000) *The Star System: Hollywood's Production of Popular Identities*. London: Wallflower.

McDonald, P. (2008) 'The Star System: Producing Hollywood Stardom in the Post-Studio Era', in P. McDonald and J. Wasko, eds, *The Contemporary Hollywood Film Industry*. Oxford: Blackwell.

McFall, E. (2004) *Advertising: A Cultural Economy*. London: Sage.

McGuigan, J. (1997) 'Cultural Populism Revisited', in M. Ferguson and P. Golding, eds, *Cultural Studies in Question*. London: Sage.

McGuigan, J. (2009) *Cool Capitalism*. London: Pluto Press.

McKendrick, N., Brewer, J., and Plumb, J. (1982) *The Birth of a Consumer Society: The Commercialization of Eighteenth-Century England*. London: Europa.

MacKenzie, D. (2004) 'The Big Bad Wolf and the Rational Market: Portfolio Insurance, the 1987 Crash and the Performativity of Economics', *Economy and Society*, 33(3): 303–34.

MacKenzie, D., and Wajcman, J., eds (1999) *The Social Shaping of Technology*. 2nd edn, Buckingham: Open University Press.

McLachlan, S., and Golding, P. (2000) 'British Newspapers, 1952–1997', in C. Sparks and J. Tulloch, eds, *Tabloid Tales: Global Debates Over Media Standards*. Oxford: Rowman & Littlefield.

McNair, B. (2003) *An Introduction to Political Communication*. 3rd edn, London: Routledge.

McQuail, D. (2000) *McQuail's Mass Communications Theory*. 4th edn, London: Sage.

McRobbie, A. (1998) *British Fashion Design: Rag Trade or Image Industry?* London: Routledge.

Maffesoli, M. (1991) *The Time of the Tribes: The Decline of Individualism in Mass Society*. London: Sage.

Magleby, D. (2011) 'Adaptation and Innovation in the Financing of the 2008 Election', in D. Magleby and A. Corrado, eds, *Financing the 2008 Election*. Washington, DC: Brookings Institution.

Mann, D. (2008) *Hollywood Independents: The Postwar Talent Takeover*. Minneapolis: University of Minnesota Press.

Manning, P. (1998) *Spinning for Labour: Trade Unions and the New Media Environment*. Aldershot: Ashgate.

Manning, P. (2000) *News and News Sources*. London: Sage.

Marchand, R. (1998) *Creating the Corporate Soul*. Berkeley: University of California Press.

Marcuse, H. (1964) *One-Dimensional Man*. Boston: Beacon Press.

Marsh, D., ed. (1998) *Comparing Policy Networks*. Buckingham: Open University Press.

Marsh, D., and Rhodes, R. (1992) *Policy Networks in British Government*. Oxford: Clarendon Press.

Marshall, D. (1997) *Celebrity and Power: Fame in Contemporary Culture*. Minneapolis: University of Minnesota Press.

Martin, A., Culey, C., and Evans, S. (2006) *Make Poverty History 2005 Campaign Evaluation*. London: Firetail.

Marx, K. (1974) *The Economic and Philosophic Manuscripts of 1844*. Moscow: Progress.

Marx, K. (1976) *Capital: A Critique of Political Economy*, Vol. 1. Harmondsworth: Penguin.

Marx, K., and Engels, F. (1976) *The German Ideology*. Moscow: Progress.

Mazzoleni, G., and Schulz, W. (1999) '"Mediatization of Politics": A Challenge for Democracy', *Political Communication*, 16(3): 247–61.

Meehan, E. (1991) '"Holy Commodity Fetish, Batman!": The Political Economy of a Commercial Intertext', in R. Pearson and W. Uricchio, eds, *The Many Lives of the Batman: Critical Approaches to a Superhero and his Media*. New York: Routledge.

Meehan, E. (2005) *Why TV is Not our Fault: Television Programming, Viewers, and Who's Really in Control*. Lanham, MD: Rowman & Littlefield.

Meyer, T. (2002) *Media Democracy: How the Media Colonize Politics*. Cambridge: Polity.

Meyrowitz, J. (1985) *No Sense of Place: The Impact of Electronic Media on Social Behaviour*. New York: Oxford University Press.

Michels, R. (1967 [1911]) *Political Parties*. New York: Free Press.

Miege, B. (1989) *The Capitalization of Cultural Production*. New York: International General.

Miliband, R. (1969) *The State in Capitalist Society*. London: Weidenfeld & Nicolson.

Miller, D. (1987) *Material Culture and Mass Consumption*. Oxford: Blackwell.

Miller, D. (1994) *Don't Mention the War: Northern Ireland, Propaganda and the Media*. London: Pluto Press.

Miller, D. (1998) *A Theory of Shopping*. Cambridge: Polity.

Miller, D., ed. (2004) *Tell Me Lies: Propaganda and Media Distortion in the Attack on Iraq*. London: Pluto Press.

Miller, D. (2008) *The Comfort of Things*. Cambridge: Polity.

Miller, D. (2010) *Stuff*. Cambridge: Polity.

Miller, D., and Dinan, W. (2000) 'The Rise of the PR Industry in Britain, 1979–98', *European Journal of Communication*, 15(1): 5–35.

Miller, D., and Dinan, W. (2008) *A Century of Spin: How Public Relations Became the Cutting Edge of Corporate Power*. London: Pluto Press.

Miller, P. (1998) 'The Margins of Accounting', in M. Callon, ed., *The Laws of the Markets*. Oxford: Blackwell.

Millett, K. (1970) *Sexual Politics*. New York: Doubleday.

Minsky, H. P. (1982) *Can 'It' Happen Again? Essays on Instability and Finance*. Armonk, NY: M. E. Sharpe.

Mintel (1995) *Financial Public Relations*. London: Mintel Marketing Intelligence.

Mitchell, N. J. (1997) *The Conspicuous Corporation: Business, Public Policy, and Representative Democracy*. Ann Arbor: University of Michigan Press.

Moi, T. (1985) *Sexual/Textual Politics: Feminist Literary Theory*. London: Routledge.

Molotch, H. (2003) *Where Stuff Comes From: How Toasters, Toilets, Cars, Computers, and Many Other Things Come to be as They Are*. New York: Routledge.

Monbiot, G. (2006) *Heat: How to Stop the Planet Heating Up*. London: Allen Lane.

Moor, L. (2007) *The Rise of Brands*. Oxford: Berg.

Moran, J. (2000) *Star Authors: Literary Celebrity in America*. London: Pluto Press.

Moran, M. (2007) *The British Regulatory State: High Modernism and Hyper-Innovation*. Oxford: Oxford University Press.

Moritz, M. (2009) *Return to the Little Kingdom: Steve Jobs, the Creation of Apple and How it Changed the World*. London: Duckworth Overlook.

Morley, D. (1980) *The Nationwide Audience*. London: BFI.

Morley, D. (1992) *Television, Audiences and Cultural Studies*. London: Routledge.

Morley, D. (1996) 'Populism, Revisionism and the "New" Audience Research', in J. Curran, D. Morley and V. Walkerdine, eds, *Cultural Studies and Communication*. London: Arnold.

Mosco, V. (2009) *The Political Economy of Communication*. London: Sage.

MPAA (2010) Motion Picture Association of America, website at www.mpaa.org.

Murdock, G., and Wasko, J. (2007) *Media in the Age of Marketization*. Cresskill, NJ: Hampton Press.

Murray, R. (1989) 'Benetton Britain', in S. Hall and M. Jacques, eds, *New Times*. London: Lawrence & Wishart.

Murray, S., and Ouellette, L. (2009) *Reality TV: Remaking Television Culture*. New York: New York University Press.

Myers, G. (1999) *Ad Worlds: Brands, Media, Audiences*. London: Arnold.

Nava, M. (1988) 'Targeting the Young: What Do Marketeers Think?', unpublished paper for the Gulbenkian Enquiry into Young People and the Arts, London.

Nava, M. (1992) *Changing Cultures: Feminism, Youth and Consumerism*. London: Sage.

Nava, M. (1997) 'Framing Advertising: Cultural Analysis and the Incrimination of Visual Texts', in M. Nava, A. Blake, I. MacRury and B. Richards, eds, *Buy This Book: Studies in Advertising and Consumption*. London: Routledge.

Negran-Muntaner, F. (1997) 'Jennifer's Butt', *Aztlan Journal of Chicano Studies*, 22(2): 181–93.

Negrine, R. (2008) *The Transformation of Political Communication: Continuities and Changes in Media and Politics*. Basingstoke: Palgrave Macmillan.

Negroponte, N. (1996) *Being Digital*. London: Hodder & Stoughton.

Negus, K. (1992) *Producing Pop: Culture and Conflict in the Popular Music Industry*. London: Arnold.

Negus, K. (1997) 'The Production of Culture', in P. du Gay, ed., *Production of Culture/Cultures of Production*. London: Sage/Open University Press.

Negus, K. (1999) *Music Genres and Corporate Cultures*. London: Routledge.

Neill, Lord (1998) *5th Report of the Committee on Standards in Public Life: The Funding of Political Parties in the United Kingdom*, Cm 4057-1. London: HMSO.

Nelson, J. (1989) *Sultans of Sleaze: Public Relations and the Media*. Toronto: Between the Lines.

Nessman, K. (1995) 'Public Relations in Europe: A Comparison with the United States', *Public Relations Review*, 21: 151–60.

Newman, B., ed. (1999) *The Handbook of Political Marketing*. Thousand Oaks, CA: Sage.

Newman, K. (1984) *Financial Marketing and Communications*. London: Holt, Rinehart & Winston.

Newsom, D., Van Slyke, T., and Kruckeberg, D. (2007) *This is PR: The Realities of Public Relations*. 9th edn, Belmont, CA: Thompson.

Nichols, J., and McChesney, R. (2009) 'The Death and Life of Great American Newspapers', *The Nation*, 6 April.

Nixon, S. (1996) *Hard Looks*. London: UCL Press.

Norris, J. (1990) *Advertising and the Transformation of American Society, 1865–1920*. New York: Greenwood Press.

Norris, P., ed. (1999) *Critical Citizens: Global Support for Democratic Government*. Oxford: Oxford University Press.

Norris, P. (2002) *A Virtuous Circle*. Cambridge: Cambridge University Press.

Norris, P. (2004) 'Global Political Communication: Good Governance, Human Development, and Mass Communication', in F. Esser and B.

Pfetsch, eds, *Comparing Political Communication: Theories, Cases and Challenges*. Cambridge: Cambridge University Press.

Norris, P., Curtice, J., Sanders, D., Scammell, M., and Semetko, H. (1999) *On Message: Communicating the Campaign*. London: Sage.

NUJ (1994 and 2006) *National Union of Journalists Surveys of Members*. London: NUJ.

O'Neill, D. (2007) 'From Hunky Heroes to Dangerous Dinosaurs', *Journalism Studies*, 8(5): 813–30.

OccupyArrests (2012) website at http://occupyarrests.moonfruit.com/.

Odih, P. (2007) *Advertising in Modern and Postmodern Times*. Los Angeles: Sage.

Ofcom (2007) *New News, Future News: The Challenges for Television News after Digital Switchover*. London: Ofcom.

Offe, C. (1984) *Contradictions of the Welfare State*, ed. J. Keane. Cambridge, MA: MIT Press.

Offe, C., and Wiesenthal, H. (1985) 'Two Logics of Collective Action', in C. Offe, *Disorganized Capitalism: Contemporary Transformations of Work and Politics*, ed. J. Keane. Cambridge: Polity.

Olson, M. (1965) *The Logic of Collective Action*. Cambridge, MA: Harvard University Press.

Ommundsen, W. (2007) 'From the Altar to the Market-Place and Back Again: Understanding Literary Celebrity', in S. Redmond and S. Holmes, eds, *Stardom and Celebrity: A Reader*. London: Sage.

ONS (UK Office of National Statistics) (2011) website at www.statistics.gov.uk/hub/index.html.

Opensecrets (2012) website at www.opensecrets.org/index.php.

Orwell, G. (1948) *1984*. Harmondsworth: Penguin.

Owen, D. (2010) 'Media in the 2008 Election: 21st-Century Campaign, Same Old Story', in L. Sabato, ed., *The Year of Obama: How Barack Obama won the White House*. New York: Longman.

Packard, V. (1957) *The Hidden Persuaders*. New York: Pocket Books.

Palley, T. (2007) *Financialization: What it is and Why it Matters*, Political Economy Research Institute Working Paper 153. Amherst: University of Massachusetts Press.

Parenti, M. (1993) *Inventing Reality: The Politics of News Media*. 2nd edn, New York: St Martin's Press.

Pareto, V. (1935) *The Mind and Society*. New York: Dover.

Parish, J. (2006) *Jennifer Lopez: Actor and Singer*. New York: Infobase.

Parry-Giles, S., and Parry-Giles, T. (2002) *Constructing Clinton: Hyperreality and Presidential Image-Making in Postmodern Politics*. New York: Peter Lang.

Parsons, W. (1989) *The Power of the Financial Press: Journalism and Economic Opinion in Britain and America*. London: Edward Elgar.

Patterson, T. (1994) *Out of Order*. London: Vintage Books.

Peirce, C. S. (1931–58) *Collected Writings*, 8 vols, ed. C. Hartshorne, P. Weiss and A. Burks. Cambridge, MA: Harvard University Press.

Pels, D. (2003) 'Aesthetic Representation and Political Style: Re-Balancing Identity and Difference in Media Democracy', in J. Corner and D. Pels, eds, *Media and the Restyling of Politics: Consumerism, Celebrity and Cynicism*. London: Sage.

Peterson, R. (1994) 'Measured Markets and Unknown Audiences: Case Studies from the Production and Consumption of Music', in J. Ettema and D. Whitney, eds, *Audiencemaking: How the Media Create the Audience*. London: Sage.

Pew (2009a) *Dissecting the 2008 Electorate: Most Diverse in US History*, 30 April. Washington, DC: Pew Research Center.

Pew (2009b, 2011 and 2012) *The State of the News Media*. Washington, DC: Pew Project for Excellence in Journalism [annual reports].

Pew News Coverage Index (2011) website at www.journalism.org/news_index/99.

Pharr, J., and Putnam, R., eds (2000) *Disaffected Democracies: What's Troubling the Trilateral Countries?* Princeton, NJ: Princeton University Press.

Philips, K. (2006) *American Theocracy: The Peril and Politics of Radical Religion, Oil and Borrowed Money in the 21st Century*. Harmondsworth: Penguin.

Philo, G., and Berry, M. (2004) *Bad News from Israel*. London: Pluto Press.

Phizacklea, A. (1991) *Unpacking the Fashion Industry*. London: Routledge.

Piore, M., and Sabel, C. (1984) *The Second Industrial Divide*. New York: Basic Books.

PIPA (Programme on International Policy Attitudes), (2006) website at www.pipa.org.

Polanyi, K. (1944) *The Great Transformation*. Boston: Beacon Press.

Polling Report, website at www.pollingreport.com/politics.htm.

Posner, H. (2011) *Marketing Fashion*. London: Laurence King.

Potter, J. (1996) *Representing Reality: Discourse, Rhetoric and Social Construction*. Thousand Oaks, CA: Sage.

Potter, J., and Wetherell, M. (1987) *Discourse and Social Psychology: Beyond Attitudes and Behaviour*. London: Sage.

Poulantzas, N. (1975) *Classes in Contemporary Capitalism*. London: New Left Books.

PR Week (1993, 1999) In-House Surveys, *PR Week*, 27 May 1993, 20 August 1999.

PR Week (1994, 2011) *PR Week*, 1 July 1994, 14 July 2011.

Protess, D., Cook, F. L., Doppelt, J. C., Ettema, J. S., Gordon, M. T., Leff, D. R., and Miller, P. (1991) *The Journalism of Outrage: Investigative Reporting and Agenda Building in America*. New York: Guilford Press.

PRSA (Public Relations Society of America) website at www.prsa.org/.

Putnam, R., ed. (2002) *Democracies in Flux: The Evolution of Social Capital in Contemporary Societies*. Oxford: Oxford University Press.

Quarmby, K. (2005) 'Why Oxfam is Failing Africa', *New Statesman*, 30 May.

Radway, J. A. (1984) *Reading the Romance: Women, Patriarchy and Popular Literature*. London: Verso.

Rampton, S., and Stauber, J. (2002) *Trust Us, We're Experts! How Industry Manipulates Science and Gambles with your Future*. New York: Jeremy P. Tarcher/Putnam.

Rawnsley, A. (2001) *Servants of the People: The Inside Story of New Labour*. Harmondsworth: Penguin.

Rees-Mogg, W. (2005) 'The Tories' Future? It's up to Gordon Brown', *Mail on Sunday*, 2 October.

Reich, R. (1991) *The Work of Nations*. New York: Simon & Schuster.

Reilly, F. K., and Brown, K. C. (2000) *Investment Analysis and Portfolio Management*. 6th edn, Fort Worth, TX: Dryden Press.

Rios, D., and Reyes, X. (2007) 'Jennifer Lopez and a Hollywood Latina Romance Film: Mythic Motifs in *Maid in Manhattan*', in M. Galician and D. Merskin, eds, *Critical Thinking about Sex, Love and Romance in the Mass Media*. Mahwah, NJ: Lawrence Erlbaum.

Ritzer, G. (1998) *The McDonaldization Thesis*. London: Sage.

Ritzer, G. (2004) *The McDonaldization of Society*. Thousand Oaks, CA: Pine Forge Press.

Robbins, K., and Cornford, J. (1992) 'What is "Flexible" about Independent Producers?', *Screen*, 33(2): 190–200.

Rojek, C. (2001) *Celebrity*. London: Reaktion Books.

Rosen, R. (2011) 'Occupy: You Can't Evict an Idea', *OpenDemocracy*, 12 December, at: www.opendemocracy.net/5050/ruth-rosen/occupy-you-can%E2%80%99t-evict-idea.

Rosenthal, L. (2011) 'Occupy Wall Street and the Tea Party: Bedfellows?', *OpenDemocracy*, 4 November, at: www.opendemocracy.net/lawrence-rosenthal/occupy-wall-street-and-tea-party-bedfellows.

Ross, S. (2004) *Toward New Understandings: Journalists and Humanitarian Relief Coverage*. New York: Fritz Institute/Reuters Foundation.

Sacks, H. (1972) 'An Initial Investigation of the Usability of Conversational Data for Doing Sociology', in D. Sudnow, ed., *Studies in Social Interaction*. New York: Free Press.

Said, E. (1980) *Orientalism*. Harmondsworth: Penguin.

Santo, A. (2008) 'Para-Television and Discourses of Distinction: The Culture of Production of HBO', in M. Leverette, B. Ott and C. Buckley, eds, *It's Not TV: Watching HBO in the Post-Television Era*. New York: Routledge.

Sassatelli, R. (2007) *Consumer Culture: History, Theory and Politics*. London: Sage.

Saussure, F. de (1974 [1916]) *Course in General Linguistics*, trans. W. Baskin. London: Fontana/Collins.

Savigny, H. (2008) *The Problem of Political Marketing*. London: Continuum.

Scammell, M. (1995) *Designer Politics: How Elections Are Won*. London: Macmillan.

Scammell, M. (1999) 'Political Marketing: Lessons for Political Science', *Political Studies*, 47(4): 718–39.

Scammell, M. (2003) 'Citizen Consumers: Towards a New Marketing of Politics?', in J. Corner and D. Pels, eds, *Media and the Restyling of Politics: Consumerism, Celebrity and Cynicism*. London: Sage.

Schatz, T. (2008) 'The Studio System and Conglomerate Hollywood', in P. McDonald and J. Wasko, eds, *The Contemporary Hollywood Film Industry*. Oxford: Blackwell.

Schlesinger, P. (1990) 'Rethinking the Sociology of Journalism: Source Strategies and the Limits of Media-Centrism', in M. Ferguson, ed., *Public Communication: The New Imperative*. London: Sage.

Schlesinger, P., and Tumber, H. (1994) *Reporting Crime: The Media Politics of Criminal Justice*. Oxford: Clarendon Press.

Schudson, M. (1984) *Advertising, the Uneasy Persuasion: Its Dubious Impact on American Society*. London: Routledge.

Schudson, M. (1996) 'The Sociology of News Production Revisited', in J. Curran and M. Gurevitch, eds, *Mass Media and Society*. London: Arnold.

Schudson, M. (2001) 'The Objectivity Norm in American Journalism', *Journalism: Theory, Criticism and Practice*, 2(2): 149–70.

Schudson, M. (2003) *The Sociology of News*. New York: W. W. Norton.

Schudson, M. (2006) *Why Democracies Need an Unlovable Press*. Cambridge: Polity.

Scott, D. (2010) *The New Rules of Marketing and PR*. 2nd edn, Hoboken, NJ: John Wiley.

Seaton, J. (1991) 'Trade Unions and the Media', in B. Pimlott and C. Cook, eds, *Trade Unions in British Politics: The First 250 Years*. Harlow: Longman.

Selden, R., and Widdowson, P. (1993) *A Reader's Guide to Contemporary Literary Theory*. 3rd edn, New York: Harvester Wheatsheaf.

Sennett, R. (2006) *The Culture of the New Capitalism*. New Haven, CT: Yale University Press.

Shiller, R. (1989) *Market Volatility*. Cambridge, MA: MIT Press.

Shiller, R. (2001) *Irrational Exuberance*. Princeton, NJ: Princeton University Press.

Shlosser, E. (2002) *Fast Food Nation*. Harmondsworth: Penguin.

Shoemaker, P. (1989) 'Public Relations versus Journalism: Comments on Turrow', *American Behavioural Scientist*, 33(2): 213–15.

Siegal, J. (1998) *Stocks in the Long Run*. 2nd edn, New York: McGraw-Hill.

Sigal, L. V. (1973) *Reporters and Officials: The Organization and Politics of Newsmaking*. Lexington, MA: Lexington Books.

Simmel, G. (1904) 'Fashion', *International Quarterly*, 10: 130–55.

Simmel, G. (2002 [1903]) 'The Metropolis and Mental Life', repr. in G. Bridge and S. Watson, eds, *The Blackwell City Reader*. Oxford: Wiley-Blackwell.

Simmons, J. (2003) 'Popular Culture and Mediated Politics', in J. Corner and D. Pels, eds, *Media and the Restyling of Politics: Consumerism, Celebrity and Cynicism*. London: Sage.

Sireau, N. (2009) *Make Poverty History: Political Communication in Action*. Basingstoke: Palgrave Macmillan.

Sireau, N., and Davis, A. (2007) 'Interest Groups and Mediated Mobilisation: Communication in the Make Poverty History Campaign', in A. Davis, *The Mediation of Power: A Critical Introduction*. London: Routledge.

Slater, D. (1997) *Consumer Culture and Modernity*. Cambridge: Polity.

Slater, D. (2002) 'Capturing Markets from the Economists', in P. du Gay and M. Pryke, eds, *Cultural Economy*. London: Sage.

Slaughter, A. (2000) 'Governing the Global Economy through Government Networks', in M. Byers, ed., *The Role of Law in International Politics*. Oxford: Oxford University Press.

Smelser, N., and Swedberg, R., eds (2005) *The Handbook of Economic Sociology*. 2nd edn, Princeton, NJ: Princeton University Press.

Snow, N. (2004) 'Brainscrubbing: The Failures of US Public Diplomacy after 9/11', in D. Miller, ed., *Tell Me Lies: Propaganda and Media Distortion in the Attack on Iraq*. London: Pluto Press.

Sola Pool, I. de (1983) *Technologies of Freedom*. Cambridge, MA: Harvard University Press.

Sola Pool, I. de (1990) *Technologies without Boundaries: On Telecommunications in a Global Age*. Cambridge, MA: Harvard University Press.

Sombart, W. (1922) *Luxury and Capitalism*. Ann Arbor: University of Michigan Press.

Soros, G. (1994) *The Alchemy of Finance: Reading the Mind of the Market*. 2nd edn, London: Wiley.

Spanier, G. (2011) 'Apple's Own Ad Agency and Other Secrets of a Stellar Brand', *Evening Standard*, 10 October.

Sparks, C., and Tulloch, J. (2000) *Tabloid Tales: Global Debates Over Media Standards*. Oxford: Rowman & Littlefield.

Spinwatch, website at www.spinwatch.org.

Spurgeon, C. (2008) *Advertising and New Media*. London: Routledge.

Stacey, J. (1994) *Star Gazing: Hollywood Cinema and Female Spectatorship*. London: Routledge.

Stanyer, J. (2007) *Modern Political Communication: Mediated Politics in Uncertain Times*. Cambridge: Polity.

Starn, O. (2011) *The Passion of Tiger Woods: An Anthropologist Reports on Golf, Race and Celebrity Scandal*. Durham, NC: Duke University Press.

Stauber, J., and Rampton, S. (1995) *Toxic Sludge is Good For You: Lies, Damn Lies and the Public Relations Industry*. Monroe, ME: Common Courage Press.

Stauber, J., and Rampton, S. (2003) *Weapons of Mass Deception: The Uses of Propaganda in Bush's War on Iraq*. New York: Tarcher/Penguin.

Stern, N. (2007) *The Economics of Climate Change: The Stern Review*. Cambridge: Cambridge University Press.

Stiglitz, J. (2002) *Globalization and its Discontents*. Harmondsworth: Penguin.

Stiglitz, J. (2010) *Freefall: Free Markets and the Sinking of the Global Economy*. Harmondsworth: Penguin.

Strange, S. (1996) *The Retreat of the State: The Diffusion of Power in the World Economy*. Cambridge: Cambridge University Press.

Strasser, S. (2003) 'The Alien Past: Consumer Culture in Historical Perspective', *Journal of Consumer Policy*, 26(4): 375–93.

Street, J. (2003) 'The Celebrity Politician: Political Style and Popular Culture', in J. Corner and D. Pels, eds, *Media and the Restyling of Politics: Consumerism, Celebrity and Cynicism*. London: Sage.

Sussman, G. (2011) *The Propaganda Society: Promotional Culture and Politics in Global Context*. New York: Peter Lang.

Swanson, D., and Mancini, P., eds (1996) *Politics, Media and Modern Democracy: An International Study of Innovations in Electoral Campaigning and their Consequences*. New York: Praeger.

Swedberg, R. (2003) *Principles of Economic Sociology*. Princeton, NJ: Princeton University Press.

Tagg, J. (1988) *The Burden of Representation: Essays on Photographies and Histories*. Basingstoke: Macmillan.

Taibbi, M. (2011) 'Why Isn't Wall Street in Jail?', *Rolling Stone*, 3 March.

Tellis, G. (2004) *Effective Advertising: Understanding When, How and Why Advertising Works*. Thousand Oaks, CA: Sage.

Thompson, J. (1995) *The Media and Modernity: A Social Theory of the Media*. Cambridge: Polity.

Thompson, J. (2000) *Political Scandal*. Cambridge: Polity.

Thornton, S. (1995) *Clubcultures: Music, Media and Subcultural Capital*. Cambridge: Polity.

Thornton, S. (2008) *Seven Days in the Art World*. London: Granta.

Thussu, D. (2008) *News as Entertainment: The Rise of Global Infotainment*. London: Sage.

Thussu, D., and Freedman, D., eds (2003) *War and the Media Reporting Conflict 24/7*. London: Sage.

Tiffen, R. (1989) *News and Power*. Sydney: Allen & Unwin.

Toffler, A. (1971) *Future Shock*. London: Random House.

Toffler, A. (1980) *The Third Wave*. London: Collins.

Tomlinson, A., ed. (1990) 'Introduction', in A. Tomlinson, ed., *Consumption, Identity and Style: Marketing, Meanings and the Packaging of Pleasure*. London: Comedia.

Tormey, S. (2012) 'Occupy Wall Street: From Representation to Post-Representation', *Journal of Critical Global Studies*, no. 5: 132–7.

Toynbee, J. (2000) *Making Popular Music: Musicians, Creativity and Institutions*. London: Arnold.

Tracy, K. (2008) *Jennifer Lopez: A Biography*. Westport, CT: Greenwood Press.

Truman, D. (1951) *The Governmental Process*. New York: Alfred A. Knopf.

Tulloch, J. (1993) 'Policing the Public Sphere: The British Machinery of News Management', *Media, Culture and Society*, 15(3): 363–84.

Tumber, H., and Palmer, J. (2004) *Media at War: The Iraq Crisis*. London: Sage.

Tungate, M. (2005) *Fashion Brands: Branding Style from Armani to Zara*. London: Kogan Page.

Tunstall, J. (1971) *Journalists at Work*. London: Sage.

Tunstall, J. (1996) *Newspaper Power: The National Press in Britain*. Oxford: Oxford University Press.

Turner, A. (2011) 'Credit Creation and Social Optimality', speech given at Southampton University, 29 September.

Turner, G. (2004) *Understanding Celebrity*. London: Sage.

Turner, G. (2008) *The Credit Crunch: Housing Bubbles, Globalisation and the Worldwide Economic Crisis*. London: Pluto Press.

Turner, G. (2009) *Ordinary People and the Media: the Demotic Turn*. London: Sage.

Turner, G., Bonner, F., and Marshall, P. (2000) *Fame Games: The Production of Celebrity in Australia*. Cambridge: Cambridge University Press.

Turrow, J. (2009) 'Advertisers and Audience Autonomy at the End of Television', in J. Turrow and M. McAllister, eds, *The Advertising and Consumer Culture Reader*. New York: Routledge.

Turrow, J. (2011) *The Daily You: How the Advertising Industry is Defining Your Identity and Your World*. New Haven, CT: Yale University Press.

Tuten, T. (2008) *Advertising 2.0: Social Media Marketing in a Web 2.0 World*. Westport, CT: Praeger.

Twitchell, J. (1996) *Adcult USA: The Triumph of Advertising in American Culture*. New York: Columbia University Press.

Tye, L. (1998) *The Father of Spin: Edward L. Bernays and the Birth of Public Relations*. New York: Crown.

UK Electoral Commission (2012) website at www.electoralcommission.org. uk/.

UNCTAD (2009) *The Global Economic Crisis: Systemic Failures and Multilateral Remedies*, UNCTAD/GDS/2009/1. New York: United Nations Conference on Trade and Development.

US Bureau of Labor Statistics (2010) *National Employment Matrix*. Washington, DC: US Bureau of Labor Statistics.

US Senate (2008) *Report on Whether Public Statements Regarding Iraq by United States Government Officials Were Substantiated*. Washington, DC: US Government Printing Office.

Van Dijk, T. (1987) *Communicating Racism: Ethnic Prejudice in Thought and Talk*. Newbury Park, CA: Sage.

Van Dijk, T. (2008) *Discourse and Context: A Sociocognitive Approach.* Cambridge: Cambridge University Press.

Veblen, T. (1899) *The Theory of the Leisure Class: An Economic Study of Institutions.* New York: Macmillan.

Veljanovski, C., ed. (1989) *Freedom in Broadcasting.* London: Institute of Economic Affairs.

Wade, J. B., Porac, J. F., Pollock, T. G., and Graffin, S. D. (2006) 'The Burden of Celebrity: The Impact of CEO Certification Contests in CEO Pay and Performance', *Academy of Management Journal*, 9(4): 643–60.

Wainwright, H. (2012) 'An Excess of Democracy', *OpenDemocracy*, 24 February, at: www.opendemocracy.net/ourkingdom/hilary-wainwright/excess-of-democracy.

Wallace, J., and Erickson, J. (1992) *Hard Drive: Bill Gates and the Making of the Microsoft Empire.* New York: Wiley.

Wasko, J. (2001) *Understanding Disney: The Manufacture of Disney.* Cambridge: Polity.

Wasko, J. (2003) *How Hollywood Works.* London: Sage.

Waters, M. (1995) *Globalization.* London: Routledge.

Watts, E., and Orbe, M. (2002) 'The Spectacular Consumption of "True" African American Culture: "Whassup" with the Budweiser Guys?', *Critical Studies in Media Communication*, 19(1): 1–20.

Webb, P. (2000) *The Modern British Party System.* London: Sage.

Weber, M. (1948) *From Max Weber: Essays in Sociology*, ed. H. H. Gerth and C. Wright Mills. London: Routledge.

Webster, F. (2006) *Theories of the Information Society.* 3rd edn, London: Routledge.

Wernick, A. (1991) *Promotional Culture: Advertising, Ideology and Symbolic Expression.* London: Sage.

West, D., and Orman, J. (2003) *Celebrity Politics.* Upper Saddle River, NJ: Prentice Hall.

Wetherilt, A. V., and Weeken, O. (2002) 'Equity Valuation Measures: What Can They Tell Us?', *Bank of England Quarterly Bulletin*, 42(4): 391–403.

Whittaker, M., and Savage, L. (2011) *Missing Out: Why Ordinary Workers are Experiencing Growth without Gain.* London: Resolution Foundation.

Wigley, B. (2008) *London: Winning in a Changing World.* London: Merrill Lynch Europe.

Willetts, P. (2008) 'Transnational Actors and International Organizations in Global Politics', in J. Baylis, S. Smith and P. Owens, eds, *The Globalization of World Politics: An Introduction to International Relations.* 2nd edn, Oxford: Oxford University Press.

Williams, R. (1980) 'Advertising: The Magic System', in R. Williams, *Problems in Materialism and Culture: Selected Essays.* London: Verso.

Williamson, J. (2002 [1978]) *Decoding Advertisements: Ideology and Meaning in Advertising.* London: Marion Boyars.

Williamson, J. (1986) 'The Problem with Being Popular', *New Socialist*, September: 14–16.

Willis, P. (1990) *Common Culture: Symbolic Work at Play in the Everyday Cultures of the Young*. Milton Keynes: Open University Press.

Wilmshurst, J., and Mackay, A. (1999) *The Fundamentals of Advertising*. Oxford: Butterworth-Heinemann.

Wilson, D. (1984) *Pressure: The A to Z of Campaigning in Britain*. London: Heinemann.

Wilson, E. (2003) *Adorned in Dreams: Fashion and Modernity*. 2nd edn, London: I. B. Tauris.

Wilson, K. (2000) 'Communicating Climate Change through the Media: Predictions, Politics and Perceptions of Risk', in S. Allan, B. Adam and C. Carter, eds, *Environmental Risks and the Media*. London: Routledge.

Wilson, R., and Pickett, K. (2009) *The Spirit Level: Why Equal Societies Almost Always Do Better*. London: Allen Lane.

Winseck, D. (2011) 'Introductory Essay: The Political Economies of Media and the Transformation of the Global Media Industries', in D. Winseck and D. Jin, eds, *The Political Economies of Media: The Transformation of the Global Media Industries*. London: Bloomsbury.

Winston, B. (1998) *Media, Technology and Society: A History from Telegraph to the Internet*. London: Routledge.

Wodak, R., and Meyer, M. (2009) 'Critical Discourse Analysis: History, Agenda, Theory and Methodology', in R. Wodak and M. Meyer, eds, *Methods of Critical Discourse Analysis*. 2nd edn, Los Angeles: Sage.

Woodward, B. (2004) *Plan of Attack*. New York: Pocket Books.

Woodward, B. (2006) *State of Denial: Bush at War, Part III*. New York: Simon & Schuster.

Woog, A. (2008) *Jennifer Lopez: The Great Hispanic Heritage*. New York: Infobase.

Wring, D. (2005) *The Politics of Marketing the Labour Party*. London: Palgrave.

Wyatt, J. (1994) *High Concept: Movies and Marketing in Hollywood*. Austin: University of Texas Press.

Zelizer, B. (2004) *Taking Journalism Seriously: News and the Academy*. Thousand Oaks, CA: Sage.

Zorn, D., Dobbin, F., Dierkes, J., and Kwok, M. (2005) 'Managing Investors: How Financial Markets Reshaped the American Firm', in K. Knorr Cetina and A. Preda, eds, *The Sociology of Financial Markets*. Oxford: Oxford University Press.

Index

1 per cent, the 68, 169
9/11 141–2

Abbot Mead Vicker (AMV) 166–7
accountancy 174, 186, 198
actor network theory (ANT) 9, 178
Adam and Eve 54
Adorno, T. 121
advertising agents and agencies 16–18
Advertising Association 17
Advertising Effectiveness awards 18
Advertising Standards Authority 17
Aegis 68
agenda-setting 151–2, 160–1
agents, personal/talent 6, 92, 100,
        106–8, 114
Agins, T. 76, 80, 85–6
Ahmadinejad, Mahmoud 61
Aims of Industry 30
Air Jordan 119
Alberoni, F. 117–18, 121
ALMAs 127
al-Qaeda 141–2
Amazon 20, 39
American dream 129
American Idol 102, 128
American Marketing Association
        (AMA) 17–19
American Tobacco 26
Amnesty 162
Anderson, Lindsay 38
Andrews, D. 122, 130
Anglo-American New Criticism 56

Anglo-American promotional
        capitalism 197–9
Apple Inc. 5, 10, 48, 54, 88–91
    iMac 91
    iPad, iPhone, iPod 90
    iTunes 90
Arab Spring 168, 170
Arcadia Group 75, 86
art
    art market 176, 179
    art, promotional culture as 37
Arvidsson, A. 36, 38, 48
astro-turf campaign groups 26, 94,
        201
audience studies 3, 8, 34–50
Australian Women's Weekly 115

Bacall, Lauren 121
banking crisis (2007–) 31, 174,
        186–9
Barker, M. 52
Barnum, P. T. 7, 18, 27
Barthes, Roland 38, 40, 53, 59, 62
Barton, Bruce 25, 80
Baudrillard, J. 65–6
Bauman, Z. 5, 46, 49
Bear Stearns 188
behavioural economics 177
Bell, D. 87
Bell, Tim 30, 164
Bennett, T. 63
Benson, S. H. 30
Berger, J. 37, 60

Bernays, Edward 18, 25–6
Betamax video 82
Beyoncé 122
Bieber, Justin 202
Bird, S. 114
Blair, Tony 22, 56, 61–2, 122, 125,
　　197
Blair Witch Project, The 107
Bloomberg, Michael 169
Blumer, H. 83
Boase Massimi Pollitt 17
Bocock, R. 35, 36
Boltanski, L. 45
Bond, James 63
Bono 165–7
Boorstin, Daniel 25, 117
Boston University 18
Bottom-up culture 73, 75–7, 83
Bourdieu, P. 2, 42, 119
　　fields 119–23
　　forms of capital 42, 119–23
　　habitus 42
Braham, P. 83–4
brand equity 48, 78–9, 119
BRIC economies 179–80
Brierly, S. 56–7
British Medical Association (BMA)
　　162
Bronx 127
Brukheimer, Jerry 119
Buckingham Palace 155
budgets, promotional 4–5, 19
　　in civil society 159–60
　　in film 107–9
　　in politics 138–9, 146–7
Bureau of Investigative Journalism
　　180
Burson Marsteller 26
Burston, J. 101
Bush, George W. 122, 145, 147–8,
　　184, 197
Bush family 120
business news *see* news media
business-to-business promotion 10,
　　77, 80–2, 85–6
Butler, Ralph Starr 17

Callon, M. 178
Cameron, David 10, 97–8, 123–6,
　　150

campaign costs *see* budgets,
　　promotional
Campbell, C. 41
Canadian elections 136
Carl Byoir 26
Carlton Communications 125, 150
Cashmore, E. 122, 128
CBS 102
celebrity 10, 52, 75, 83, 112–32,
　　167–8, 194, 197
　　typographies of 117
celetoids 116–18, 194
Central Office of Information 24,
　　138–9
Champs-Elysées 79
Chandler, D. 52
charismatic authority 113
Chartered Institute of Marketing
　　(CIM) 17–19, 21
Chartered Institute of Public
　　Relations (CIPR) 18–19, 24, 156
Chartered Marketer awards 18
Chaudhuri, M. 32
Cheskin, Louis 25
Chiapello, E. 45
Chomsky, N. 53, 60, 160 169, 171
Christopherson, S. 106, 110
Chung, K. 131
Citigroup 188
citizen representation 11, 136–8,
　　141–3, 149–50
City of London 182–6
civil society 11, 154–71
Claiborne, Liz 80
Clarke, Basil 24
Clarke, Ken 124
Clegg, Nick 150
Clerks 107
Clifton, R. 23
Clinton, Bill 145, 184
Clooney, George 167, 202
Coalition for Health Insurance
　　Choices 26
Coca-Cola 49
Cochoy, F. 81
codes of practice, promotional
　　industries 17–19
Cole, C. 122, 130
collective tastes 76
Comic Relief 165–7

commercial intertexts 109, 112, 192, 199
commodity fetishism 27–8, 49, 63
commodity self 5, 49, 128–9, 194
Confederation of British Industry (CBI) 156
conglomerates 158
  fashion 75
  media and promotional 19, 45, 67, 93, 98–105, 108–10, 198
Connell, I. 118
Conservative Party 22, 30, 123–6, 138, 150–3, 163–5, 180
conspicuous consumption 42–3
consultancy sector (public relations) 155, 163–5
consumer society, the 9, 34–50
  consumer-generated content 48
  early (17th, 18th, 19th centuries) 35–6, 74
  20th century 36–7, 74
  in India 43
  working conditions in 46–9
consumer sovereignty 9, 36, 46
consumer studies 3, 8, 34–50
  and identity 41–3, 63–4, 67, 113, 196
  opposition and resistance 43–4
content analysis, quantitative 53
Cook, G. 56–7
Coombe, R. 38–9, 114
copyright law 48
Cosby, Bill 122
Coulson, Andy 98
counter-cultures (1960s–) 45–6
couturiers 74
Cowell, Simon 119
Cracknell, J. 160
Crane, D. 63
creativity 98–105, 199–200
CRESC 180
crisis of democracy 136–7
critical discourse analysis (CDA) 55–6, 61–2
Cronin, A. 63–4
cross-media promotion 97, 108–9, 116, 199
Cruise, Tom 106, 108
cultural economy 9, 11, 73, 77–82, 174, 177–8

cultural industries 31, 37, 98–111
cultural intermediaries 2, 37, 75
cultural turn 44
cultures of production 103–4
Curran, J. 94, 180
Curtis, Richard 165–7
Cutlip, S. 25
CWU see UCW

D'Acci, J. 101
Dahl, R. 157
Daily Herald 94
Dallas (television programme) 38
Dalton, R. 136–7
Danesi, M. 57
Davies, N. 96
Davis, A. 29, 120, 163, 180
Davis, David 123–6
Davis, F. 76–7, 83–4
de Certeau, M. 40, 43
Deacon, D. 142, 156
debt 47, 180, 186–9, 193
  sovereign debt 47, 158, 165–7, 180, 186–9
DeCordova, R. 114
democracy, and promotion 21–2, 118, 136–40, 200–2
Democratic Party (US) 18, 30, 145–8
denotative and connotative, semiotics 55
Department for Education and Skills 17
Department of Trade and Industry 163–5
Depression, the Great (1930s) 25
deregulation see regulation
derivatives 180, 187
Designers and Art Directors Association 17
Dichter, Ernest 25
Dickens, Charles 113
digital media, and promotion 20–1, 29, 39, 45, 95, 100, 102, 108–9, 141, 145–6, 169, 199
Dinan, W. 26, 30
discourse analysis (DA) 52–3, 55–6
Disney/Disneyland 5, 65, 108–10
distinction and consumption 42, 83–4
dominant codes 44, 62, 127–9
Dorothy Perkins 86

dotcom bubble 11, 174, 185–6
Douglas, M. 35, 42–3
Dover, E. 146
Dow Jones 186
Dowd, Matthew 145
Drake, P. 108–9
Dutch tulip bulbs 176
Dyer, G. 56, 60
Dyer, R. 113

Economic League 30
economic sociology 9, 11, 73, 77–82,
    174, 177–8
economics
    heterodox 11, 174, 177
    neo-classical 3, 11, 173–6
    orthodox see neo-classical
Economics Advisory Group 164
economy and promotion 20–1, 23
Edelman, Dan 24
Edison, Thomas 87
education, for promotional industries
    16–18
Efficient Market Hypothesis (EMH)
    175–6, 183
El Mariachi 107
election campaigns 30, 116, 138–9,
    142–8, 201
'electoral-professional' parties 29, 138
emotional labour 49
Empire Marketing Board 18, 24
encoding/decoding 38, 62–3
Engelen, E. 180
entertainment industry see cultural
    industries
environmental issues and critique 23,
    47, 68, 193
Epstein, E. 108–9
equality (class, race, gender) 24, 118,
    121–2
Erickson, J. 89
estrangement of labour 27–8
ethics, promotional industry codes of
    16–19
ethnicity 127–9, 146–8
European Parliament 30
Evans 86
Ewen, S. 25–6
Excellence in Public Relations awards
    18

exchange value see value
expenditure on promotion see
    budgets, promotional

Facebook 39, 126, 146, 196
Fairclough, N. 56, 61–2
FairVote 145–6
fan fiction/fan cultures 38–9, 49
Fannie Mae 188
Farrar-Myers, V. 147
fashion 83–6
fashion designers 84–6
fashion journalism see news media
feminist critiques see gender critique
Ferguson, C. 181, 184
fetishism see commodity fetishism
fields, field theory 120–3
Fiennes, Ralph 128
film studios, Hollywood 105–11
financial investors 80–1, 120, 182–9
financial lobby, the 11, 174, 180–5
financial markets 11, 158, 174–6,
    179–89
Financial Services Act 184
Financial Services Authority (FSA)
    184, 186
Financial Times 56, 180
financialization 158, 174, 181–5, 191,
    197–8
Fiske, J. 39, 41, 43, 45, 63, 76, 118
Fleishman, Alfred 24
Fleishman Hillard 24
Fletcher, W. 22, 24, 30, 37
Flickr 39
Forbes 119, 126, 129–31
Ford, Henry 20, 37, 74, 87, 194
Fordism/Fordist mass production 20,
    36, 46, 87
forms of capital (economic, cultural,
    social) 42, 112, 119–23
Foucault, M. 55, 59
Fowles, J. 38, 63
Fox, Liam 124
Fox Film Corporation 109–10
Frank, T. 45

Frankfurt School 31, 101–3, 111, 121
Franklin, B. 96, 155
Frears, Stephen 38
Freddy Mac 188

Friedman, Milton 7
Frith, K. 32, 53
Froud, J. 80–1, 120
fund managers *see* financial investors

G8 165–7
Galbraith, J. K. 28
Gallup, George 17
Gallup polls 17, 148
Gamson, J. 121
Gap Inc. 5, 90–1
Gates, Bill 87–9
Gaultier, John Paul 7
Geldof, Bob 165–8
gender critique of advertising 9, 24,
     32, 41, 57, 60, 63–4, 67, 121–2,
     127–9
General Electric 80–1
general intellect, the 48
General Motors 20, 80, 130
German election (2002) 145
Gibbons, G. 19, 21
Gillan, J. 102
Giroux, H. 148
Gitlin, T. 31, 100–2, 160, 169–70
Glasgow University Media Group
     61
Glass–Steagall Act (1933) 184
globalization 61–2, 66–7, 95, 168–71,
     182–3, 191
GM crops 56
Goddard, A. 57
Goffman, E. 56–7
Goldenberg, E. 160
Golding, P. 115
Goldman, R. 28, 59–60, 66–8
golf 129–31
Goodman, R. 32
Google 20, 22, 39, 54, 95, 196
Gore, Al 147
Grammy awards 127
Gramsci, A. 45
Granovetter, M. 82, 88, 178
Grant, Ulysses S. 113
Grant, W. 157
Gray, J. 102
Grunig, J. 22
Guber, Peter 108
Gulf War 25, 141–2
Gummer, Peter 30

Hall, S. 38, 62–3
Hanks, Tom 106, 108
Harry Potter 39, 109, 120
Hartley, J. 63
Harvey, D. 67
Hasbro 109
haute couture fashion 7, 10, 83–6
Havas 68
Havel, Vaclav 121
HBO 102, 104
Hebdige, D. 38, 40–1
Heinz 78
Herman, E. 53, 60, 61, 160
Heseltine, Michael 163–5
Hesmondhalgh, D. 99–100, 104
Hilfiger, Tommy 86
Hill and Knowlton 24, 26
Hispanic community (US) 127–8
Hobson, D. 35
Hochschild, A. 47, 49
Hodkinson, S. 167
Hoedeman, O. 30
Hollywood 4, 5, 7, 10, 31, 93,
     105–10, 200
Home Office 124
homogenization 101–3
Hooper audience ratings 17
Hope, Bob 130
Horkheimer, M. 121
Horton, D. 116
House of Representatives (US)
     139
House of Un-American Activities
     Committee 26
Howard, Michael 123
Hudson, Hugh 38

IBM 88–9
identity *see* consumer studies
ideology 58–9, 67–8, 126–9
     in politics 144
IMF 198
IMG agency 130
immaterial labour 48
independent producers 104–11
Indignados 168
individualism 29, 121, 193–5
industrialization and relations 20,
     61
industry historians 15–23

inequality (class, race, gender) 8,
    27–8, 57–9, 67–9, 127–9, 158,
    169–71, 193, 197–8
information subsidies 29, 95–8,
    159–61
Inland Revenue (UK) 155
insider–outsider interest groups 154,
    157–8, 165–8
Institute of Public Relations (IPR)
    see Chartered Institute of Public
    Relations
institutional investors see financial
    investors
interest groups 154–62, 165–8
internalization of promotion 3, 5, 49,
    191
Interpublic 68
Investment Management Association
    183
Ipsos-MORI 137, 151
Iran 61
Iraq 24–5, 141–2
Irish Republicans 24
Isaacson, W. 91
Isherwood, B. 35, 42–3
ITV 22

J. Walter Thompson 17
Jackson, Andrew 113
Jackson, T. 84, 86
Jameson, F. 67
Japanese election (1995) 136
jeans 77, 84
Jhally, S. 28, 53, 122
Jobs, Steve 7, 37, 87–91, 194
Johnson, Boris 202
Jordan, M. 119
jouissance 41
journalists 93–8, 125–6, 148–53, 161
JVC 82

Kantola, A. 56, 61
Karan, Donna 75, 80, 86
Kardashian, Kim 202
Karmak, E. 80
Katz, E. 38
Kellner, D. 67, 121
Kelly, A. 37
Kennedy family 120
Kenski, K. 147

Kerry, John 147
Keynes, John Maynard 7
Khan, N. 85
Khurana, R. 120
King, G. 110
Klein, N. 28, 46
Knittel, C. 131
Kodak 59
Kovach, B. 96
Krotz, F. 149
Kull, S. 142
Kumar, D. 61
Kuwaiti government 24

Labour Party 22, 30, 56, 61–2, 138,
    150–3, 164–6
Lady Gaga 67, 119
Lambiase, J. 128
Lash, S. 66, 78
Latina see Hispanic
Lauren, Ralph 86, 91
Lawson, Max 167
Lears, T. 41, 46–7
Lee, Ivy 18, 26
Lee, M. 36
Lees-Marshment, J. 21–2, 143–4
Leeson, Nick 190
legitimacy, in media 136, 160–2, 164
Lego 80
Leiss, W. 20, 23, 42, 66
leisure class, the 42
L'Etang, J. 24, 26
Leveson Inquiry 97–8
Levi's 5, 48, 57
Lewis, B. 179
Lewis, J. 60, 97, 122
Liberty 162
Lichter, S. 161
Liebes, T. 38
Lim, G. 127, 129
literary criticism 56, 59, 62
Live 8 165–7
Livingstone, S. 39
lobbying 6, 30–1, 180–5, 201
Lockhart, T. 128
London Economics 164
London School of Economics 17
London Stock Exchange 182–9
Lopez, Jennifer 10, 126–9
Lord of the Rings 39, 109

Lotz, A. 39
Louis Vuitton 48, 75
Lowe Bell 30, 138, 164
Ludlow Massacre 26
Lunt, P. 39
Lury, C. 36, 40, 42, 44, 48, 66, 78
LVMH 75

McCain, John 147
McChesney, R. 96–7
MacDonald, M. 114
McDonald, P. 107, 114, 119
McDonald's Corp. 49, 59
McDonaldization 96
McFall, L. 81
McGuigan, J. 45–6
McGuire, P. 88
Mackay, A. 23
McLachlan, S. 115
McRobbie, A. 83, 85
Madison Avenue 45, 79
Madoff, Bernie 190
Madonna 45, 67, 121
Maid in Manhattan 128
Major, John 163
Make Poverty History 11, 154, 165–8, 197
manipulation 8, 25
Mann, D. 106
Marchand, R. 20, 25, 41
marginal utility 175
Marketing (magazine) 17
Marketing and Sales Standards Setting Body 17
marketization 197–9
market-oriented parties (MOPs) 21–2, 144
Marx, Karl 27–8, 174–5
Marxist (including post-Marxist) critiques 8–9, 23–33, 45, 58–60, 64
media capital 196–7
media co-option 165–7
media effects 3, 37, 151
media logic *see* mediatization
media management 140–3, 201–2
mediation *see* mediatization
mediatization 11, 27, 148–53, 196–7
mergers, acquisitions and takeovers 79, 81, 120, 184

Merrill Lynch 188
methods of textual analysis 52–6
Metropolitan Police 4, 97–8, 155
Meyer, M. 53
Meyer, T. 149
Microsoft Corp. 10, 88–90
Mike Douglas Show 130
Miliband, Ed 98, 150
Milken, Michael 190
Miller, Daniel 35, 40–4
Miller, David 26, 30, 160
Ministry of Defence 4
Ministry of Health 18
Ministry of Information 24
Miramax 106
Mizrahi, Isaac 85
modality, in semiotics 54
Model-T car 20
modernist epistemology 64–5, 196
Molotch, H. 88
Moor, L. 48
Moran, J. 115, 122
Morgan Stanley 188
Moritz, M. 89
Morley, D. 38, 44, 63
motivational research 17, 25
Mount Pelerine Society 30
MTV 67
multi-media platforms *see* digital media
Murdoch, R. 97–8
musicals 101
Myers, G. 38, 39, 56–7

National Association of Manufacturers 30
National Association of Teachers of Advertising 17
National Enquirer 143
National Health Service (NHS) 152, 171
National Union of Journalists 96
Nationwide (television programme) 38, 63
nature in advertising 59
Nava, M. 38, 63
Nazi Party 26
negative advertising 146–7
Negran-Muntaner, F. 127
Negus, K. 79, 81, 104, 115

Nelson, J. 26
neo-liberalism 182–5, 194, 197–9
network television (US) 53, 101–2,
    104–5
New Deal 30
new economic sociology *see* economic
    sociology
New York 127, 168–9
New York Stock Exchange 80, 182–9
New York Times 53, 56, 95, 143
Newman, K. 180
News Corporation 97–8
news media 10, 31, 44, 52, 58, 60–1,
    93–8, 115, 125–6, 150–3, 168
    advertising influence on 22–3, 94,
        159
    business/financial news 61, 116,
        181
    electoral coverage 142–3, 147
    fashion journalism 83–5
    music press 115
    public relations influence on 94,
        180
    tabloid news 114–15, 118, 142, 194
News of the World 97–8
news sources 60–1, 94–8, 159–62
news values 149, 151, 161, 165, 196
Newsom, D. 18, 19, 22
Newsweek 143
NGOs *see* interest groups
Nichols, J. 96–7
Nielson audience ratings 17, 101,
    195, 200
Nike 4, 60, 66, 68, 119, 130–1
Nixon, S. 36
Norris, P. 157
Northern Rock 187

Obama, Barack 145–8, 197
Occupy movement 11, 148, 155,
    168–71, 197
Odih, P. 66–7
Ofcom 17, 143
Office of Global Communications
    141
Office of National Statistics 2
Office of Strategic Influence 141
oil prices 176
Ommundson, W. 122
Omnicom 68

Omo 59
ontological insecurity 67, 195–6
Opensecrets 30
Orientalism 59
Orman, J. 117, 120
Orwell, George 25
outsourcing work abroad 46–7
Oxfam 165, 167

Packard, Vance 25
Papson, S. 59–60, 66–8
Paramount (1948 ruling) 105–6
para-social relations 113
Parker, Alan 38
Parlin, Charles Coolidge 17
Parsons, Talcott 177
Parsons, W. 180
P/E ratios 186
Pears 78
Peirce, C. S. 52–5
People (magazine) 128
Pepsi 109
performativity 64, 81, 178
Persil 59
Peterson, D. 61
Peterson, R. 81
Pew 96, 143, 146
PGA 129
Phantom Menace, The 109
phone hacking 97–8
Pickford, Mary 114, 119
Piore, M. 87
Pixar 5
pleasure (*plaisir*) of consumption 41
pluralism/plurality 11, 154–71
Polanyi, K. 177
policy communities/networks 157
political capital 120, 123
political co-option 166–8
political economy 174–5 (*see also*
    Marxist critiques)
political field 120–1, 123–6
political marketing 21–2, 135,
    139–40, 143–8
political parties 123–6, 135–40, 143–8
    communication 10, 21–2, 37, 52,
        143–8
    party leaders 120, 143–53
    party members, 123–6, 137, 144,
        157

polysemy 38, 44, 62–3
Ponzi schemes 188–90
popular culture 10
    music 98–105
    promotional culture as 37–8, 76
    television 98–105
Post Office (UK) 154, 163–5, 171
post-Fordism 20, 65, 87, 106
post-industrialism *see* post-Fordism
postmodernism 9, 64–7, 195
poststructuralism 9, 64–7
powerless elite 116–18
pressure groups *see* interest groups
priceline.com 186
primary definers 160–2
privatization 11, 31, 158, 163–5, 198
productionist thesis 34–7
productive consumption 40
productive interface, promotional
        culture as 34
professionalization
    of political parties 135–40, 143–53
    of promotional industries 15–19,
        24–7
promotional culture, definition 1–3
promotional industries 1–3, 6, 8,
        15–33
promotional intermediaries, definition
        1–3
promotional texts, definition 51–2
propaganda, promotion as 24–7,
        60–1, 141–2, 193
    propaganda model 60–1, 95
property market 11, 176
prosumers 39
pseudo-events 25, 29, 94, 117, 142,
        196
pseudo-individuality 31, 101–2, 121
public information 140–3, 201–2
public interest 15, 58, 93–4, 161
Public Relations Consultants
        Association 180
Public Relations Society of America
        (PRSA) 18, 22, 141
public sphere 29, 136, 140
Publicis 68
Putnam, R. 137

Quintanilla-Perez, Selena 127
QWERTY keyboard 82

race, critique of promotional culture
        24, 32, 127–9, 146–8
Radcliffe, Daniel 119
Radway, J. 41
Rampton, S. 26, 30
reader-oriented theory 62
Reagan, Ronald 121, 184
real estate market *see* property market
reality television 102, 116
Rees-Mogg, William 125
reflectionist accounts of texts 56–8
regulation
    deregulation of industry 31, 158,
        183–5, 197–8
    of finance 181–5, 187
    of promotional industries 16
Republican Party (US) 18, 30, 145–8,
        169–70
Reyes, X. 128
Ricardo, David 174–5
Rios, D. 128
risk and unpredictability, 199–200
    cultural industries 98–100, 108,
        119
    finance 186–9
Ritzer, G. 46
Roberts, Julia 108, 119
Rockefeller, John D. 26, 194
Rojek, C. 117–18, 121
Romney, Mitt 148
Roosevelt, Franklin D. 30
Rosen, R. 171
Rothman, S. 161
Russell, Ken 38
Russian Formalists 56

Saatchi, Charles 179
Saatchi and Saatchi 30, 138, 179
Sabel, C. 87
St Paul's Cathedral 169
Sarkozy, Nicolas 197
Sassatelli, R. 35, 40
Saussure, F. 52–4
Savage, L. 69
Savile Row 79
Schatz, T. 108
Schlesinger, John 38
Schröder, Gerhard 145
Schwarzenegger, Arnold 108, 121
science and technology studies 88

Scott, Ridley 38, 106
Scott, Walter Dill 17
search engines 20, 39
securitization 187–8
self-promotion 3, 5, 191–4
Selfridges 75, 86
semiotic guerrillas 43
semiotics (signs, signifiers, signifieds)
    38, 52–5, 62, 64–7
Sennett, R. 46
Shandwick, 30, 138
Shaw, D. 84, 86
Sherlock Holmes 39
She's Gotta Have It 107
shopping malls/spaces 39, 43, 79
Sigal, L. 95
Simmel, G. 35, 41, 42, 74, 79, 83
Sinn Fein 160
Skilling, Jeffrey 190
Slater, D. 35, 43, 81–2
Smelser, N. 177
Smith, Adam 174–5
social media/networking 5, 23, 29, 39,
    49, 52, 169, 196, 199
social movements 154–62, 168–71
social shaping 4, 9, 88
Sola Pool, I. de 87
Sombart, W. 42
Sony 79–80, 82, 104, 108, 110
soundbites 29, 142, 149
South Sea stock bubble 176
Spanier, G. 89
Spiderman 109
spin doctors 29, 142
sponsorship 130–1
Spurgeon, C. 39
Stacey, J. 41, 113, 121
stakeholder elites 182
standardization 31, 88, 93, 101–3
Stango, V. 131
Star Trek 38–9
Star Wars 109
stars 52, 113–14, 117, 126
Stauber, J. 26, 30
Stewart, James 130
Stirling University 18
stock markets 185–6
Stoiber, Edmund 145
Storper, M. 106
Strasser, S. 47–8

subprime mortgages 188, 200
Sundance film festival 106, 110
Swatch 66, 78
Swedberg, R. 82
swing voters/states 126, 140, 201
symbolic, iconic, indexical 54
symbolic capital 10, 112, 119–31,
    162, 202
symbolic power 10, 112–31
symbolic value *see* value
synergies 79–80, 100, 108–9, 199

Taibbi, M. 181
tax and tax cuts 31, 142, 158, 182–3,
    187
Tea Party 148, 169–70
technological determinism 87
Tellis, G. 21
Thatcher, Margaret 22, 164
think tanks 164, 168, 201
Thornton, S. 179
time/space compression 65, 195
top-down culture 73–5, 83
Topshop 86
Torches of Freedom March 26
Tormey, S. 168, 170
Tourre, Fabrice 190
Toy Story 66
Toynbee, J. 104
trade unions 11, 24, 61, 154–65
Treasury (UK) 124
Truman, D. 157
trust 137, 143, 195–6
Tungate, M. 76, 83–6
Tunstall, J. 96
Turner, Adair 184
Turner, G. 115, 117–18
Tuten, T. 23
Twain, Mark 113
Twilight 39
Twitter 39, 126, 196
two-way symmetrical public relations
    22, 141

UCW union 154, 163–5
UGC (user-generated content) 48
Unilever 59
United Fruit 26
Urry, C. 78
US Air Force 160

US Bureau of Labour Statistics 2
US Congress 30
US elections/candidates 4, 11,
    142–8

value 11, 173–81
    exchange value 9, 27–8, 175–7
    natural 174
    sign value 78, 177
    symbolic value 7, 9, 65–8, 177
    use value 9, 28, 41, 65–6, 83, 90,
        175–7
Veblen, T. 35, 42, 74
Ventura, Jesse 121
voters/voter turnout 136–7, 145–8

Wade, J. 120, 122
Wainright, H. 170
Wall Street 182
    crash (1929) 176, 184
Wall Street Journal 95, 143
Wallace, J. 89
Wallis, Neil 98
Walton, Sydney 24
war on terror 95
War on Want 166
war-time propaganda *see* propaganda
Washington, George 113
Washington Post 60
Wasko, J. 31, 106
Wattenberg, M. 136–7
weapons of mass destruction 60–1,
    68, 142
Wedgwood, Josiah 78

Welch, Jack 80–1, 194
Wernick, A. x, 1, 66–7, 78
West, D. 117, 120
Westminster 124, 152
Whittaker, M. 69
Wilde, Oscar 113
Williams, R. 28–9
Williamson, J. 45, 59
Willis, P. 45
Wilmshurst, J. 23
Wilson, E. 83
Winfrey, Oprah 119, 130
Winston, B. 87
Wodak, R. 53
Wohl, R. 116
Woods, Tiger 10, 129–31
Woog, A. 127
Woollacott, J. 63
workers, cultural industries 98–110
World Bank 198
World Development Movement 166
World Wildlife Fund 162
Worth, Charles Frederick 84
WPP 19, 68
Wrigley's 57
writerly texts 62

Yahoo 95
Young British Art 179
YouTube 39, 146, 196

Zara 76, 84
Zawawi, C. 97
Zuccotti Park 168–9